FROMMER'S

MOTORIST'S PHRASE BOOK

FROMMER'S
MOTORIST'S
PHRASE BOOK

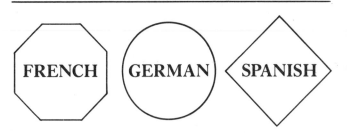

FRENCH GERMAN SPANISH

First Published in UK Edition 1983

This edition first published 1986 by
Frommer/Pasmantier Publishers
A Division of Simon & Schuster, Inc.
1230 Avenue of the Americas
New York, NY 10020

ISBN 0-671-62431-8

Contributors
Edwin Carpenter, Valerie M. McNulty
Anne Dickinson

Philippe Patry, Marlies Pfeiffer, Ulrike Seeberger
Carmen Billinghurst, Isabel Carrera

Contents

Contents

Introduction

This is a new type of phrase book, specially written with the motorist in mind. By combining French, German and Spanish in one volume it is of particular use to anyone touring any or all of the countries where these languages are spoken, but we hope it will be just as useful if you're driving around one area.

We've tried to cover as many aspects of touring by car as possible — for motorists taking their accommodation with them, there's a comprehensive section on camping and travelling with a trailer, with general information on camping abroad; if you prefer to let others do the work, you'll find the phrases you need in the "Hotels" chapter. The book will tell you how to ask the way (and how to make sense of the answer!), how to ask for a parking ticket or 15 litres of 4-star petrol; and if anything goes wrong with the car, the "Breakdowns" section will help you out.

While catering specifically for the needs of the motorist abroad, we haven't neglected all the other aspects of your holiday, such as sightseeing, keeping the children amused, relaxing over a drink in the local café, and eating out. And there are guides to food and wine so you'll know what to choose. There's also a comprehensive shopping section, with a list of shop names to help you find your way around, whether you're buying postcards or potatoes, as well as conversion tables for everything from tire pressures to shoe sizes.

The phrases are simple but idiomatic, with an easy-to-read pronunciation immediately following. You will also find lists of useful words (similarly followed by their pronunciation) in several sections. So once you have pinpointed the phrase you want you can ring the changes to suit your specific needs — for example, in the section on shopping for food, you will find the phrase "I would like a pound of tomatoes" and on the following pages a list of likely items that you can simply substitute for "tomatoes".

Have a nice trip!

Pronunciation Guide

We've tried to make the pronunciation aids under the phrases as simple as possible, breaking them into syllables to make them easier to read. Here we want to give some advice about sounds which often cause English-speakers problems.

French (*see also page 9*)

In English, the letter *r* is often ignored; not so in French. In *bar*, for example, the *r* has to be properly pronounced, rolled slightly at the back of the mouth.

Some French sounds are completely different from any English ones, such as the vowel in *rue*. To pronounce it you have to purse your lips as if to say *oo* and then try to say *ee*.

French also has nasal vowels, vowels followed by *n* or *m*; you sometimes hear this sort of sound at the end of the English word *restaurant*. You make these sounds by almost, but not quite, adding *ng* after the vowel.

The letter *e* in French often has a very weak sound, rather like the *a* in *above*; we've shown this as *uh*.

German (*see also page 10*).

The most obvious difference between German and English is that all German nouns begin with capital letters. German also has an extra letter – ß – which is like *ss*.

The sign ¨ (the umlaut) which often appears over German vowels changes their sound, and most of these changes are explained in the table on page 10; however, *ö* and *ü* are different from any English sounds. We show *ö* as *ur'* because it is like the sound in *hurt*, without sounding the *r*. The *ü* sound, shown as o͞o, can be made by pursing your lips as if to say *oo* and then trying to say *ee*.

Spanish (*see also page 11*)

The letter *r* must be rolled, not ignored as it often is in English; the double *r* is rolled even more strongly.

Vowels are always single sounds: when you find two together, as in *aceite*, you have to pronounce both of them in quick succession: a-**the**-ee-tay.

Finally, remember that for all the languages pronunciations have to be taken at face value: *s* is always pronounced *s*, never *z*, and *e* never represents *ee*. Be careful when a pronunciation looks like an English word: for example, the French *poste* is shown as *post*, but it rhymes with *lost*, not *most*.

French spelling	Closest English sound	Shown here by	Example	
ch	*ship*	*sh*	chat	*sha*
ç	*sat*	*s*	façon	*fa-soñ*
g	*before a, o, u,* got	*g*	gâteau	*ga-tõ*
	before e, i, measure	*zh*	rouge	*roozh*
gn	compa*ni*on	*ny*	vigne	*vee-nyuh*
h	*not pronounced*		homme	*om*
j	*measure*	*zh*	joue	*zhoo*
qu	*kick*	*k*	quel	*kel*
r	carro*t* (*see p8*)	*r*	rouge	*roozh*
w	*vase*	*v*	wagon	*va-goñ*
a, â	*father*	*ah*	plage	*plahzh*
a, à	*fat*	*a*	chat	*sha*
ai	*play*	*ay*	quai	*kay*
	or s*e*t	*e*	mais	*me*
ail, eil	*buy*	*ye*	travail	*tra-vye*
au, eau	*boat*	*õ*	faux	*fõ*
e, è	*set*	*e*	mets	*me*
é	*play*	*ay*	été	*ay-tay*
eu, œu	*thud*	*uh*	pleut	*pluh*
i	*meet*	*ee*	vide	*veed*
	or yet	*y*	bien	*byañ*
o	*UK* p*o*t, *US* thought	*o*	bol	*bol*
	or boat	*õ*	trop	*trõ*
oi	*UK* suave	*wah*	mois	*mwah*
ou	*boot*	*oo*	bout	*boo*
u	*see p8*	*ōō*	rue	*rōō*
y	*meet*	*ee*	cycle	*see-kluh*
an, en *etc*	*see p8*	*oñ etc*	plan	*ploñ*

Pronunciation Guide
German

German spelling	Closest English sound	Shown here by	Example	
a	cat	a	das	das
	or father	ah	haben	**hah**-bèn
ä	met	e	Äpfel	**ep**-fèl
	or gate	ay	Käse	**kay**-zè
au	cow	ow	braun	brown
äu	boy	oy	Geräusch	gè-**roysh**
e	met	e	Hotel	ho-**tel**
	or gate	ay	geben	**gay**-bèn
	or garden	è	Woche	**vokh**-è
ei	wine	i...e	Wein	vine
	or ye		frei	frye
	or eye		Eier	**eye**-èr
eu	boy	oy	heute	**hoy**-tè
i	bit	i	bitte	**bit**-è
	or meet	ee	ihn	een
ie	meet	ee	Sie	zee
o	not	o	Woche	**vokh**-è
	or note	ō	wo	vō
ö	hurt	ur'	möchte	**mur'kh**-tè
u	hook	oo	Nuß	noos
ü	see p8	ōō	über	**ōō**-bèr
ch	*Scottish* loch	kh	Woche	**vokh**-è
d	date	d	die	dee
	or cat	t	Bad	baht
g	give	g	geben	**gay**-bèn
	or take	k	Zug	tsook
j	yes	y	jemand	**yay**-mant
qu	k + v	kv	Qualität	kva-li-**tayt**
s	sat	s	das	das
	or zero	z	Sie	zee
sch	shout	sh	Schuhe	**shoo**-è
sp	sh + p	shp	sprechen	**shprekh**-èn
ß	loss	s	Nuß	noos
st	sh + t	sht	Stadt	shtat
	or last	st	nächste	**naykh**-stè
v	fat	f	von	fon
w	vine	v	Wein	vine
z	cats	ts	zu	tsoo

The syllable to be stressed is shown in heavy type.

Spanish spelling	Closest English sound	Shown here by	Example	
a	father	a	padre	**pa**-dray
e	gate	ay	peseta	pe-**say**-ta
	or pet	e	pero	**pe**-rō
i	feed	ee	litro	**lee**-trō
	or yet	y	tiene	**tyay**-nay
o	note	ō	como	**kō**-mō
	or UK pot	o	dónde	**don**-day
	US thought			
u	moon	oo	algún	al-**goon**
	or quick	w	cuando	**kwan**-dō
y	you	y	yo	yō
c	before a, o, u, cat	k	calle	**ka**-lyay
	before e, i, thin	th	centro	**then**-trō
g	before a, o, u, got	g	gato	**ga**-tō
	before e, i, loch (Scottish)	kh	gente	**khen**-tay
j	loch	kh	jueves	**khway**-bays
ll	million	ly	calle	**ka**-lyay
ñ	onion	ny	niño	**nee**-nyō
qu	quay	k	queso	**kay**-sō
r	carrot (*rolled*)	r	ropa	**rō**-pa
rr	*see p8*	rr	cerrado	the-**rra**-dō
s	sat	s	sábado	**sa**-ba-dō
v	bat	b	vino	**bee**-nō
z	thin	th	zumo	**thoo**-mō

The syllable to be stressed is shown in heavy type.

Everyday Phrases

French	German
Bonjour Monsieur (*to a man*) *boñ-zhoor muh-syuh* Madame (*to a woman*) *ma-dam* Mademoiselle (*to a girl*) *mad-mwah-zel*	Guten Morgen **goo**-tèn **mor**-gèn
Bonjour *boñ-zhoor*	Guten Tag **goo**-tèn tahk
Bonsoir *boñ-swar*	Guten Abend **goo**-tèn **ah**-bènt
Bonne nuit *bon nwee*	Gute Nacht **goo**-tè nakht
Au revoir *ō ruh-vwar*	Auf Wiedersehen owf **vee**-dèr-zay-èn
Oui *wee*	Ja *yah*
Non *noñ*	Nein *nine*
Comment allez-vous? *ko-moñ ta-lay-voo?*	Wie geht es Ihnen? *vee gayt es **een**-èn?*
Très bien, merci *tre byañ mer-see*	Es geht mir sehr gut *es gayt meer zayr goot*
S'il vous plaît *see voo play*	Bitte **bit**-è
Oui merci *wee mer-see*	Ja, bitte *yah,* **bit**-è
Merci *mer-see*	Danke **dang**-kè
Non merci *noñ mer-see*	Nein, danke *nine,* **dang**-kè
C'est très gentil à vous *say tre zhoñ-tee a voo*	Das ist sehr freundlich von Ihnen *das ist zayr **froynt**-likh fon **een**-èn*
Je vous en prie *zhuh voo zoñ pree*	Keine Ursache! **kine**-è **oor**-zakh-è!
Pardon *par-doñ*	Es tut mir leid *es toot meer lite*
Excusez-moi *ex-kōō-zay mwah*	Entschuldigung *ent-**shool**-di-goong*
Ça ne fait rien *sa nuh fay ryañ*	Das macht nichts *das makht nikhts*
Il fait beau *eel fay bō*	Schönes Wetter heute **shur'n**-ès **ve**-tèr **hoy**-tè

Spanish

Buenos días **bway**-nōs **dee**-as	Good morning
Buenas tardes **bway**-nas **tar**-days	Good afternoon
Buenas tardes **bway**-nas **tar**-days	Good evening
Buenas noches **bway**-nas **no**-chays	Good night
Adiós a-**dyōs**	Goodbye
Sí see	Yes
No nō	No
¿Cómo está usted? **ko**-mō es-**ta** oos-**ted**?	How are you?
Estoy muy bien es-**toy** mwee byen	I'm very well
Por favor por fa-**bor**	Please
Sí, por favor see, por fa-**bor**	Yes please
Gracias **gra**-thyas	Thank you
No, gracias nō, **gra**-thyas	No thank you
Se lo agradezco mucho say lō a-gra-**deth**-kō **moo**-chō	That's very kind of you
De nada day **na**-da	You're welcome
Lo siento lō **syen**-tō	I'm sorry
Oiga, por favor **oy**-ga, por fa-**bor**	Excuse me
No importa nō eem-**por**-ta	It doesn't matter
Hace un día estupendo **a**-thay oon **dee**-a es-too-**pen**-dó	It's a lovely day

Everyday Phrases

French	German
Est-ce que vous pouvez m'aider, s'il vous plaît? *es-kuh voo poo-vay me-day, see voo play?*	Können Sie mir bitte helfen? ***kur'n**-èn zee meer **bit**-è **hel**-fèn?*
Est-ce que vous pouvez venir avec moi, s'il vous plaît? *es-kuh voo poo-vay vuh-neer a-vek mwah, see voo play?*	Würden Sie bitte mit mir kommen? ***vōōr**-dèn zee **bit**-è mit meer **ko**-mèn?*
Répétez, s'il vous plaît *ray-pay-tay, see voo play*	Wiederholen Sie das, bitte *vee-dèr-**hō**-len zee das, **bit**-è*
Je ne comprends pas *zhuh nuh koñ-proñ pa*	Ich verstehe das nicht *ikh fer-**shtay**-è das nikht*
Je ne parle pas français *zhuh nuh parl pa froñ-say*	Ich spreche kein Deutsch *ikh **shpre**-khè kine doytsh*
Parlez-vous anglais? *par-lay voo zoñ-glay?*	Sprechen Sie Englisch? ***shpre**-khèn zee **eng**-lish?*
J'ai besoin de quelqu'un qui parle anglais *zhay buh-zwañ duh kel-kuñ kee parl oñ-glay*	Ich brauche jemanden, der Englisch spricht *ikh **brow**-khè **yay**-man-dèn, der **eng**-lish shprikht*
Où est le syndicat d'initiative? *oo ay luh sañ-dee-ka dee-nee-sya-teev?*	Wo ist das Fremdenverkehrsamt? *vō ist das **frem**-dèn-fer-**kayrz**-amt?*
Où est le poste de police? *oo ay luh post duh po-lees?*	Wo ist das Polizeirevier? *vō ist das po-lit-**sye**-re-veer?*
J'ai perdu mon passeport *zhay per-dōō moñ pas-por*	Ich habe meinen Paß verloren *ikh **hah**-bè **mine**-èn pas fer-**lōr**-èn*
Où est le Consulat américain? *oo ay luh koñ-sōō-la a-may-ree-kañ?*	Wo ist das amerikanische Konsulat? *vō ist das a-may-ri-**kah**-nish-è kon-zoo-**laht**?*
Mon passeport, s'il vous plaît *moñ pas-por, see voo play*	Bitte geben Sie mir meinen Paß wieder ***bit**-è **gay**-bèn zee meer **mine**-èn pas **vee**-dèr*
Qu'est-ce que c'est? *kes-kuh say?*	Was ist das? *vas ist das?*
Quelle heure est-il, s'il vous plaît? *kel uhr e teel, see voo play?*	Wie spät ist es, bitte? *vee shpayt ist es, **bit**-è?*
Est-ce que je peux emprunter votre stylo, s'il vous plaît? *Es-kuh zhuh puh zoñ-pruñ-tay vot-ruh stee-lō , see voo play?*	Kann ich Ihren Kuli leihen, bitte? *kan ikh **ee**-rèn **koo**-li **lye**-èn, **bit**-è?*

Everyday Phrases

¿Puede ayudarme por favor? *pway-day a-yoo-**dar**-may por fa-**bor***?	**Can you help me please?**
¿Podría usted venir conmigo, por favor? *po-**dree**-a oos-**ted** bay-**neer** kon-**mee**-gō, por fa-**bor***?	**Could you come with me please?**
¿Puede repetir eso, por favor? *pway-day ray-pay-**teer** e-sō, por fa-**bor***?	**Please repeat that**
No entiendo *nō en-**tyen**-dō*	**I don't understand**
No hablo español *nō a-blō es-pa-**nyol***	**I don't speak French/German/ Spanish**
¿Habla usted inglés? *a-bla oos-**ted** eeng-**glays***?	**Do you speak English?**
Necesito a alguien que hable inglés *nay-thay-**see**-tō a **al**-gyen kay **a**-blay eeng-**glays***	**I need someone who speaks English**
¿Dónde está la oficina de Turismo? ***don**-day es-**ta** la o-fee-**thee**-na day too-**rees**-mō?*	**Where is the Tourist Information Office?**
¿Dónde está la comisaría de policía? ***don**-day es-**ta** la ko-mee-sa-**ree**-a day po-lee-**thee**-a?*	**Where is the police station?**
He perdido el pasaporte *ay per-**dee**-dō el pa-sa-**por**-tay*	**I have lost my passport**
¿Dónde está el Consulado Americano? ***don**-day es-**ta** el kon-soo-**la**-dō a-may-ree-**ka**-nō?*	**Where is the U.S. Consulate?**
Devuélvame el pasaporte, por favor *day-**bwel**-ba-may el pa-sa-**por**-tay, por fa-**bor***	**Please give me my passport back**
¿Qué es esto? *kay es **es**-tō?*	**What is this?**
¿Qué hora es, por favor? *kay **ō**-ra es, por fa-**bor***?	**What time is it, please?**
¿Me presta su pluma, por favor? *may **pres**-ta soo **ploo**-ma, por fa-**bor***?	**May I borrow your pen, please?**

15

Crossing the Border

French	German
Voici mon passeport *vwah-see moñ pas-por*	Hier ist mein Paß *heer ist mine pas*
Ma femme et moi sommes sur le même passeport *ma fam ay mwah som sōōr luh mem pas-por*	Meine Frau und ich haben einen gemeinsamen Paß *__mine__-è frow oont ikh __hah__-bèn __ine__-èn gè-__mine__-zahm-èn pas*
Nos enfants sont sur ce passeport *nŏ zoñ-foñ soñ sōōr suh pas-por*	Unsere Kinder sind auf diesem Paß *__oon__-zè-rè __kin__-dèr zint owf __dee__-zèm pas*
Voici mon permis de conduire et la carte verte *vwah-see moñ per-mee duh koñ-dweer ay la kart vert*	Hier sind mein Führerschein und meine grüne Versicherungskarte *heer zint mine __foo__-rer-shine oont __mine__-è gr__oo__-nè fer-__zikh__-è-roongs-kar-tè*
Je reste deux semaines *zhuh rest duh smen*	Ich bleibe zwei Wochen *ikh __blye__-bè tsvye __vo__-khèn*
Je n'ai rien à déclarer *zhuh nay ryañ a day-kla-ray*	Ich habe nichts zu verzollen *ikh __hah__-bè nikhts tsoo fer-__tsol__-èn*
C'est pour ma consommation personnelle *say poor ma koñ-so-mas-yoñ per-so-nel*	Das ist für meinen persönlichen Bedarf *das ist f__oo__r __mine__-èn per-__zur'n__-likh-èn bè-__darf__*
Est-ce que je dois déclarer ça? *es-kuh zhuh dwah day-kla-ray sa?*	Muß ich das verzollen? *moos ikh das fer-__tsol__-èn?*
C'est combien? *say koñ-byañ?*	Wieviel muß ich dafür zahlen? *vee-__feel__ moos ikh da-f__oo__r tsah-lèn?*
C'est tout? *say too?*	Ist das alles? *ist das __a__-lès?*
J'ai manqué mon ferry *zhay moñ-kay moñ fe-ray*	Ich habe meine Fähre verpaßt *ikh __hah__-bè __mine__-è __fay__-rè fer-__past__*
À quelle heure est la prochaine traversée? *a kel uhr ay la pro-shen tra-ver-say?*	Wann ist die nächste Überfahrt? *van ist dee __naykh__-stè __oo__-bèr-fahrt?*

Spanish

Aquí está mi pasaporte a-**kee** es-**ta** mee pa-sa-**por**-tay	**Here is my passport**
Mi esposa y yo tenemos un pasaporte familiar mee es-**pō**-sa ee yō tay-**nay**-mōs oon pa-sa-**por**-tay fa-meel-**yar**	**My wife and I are on a joint passport**
Nuestros hijos están en este pasaporte **nwes**-trōs **ee**-khōs es-**tan** en **es**-tay pa-sa-**por**-tay	**Our children are on this passport**
Aquí está mi carnet de conducir y la carta verde a-**kee** es-**ta** mee **kar**-nay day kon-doo-**theer** ee la **kar**-ta **ber**-day	**Here is my driving license and green card.**
Me voy a quedar dos semanas may boy a kay-**dar** dos say-**ma**-nas	**I am staying for 2 weeks**
No tengo nada que declarar no **teng**-gō **na**-da kay day-kla-**rar**	**I have nothing to declare**
Eso es para mi uso personal **e**-sō es **pa**-ra mee **oo**-sō per-**sō**-**nal**	**This is for my personal use**
¿Tengo que declarar esto? **teng**-gō kay day-kla-**rar es**-tō?	**Do I have to declare this?**
¿Cuánto tengo que pagar? **kwan**-tō **teng**-gō kay pa-**gar**?	**How much do I have to pay?**
¿Está ya todo? es-**ta** ya **tō**-dō?	**Is that all?**
He perdido el ferry ay per-**dee**-dō el **fe**-ree	**I have missed my ferry**
¿A qué hora es el próximo? a kay **ō**-ra es el **prok**-see-mō?	**When is the next crossing?**

Service Station

French	German
Petrol (l'essence) comes in two varieties in France: ordinaire (2 star) and super (4 star). On Page 147 you will find tables for converting gallons to litres, and for working out your metric tyre pressures.	Petrol (das Benzin) comes in two varieties in Germany: Normal (3 star) and Super (4 star). On page 147 you will find tables for converting gallons to litres, and for working out your metric tyre pressures.
Quinze litres d'ordinaire/de super/de diesel, s'il vous plaît *kañz lee-truh dor-dee-ner/duh sōō-per/duh dee-zel, see voo play*	Fünfzehn Liter Normal/Super/Diesel, bitte *fōōnf-tsayn lee-tèr nor-mahl/zoo-pèr/dee-zèl, bit-è*
Pour cinquante francs, s'il vous plaît *poor sañ-koñt froñ, see voo play*	Für zwanzig Mark bitte *fōōr tsvan-tsikh mark bit-è*
Le plein, s'il vous plaît *luh plañ, see voo play*	Volltanken bitte *fol-tang-kèn bit-è*
Vérifiez l'huile/l'eau/la pression des pneus, s'il vous plaît *vay-reef-yay lweel/lō/la pres-yoñ day pnuh, see voo play*	Sehen Sie bitte das Öl/das Kühlwasser/den Reifendruck nach *zay-èn zee bit-è das ur'l/das kōōl-vas-èr/dayn rye-fèn-drook nahkh*
La pression devrait être de un virgule huit *la pres-yoñ duh-vray te-truh duh uñ veer-gōōl weet*	Der Reifendruck sollte eins Komma acht atü sein *der rye-fèn-drook zol-tè ines ko-ma ahkht a-tōō zine*
J'ai besoin d'eau distillée *zhay buh-zwañ dō dee-stee-yay*	Ich brauche destilliertes Wasser *ikh brow-khè des-til-eer-tès vas-èr*
Où sont les toilettes? *oo soñ lay twah-let?*	Wo sind die Toiletten? *vō zint dee tō-a-let-èn?*
Un bidon d'huile/d'huile pour la boîte de vitesses, s'il vous plaît *uñ bee-doñ dweel/dweel poor la bwaht duh vee-tes, see voo play*	Eine Dose Öl/Getriebeöl bitte *ine-è dō-zè ur'l/gè-tree-bè-ur'l bit-è*

Service Station

Spanish

Petrol (la gasolina) *comes in two varieties in Spain:
normal (2 star) and súper (4 star). On page 147
you will find tables for converting gallons to litres,
and for working out your metric tyre pressures.*

Quince litros de normal/de súper/de gas-oil por favor **keen**-thay **lee**-trōs day nor-**mal**/day **soo**-per/day gas-o-**eel** por fa-**bor**	**15 litres of 2/3 star/4 star/ diesel (fuel) please**
Mil pesetas por favor *meel pay-**say**-tas por fa-**bor***	**50 francs'/20 Marks'/1,000 pesetas' worth please**
Lleno por favor *l**yay**-nō por fa-**bor***	**Fill her up please**
Revíseme el aceite/el agua/la presión de los neumáticos por favor ray-**bee**-say-may el a-**the**-ee-tay/el **a**-gwa/la pre-**syon** day los nay-oo-**ma**-tee-kōs por fa-**bor**	**Please check the oil/the water/the tire pressures**
La presión tiene que ser de uno coma ocho la pre-**syon** t**yay**-nay kay ser day **ōō**-nō **ko**-ma **o**-chō	**The pressure should be 1.8**
Necesito agua destilada nay-thay-**see**-tō **a**-gwa des-tee-**la**-da	**I need some distilled water**
¿Dónde están los servicios? **don**-day es-**tan** los ser-**bee**-thyōs?	**Where are the toilets?**
Una lata de aceite/de aceite de cambios por favor **oo**-na **la**-ta day a-**the**-ee-tay/day a-**the**-ee-tay day **kam**-byōs por fa-**bor**	**A bottle of oil/gear oil, please**

Parking

French	German

In French towns, disc zones, where you leave a parking disc by your windscreen showing the time you arrived and when you should leave, are giving way to parking meters. Away from town centres there are streets where parking is allowed only on one side on a given day, for example during the first half of the month or on odd-numbered days.

Some German cities have adopted the system of the disc zone. You leave a parking disc by your windscreen showing when you arrived and when you should leave. Elsewhere you will find parking meters, as well as streets where parking is only allowed on one side on a given day, depending on whether it is an odd- or even-numbered date.

Où est-ce que je peux garer ma caravane?
oo es-kuh zhuh puh ga-ray ma ka-ra-van?

Wo kann ich mit meinem Wohnwagen parken?
*võ kan ikh mit **mine**-èm **võn**-vah-gèn **par**-kèn?*

Est-ce que je peux me garer ici?
es-kuh zhuh puh muh ga-ray ee-see?

Kann ich hier parken?
*kan ikh heer **par**-kèn?*

Est-ce que je peux laisser ma caravane ici?
es-kuh zhuh puh le-say ma ka-ra-van ee-see?

Kann ich meinen Wohnwagen hier lassen?
*kan ikh **mine**-èn **võn**-vah-gèn heer **las**-èn?*

Est-ce que le disque de stationnement est obligatoire?
es-kuh luh deesk duh stas-yon-moñ e to-blee-ga-twahr?

Brauche ich eine Parkscheibe?
***brow**-khè ikh **ine**-è **park**-shye-bè?*

Où trouve-t-on les disques de stationnement?
oo troov-toñ lay deesk duh stas-yon-moñ?

Wo kann ich eine Parkscheibe bekommen?
*võ kan ikh **ine**-è **park**-shye-bè bè-**kom**-èn?*

Est-ce que les feux de position sont nécessaires?
es-kuh lay fuh duh põ-zees-yoñ soñ nay-se-ser?

Muß ich das Standlicht anlassen?
*moos ikh das **shtant**-likht **an**-las-èn?*

Est-ce que le stationnement est payant ici?
es-kuh luh stas-yon-moñ e pe-yoñ tee-see?

Muß ich hier Parkgebühren bezahlen?
*moos ikh heer **park**-gè-bõõr-èn bè-**tsah**-lèn?*

Ça coûte combien?
sa koot koñ byãn?

Wieviel kostet es?
*vee-**feel** kos-tèt es?*

Je peux rester ici combien de temps?
zhuh puh res-tay ee-see koñ-byañ duh toñ?

Wie lange kann ich hier parken?
*vee **lang**-è kan ikh heer **par**-kèn?*

Le parking ferme à quelle heure?
luh par-keeng ferm a kel uhr?

Wann macht der Parkplatz zu?
*van makht der **park**-plats tsoo?*

Est-ce que le stationnement est autorisé de ce côté aujourd'hui?
es-kuh luh stas-yon-moñ e tõ-tõ-ree-zay duh suh kõ-tay õ-zhoor-dwee?

Kann ich heute auf dieser Seite parken?
*kan ikh **hoy**-tè owf **dee**-zèr **zye**-tè **par**-kèn?*

Parking

Spanish

Many Spanish towns have adopted the system of the disc zone. You leave a parking disc by your windscreen showing when you arrived and when you should leave. You are usually allowed to park for about one and a half hours. Away from town centres you will find streets where parking is only allowed on one side on a given day, for example during the first half of the month or on odd-numbered dates.

¿Dónde puedo aparcar la caravana? *don*-day **pway**-dō a-par-**kar** la ka-ra-**ba**-na?	**Where can I park with my motor home/trailer?**
¿Puedo aparcar aquí? *pway*-dō a-par-**kar** a-**kee**?	**Can I park here?**
¿Puedo dejar la caravana aquí? *pway*-dō day-**khar** la ka-ra-**ba**-na a-**kee**?	**Can I leave my motor home/ trailer here?**
¿Hace falta disco de estacionamiento limitado? *a*-thay **fal**-ta **dees**-kō day es-ta-thyo-na-**myen**-tō lee-mee-**ta**-dō?	**Do I need a parking ticket?**
¿Dónde puedo comprar un disco de estacionamiento limitado? *don*-day **pway**-dō kom-**prar** oon **dees**-kō day es-tath-yo-na-**myen**-tō lee-mee-**ta**-dō?	**Where can I get a parking ticket?**
¿Hacen falta luces de aparcamiento? *a*-then **fal**-ta **loo**-thays day a-par-ka-**myen**-tō?	**Do I need parking lights?**
¿Hay que pagar para aparcar aquí? *a*-ee kay pa-**gar** **pa**-ra a-par-**kar** a-**kee**?	**Do I have to pay to park here?**
¿Cuánto cuesta? **kwan**-tō **kwes**-ta?	**How much does it cost?**
¿Cuánto tiempo puedo estacionar aquí? **kwan**-tō **tyem**-pō **pway**-dō es-ta-thyo-**nar** a-**kee**?	**How long can I stay here?**
¿A qué hora cierra este aparcamiento? *a* kay **ō**-ra **thye**-rra **es**-tay a-par-ka-**myen**-tō?	**What time does the car park (parking lot) close?**
¿Puedo aparcar a este lado hoy? **pway**-dō a-par-**kar** a **es**-tay **la**-dō oy?	**Can I park on this side today?**

Road Conditions

French	German
The French traffic authorities signpost alternative routes on minor roads with green arrows (les flèches vertes), and in winter studded snow-tyres or chains may be compulsory.	The German traffic authorities signpost alternative routes on minor roads with blue signs, and in winter tyre chains may be compulsory.
WARNING! Pay attention to those Priorité à droite signs! Traffic from the right always has the right of way unless you see a sign saying Passage protégé. Both signs are shown inside the back cover of this book.	WARNING! Traffic from the right always has right of way unless you see the Priority Road sign shown inside the back cover of this book.

French	German
Est-ce qu'il y a beaucoup de circulation? *es-keel ya bŏ-koo duh seer-kŏŏ-la-syoñ?*	Ist viel Verkehr? *ist feel fer-**kayr**?*
Est-ce qu'il y a des bouchons? *es-keel ya day boo-shoñ?*	Gibt es Staus? *gipt es shtowz?*
Ce bouchon est provoqué par quoi? *suh boo-shoñ ay pro-vo-kay par kwah?*	Warum ist hier ein Stau? *vah-**room** ist heer ine shtow?*
Est-ce que les routes à ... sont dégagées? *es-kuh lay root a ... soñ day-ga-zhay?*	Sind die Straßen nach ... frei? *zint dee **shtrah**-sèn nahkh ... frye?*
La route sera dégagée quand? *la root suh-ra day-ga-zhay koñ?*	Wann wird die Straße wieder frei? *van virt dee **shtrah**-sè **vee**-dèr frye?*
Est-ce qu'il y a une déviation? *es-keel ya ŏŏn day-vyas-yoñ?*	Gibt es eine Umleitung? *gipt es **ine**-è **oom**-lye-toong?*
La vitesse est limitée à combien? *la vee-tes ay lee-mee-tay a koñ-byañ?*	Was ist die Höchstgeschwindigkeit? *vas ist dee **hur'khst**-gè-shvin-dikh-kite?*
Est-ce qu'il y a un péage sur cette autoroute? *es-keel ya uñ pay-azh sŏŏr set ŏ-tŏ-root?*	Ist diese Autobahn gebührenpflichtig? *ist **dee**-zè ow-tŏ-bahn gè-**bŏŏ**-ren-pflikh-tikh?*
Le péage, c'est combien? *luh pay-azh, se koñ-byañ?*	Wieviel kostet der Zoll? *vee-**feel** kos-tèt der tsol?*
Est-ce que le tunnel est ouvert? *es-kuh luh tŏŏ-nel e too-ver?*	Ist der Tunnel offen? *ist der **too**-nel o-fèn?*
Est-ce que le col est ouvert? *es-kuh luh kol e too-ver?*	Ist der Paß offen? *ist der pas o-fèn?*
Est-ce qu'il faut des chaînes? *es-keel fŏ day shen?*	Brauche ich Schneeketten? ***brow**-khè ikh **shnay**-ke-tèn?*

Spanish

WARNING! *In Spain traffic from the right has
priority unless otherwise indicated by the red and
yellow* Ceda el Paso *sign or the* Stop *sign shown
inside the back cover of this book.*

¿Hay mucho tráfico? *a-ee **moo**-chō **tra**-fee-kō?*	**Is the traffic heavy?**
¿Hay algún atasco? *a-ee al-**goon** a-**tas**-kō?*	**Are there any hold-ups (tie-ups)?**
¿Qué está produciendo este atasco? *kay es-**ta** pro-doo-**thyen**-dō **es**-tay a-**tas**-kō?*	**What's causing this hold-up?**
¿Están despejadas las carreteras a ...? *es-**tan** des-pay-**kha**-das las ka-rray-**tay**-ras a ...?*	**Are the roads to ... clear?**
¿Cuándo estará la carretera despejada? *kwan-dō es-ta-**ra** la ka-rray-**tay**-ra des-pay-**kha**-da?*	**When will the road be clear?**
¿Hay un desviamiento? *a-ee oon des-bya-**myen**-tō?*	**Is there a detour?**
¿Qué límite de velocidad hay? *kay **lee**-mee-tay day bay-lo-thee-**dad** a-ee?*	**What is the speed limit?**
¿Es esta una autopista de peaje? *es **es**-ta **oo**-na ow-tō-**pees**-ta day pay-a-**khay**?*	**Is there a toll on this motorway (highway)?**
¿Cuánto cuesta el peaje? *kwan-tō **kwes**-ta el pay-a-**khay**?*	**How much is the toll?**
¿Está abierto el túnel? *es-**ta** a-**byer**-tō el **too**-nel?*	**Is the tunnel open?**
¿Está abierto el puerto? *es-**ta** a-**byer**-tō el **pwer**-tō?*	**Is the pass open?**
¿Necesito cadenas? *nay-thay-**see**-tō ka-**day**-nas?*	**Do I need chains?**

Asking the Way

French	German
Pardon, Monsieur/Madame/ Mademoiselle, est-ce que vous pouvez m'aider, s'il vous plaît? *par-doñ, muh-syuh/ma-dam/ mad-mwa-zel, es-kuh voo poo-vay may-day, see voo play?*	Entschuldigung, können Sie mir bitte helfen? *ent-**shool**-di-goong, **kur'n**-èn zee meer **bit**-è **hel**-fèn?*
Je suis perdu *zhuh swee per-dōō*	Ich habe mich verlaufen *ikh **hah**-bè mikh ver-**low**-fèn*
Où est la station-service la plus proche? *oo ay la stas-yoñ-ser-vees la plōō prosh?*	Wo ist die nächste Tankstelle? *vō ist dee **naykh**-stè **tank**-shte-lè?*
Est-ce qu'il y a près d'ici une station-service ouverte toute la nuit? *es-keel ya pre dee-see ōōn stas-yoñ-ser-vees oo-vert toot la nwee?*	Gibt es hier in der Nähe eine Tankstelle, die nachts geöffnet ist? *gipt es heer in der **nay**-è **ine**-è **tank**-stel-è, dee nakhts ge-**ur'f**-nèt ist?*
Où sont les toilettes? *oo soñ lay twah-let?*	Wo sind die Toiletten? *vō zint dee tō-a-**le**-tèn?*
Comment est-ce que je rejoins l'autoroute/j'arrive au ferry/je sors de la zone à sens unique? *ko-moñ tes-kuh zhuh ruh-zhwañ lō-tō-root/zha-reev ō fe-ray/zhuh sor duh la zōn a soñ sōō-neek?*	Wie komme ich auf die Autobahn/zur Anlegestelle der Fähre/wieder aus dem Einbahnstraßensystem heraus? *vee **kom**-è ikh owf dee **ow**-tō-bahn/ tsoor **an**-lay-gè-shte-lè der **fay**-rè/**vee**-dèr ows daym **ine**-bahn-shtrah-sèn-sōōs-taym her-**ows**?*
Est-ce que c'est la bonne route pour aller à .../c'est la direction de...? *es-kuh say la bon root poor a-lay a .../say la dee-rek-syoñ duh...?*	Ist das die Straße nach ...?/Ist das der Weg nach (*countries, towns*)/zu (*buildings*) ...? *ist das dee **shtrah**-sè nahkh ...?/ist das der vayg nahkh/tsoo...?*
Quel est le meilleur chemin pour aller à .../la bonne route pour aller à...? *kel ay luh mye-yuhr shuh-mañ poor a-lay a .../la bon root poor a-lay a...?*	Wie komme ich am besten nach/zu ...?/Welche Straße geht nach/zu...? *vee **kom**-è ikh am **bes**-tèn nahkh/tsoo ...?/**vel**-khè **shtrah**-sè gayt nahkh/ tsoo...?*
Où va cette route? *oo va set root?*	Wo führt diese Straße hin? *vō fōōrt **dee**-zè **shtrah**-sè hin?*
Où est la poste la plus proche? *oo ay la post la plōō prosh?*	Wo ist das nächste Postamt? *vō ist das **naykh**-stè **post**-amt?*
... est à quelle distance? *... e ta kel dees-toñs?*	Wie weit ist...? *vee vite ist...?*
Est-ce que je tourne ici pour...? *es-kuh zhuh toorn ee-see poor...?*	Muß ich hier nach ... abbiegen? *moos ikh heer nahkh ... **ap**-bee-gèn?*

Asking the Way

Perdone, ¿puede usted ayudarme, por favor? per-**do**-nay, **pway**-day oos-**ted** a-yoo-**dar**-may, por fa-**bor**?	**Excuse me, can you help me please?**
Me he perdido may ay per-**dee**-dŏ	**I have lost my way**
¿Dónde está la gasolinera más próxima? **don**-day es-**ta** la ga-so-lee-**nay**-ra mas **prok**-see-ma?	**Where is the nearest service station?**
¿Hay una gasolinera abierta toda la noche por aquí cerca? **a**-ee **oo**-na ga-so-lee-**nay**-ra a-**byer**-ta **tŏ**-da la **no**-chay por a-**kee** ther-ka?	**Is there an all-night service station near here?**
¿Dónde están los servicios? **don**-day es-**tan** lŏs ser-**beeth**-yŏs?	**Where are the toilets?**
¿Por dónde se va a la autopista/al ferry/¿Cómo se sale de esta dirección única? por **don**-day say ba a la ow-tŏ-**pees**-ta/al **fe**-ree/**kŏ**-mŏ say **sa**-lay day es-ta dee-rek-**thyon oo**-nee-ka?	**How do I get on to the motorway (highway)/to the ferry/out of the one-way system?**
¿Es esta la carretera que va a .../¿Es este el camino de...? es es-ta la ka-rray-**tay**-ra kay ba a .../es es-**tay** el ka-**mee**-nŏ day...?	**Is this the right road for .../the way to...?**
¿Cuál es el mejor itinerario para ir a .../la mejor carretera para...? kwal es el may-**khor** ee-tee-nay-**ra**-ryŏ **pa**-ra eer a .../la may-**khor** ka-rray-**tay**-ra **pa**-ra...?	**Which is the best route to .../the right road for...?**
¿A dónde va esta carretera? a **don**-day ba es-ta ka-rray-**tay**-ra?	**Where does this road go to?**
¿Dónde está la oficina de correos más próxima? **don**-day es-**ta** la o-fee-**thee**-na day ko-**rray**-ŏs mas **prok**-see-ma?	**Where is the nearest post office?**
¿A qué distancia está...? a kay dees-**tan**-thya es-**ta**...?	**How far is it to...?**
¿Tuerzo aquí para ir a...? **twer**-thŏ a-**kee pa**-ra eer a...?	**Do I turn here for...?**

25

Asking the Way

French	German
Combien de temps faut-il pour y aller? *koñ byañ duh toñ fō-teel poor ee a-lay?*	Wie lange braucht man dahin? *vee lang-è browkht man dah-hin?*
Est-ce que je peux y arriver aujourd'hui? *es-kuh zhuh puh zee a-ree-vay ō-zhoor-dwee?*	Schaffe ich es heute noch dahin? *shaf-è ikh es hoy-tè nokh dah-hin?*
Est-ce que c'est loin? *es-kuh say lwañ?*	Ist es weit? *ist es vite?*
Est-ce qu'il y a un système de sens uniques? *es-keel ya uñ sees-tem duh soñ sōō-neek?*	Ist das eine Einbahnstraße? *ist das ine-è ine-bahn-shtrah-sè?*
Est-ce qu'on peut y aller à pied? *es-koñ puh tee a-lay a pyay?*	Kann man da zu Fuß hingehen? *kan man dah tsoo foos hin-gay-èn?*
Est-ce que vous pouvez me montrer sur la carte? *es-kuh voo poo-vay muh moñ-tray sōōr la kart?*	Können Sie mir das auf der Karte zeigen? *kur'n-èn zee meer das owf der kar-tè tsye-gèn?*

You may also want to ask for directions to:

French	German	Spanish	
l'aéroport *la-ay-ro-por*	der Flughafen *der flook-hah-fèn*	el aeropuerto *el a-ay-rō-pwer-tō*	**airport**
la galerie d'art *la gal-ree dar*	die Gemälde-galerie *dee gè-mel-dè-ga-lè-ree*	la galería de arte *la ga-le-ree-a day ar-tay*	**art gallery**
la banque *la boñk*	die Bank *dee bank*	el banco *el bang-kō*	**bank**
la plage *la plahzh*	der Strand *der shtrant*	la playa *la pla-ya*	**beach**
le café *luh ka-fay*	das Café *das ka-fay*	el café *el ka-fay*	**café**
le camping *luh koñ-peeng*	der Camping-platz *der kem-ping-plats*	el camping *el kam-peen*	**campsite**
l'église *lay-gleez*	die Kirche *dee kir-khè*	la iglesia *la ee-glay-sya*	**church**
le centre-ville *luh soñ-truh-veel*	das Stadtzen-trum *das shtat-tsen-troom*	el centro de la ciudad *el then-trō day la thyoo-dad*	**city centre**

Spanish

¿Cuánto se tarde en llegar? *kwan-tō say **tar**-day en lyay-**gar**?*	**How long will it take to get there?**
¿Me dará tiempo a llegar hoy? *may da-**ra tyem**-pō a lyay-**gar** oy?*	**Can I get there today?**
¿Está lejos? *es-**ta lay**-khōs?*	**Is it far?**
¿Es una zona de dirección única? *es **oo**-na **tho**-na day dee-rek-**thyon** **oo**-nee-ka?*	**Is the traffic one-way?**
¿Se puede ir andando? *say **pway**-day eer an-**dan**-dō?*	**Can you walk there?**
¿Puede indicármelo en el mapa? ***pway**-day een-dee-**kar**-may-lō en el **ma**-pa?*	**Can you show me on the map?**

French	German	Spanish	
le garage *luh ga-rahzh*	die Werkstatt *dee **verk**-shtat*	el garaje *el ga-**ra**-khay*	**garage**
l'hôpital *lō-pee-tal*	das Krankenhaus *das **krang**-kèn-hows*	el hospital *el os-pee-**tal***	**hospital**
l'hôtel *lō-tel*	das Hotel *das hō-**tel***	el hotel *el ō-**tel***	**hotel**
le parc *luh park*	der Park *der park*	el parque *el **par**-kay*	**park**
le restaurant *luh res-tō-roñ*	das Restaurant *das res-tō-**roñ***	el restaurante *el res-tow-**ran**-tay*	**restaurant**
la piscine *la pee-seen*	das Schwimm- bad *das **shvim**-baht*	la piscina *la pees-**thee**-na*	**swimming pool**
le téléphone *luh tay-lay-fon*	das Telefon *das tay-lay-**fōn***	el teléfono *el tay-**lay**-fo-nō*	**telephone**
la tour *la toor*	der Turm *der toorm*	la torre *la **to**-rray*	**tower**

Asking the Way
Things You May Hear

French	German
Vous allez tout droit/jusqu'à... *voo za-lay too drwah/zhōōs-ka...*	Gehen Sie immer geradeaus weiter/bis zu... *gay-èn zee i-mèr gè-rah-dè-ows vye-tèr/bis tsoo...*
Vous allez à droite/à gauche *voo za-lay a drwaht/à gōsh*	Gehen Sie nach rechts/nach links *gay-èn zee nahkh rekhts/nahkh links*
Tournez à droite/à gauche *toor-nay a drwaht/a gōsh*	Biegen Sie rechts ab/links ab *bee-gèn zee rekhts ap/links ap*
Prenez la première à droite/la deuxième à gauche *pruh-nay la pruhm-yer a drwaht/la duh-zyem a gōsh*	Nehmen Sie die erste (Straße) rechts/die zweite (Straße) links *nay-mèn zee dee ers-tè (shtrah-sè) rekhts/dee tsvye-tè (shtrah-sè) links*
Suivez la direction de... *swee-vay la dee-rek-syoñ duh...*	Folgen Sie den Schildern nach... *fol-gèn zee dayn shil-dèrn nahkh...*
Continuez jusqu'à/jusqu'à ce que/vers... *koñ-tee-nōō-ay zhōōs-ka/zhōōs-kas-kuh/ver...*	Gehen Sie immer geradeaus bis/bis/auf...zu *gay-èn zee i-mèr gè-rah-dè-ows bis/bis/owf...tsoo*
Traversez la rue/la place *tra-ver-say la rōō/la plas*	Gehen Sie über die Straße/den Platz *gay-èn zee ōō-bèr dee shtrah-sè/dayn plats*
Passez le passage à niveau/le pont *pa-say luh pa-sazh a nee-vō/luh poñ*	Gehen Sie über den Bahnübergang/die Brücke *gay-èn zee ōō-bèr dayn bahn-ōō-bèr-gang/dee brōō-kè*
C'est au croisement/après les feux/par là *se tō krwahz-moñ/a-pre lay fuh/par la*	Es ist an der Kreuzung/nach der Ampel/da drüben *es ist an der kroy-tsoong/nahkh der am-pèl/da drōō-bèn*
C'est juste après le coin/en face de l'église *se zhōōst a-pre luh kwañ/toñ fas duh lay-gleez*	Es ist um die Ecke/gegenüber der Kirche *es ist oom dee e-kè/gay-gèn-ōō-bèr der kir-khè*
C'est à côté du théâtre/à l'étage au-dessus *se ta kō-tay dōō tay-ah-truh/ta lay-tahzh ōd-sōō*	Es ist beim Theater/im nächsten Stock *es ist bime tay-ah-tèr/im naykh-stèn shtok*
Il faut que vous repartiez dans l'autre sens jusqu'à... *eel fō kuh voo ruh-par-tyay doñ lō-truh soñs zhōōs-ka...*	Sie müssen umkehren und zu... zurückgehen *zee mōō-sèn oom-kay-rèn oont tsoo... tsoo-rōōk-gay-èn*

Spanish

Vaya recto/hasta... *ba-ya **rek**-tō/**as**-ta...*	**You go straight ahead/as far as...**
Vaya a la derecha/a la izquierda *ba-ya a la day-**ray**-cha/a la eeth-**kyer**-da*	**You go right/left**
Tuerza *or* gire a la derecha/a la izquierda ***twer**-tha or **khee**-ray a la day-**ray**-cha/a la eeth-**kyer**-da*	**Turn right/left**
Coja la primera (calle) a la derecha/la segunda (carretera) a la izquierda *ko-kha la pree-**may**-ra (**ka**-lyay) a la day-**ray**-cha/la say-**goon**-da (ka-rray-**tay**-ra) a la eeth-**kyer**-da*	**Take the first (street) on the right/the second (road) on the left**
Siga las señales *or* indicaciones de... ***see**-ga las say-**nya**-lays *or* een-dee-ka-**thyo**-nays day...*	**Follow the signs for...**
Siga hasta/hasta que/hacia... ***see**-ga **as**-ta/**as**-ta kay/**a**-thya...*	**Keep going straight ahead as far as/until/towards...**
Cruce la calle/la plaza ***kroo**-thay la **ka**-lyay/la **pla**-tha*	**Cross the street/the square**
Cruce el paso a nivel/el puente ***kroo**-thay el **pa**-sō a nee-**bel**/el **pwen**-tay*	**Cross over the level crossing/the bridge**
Está en el cruce/después del semáforo/allá *es-**ta** en el **kroo**-thay/des-**pways** del say-**ma**-fo-rō/a-**lya***	**It's at the junction (intersection)/after the traffic lights/over there**
Está al dar la vuelta en la esquina/frente a la iglesia *es-**ta** al dar la **bwel**-ta en la es-**kee**-na/**fren**-tay a la ee-**glay**-sya*	**It's around the corner/opposite the church**
Está junto al teatro/en el próximo piso *es-**ta khoon**-tō al tay-**a**-trō/en el **prok**-see-mō **pee**-sō*	**It's next to the theatre/on the next floor**
Tiene que dar la vuelta y volver a... ***tyay**-nay kay dar la **bwel**-ta ee bol-**ber** a...*	**You'll have to turn round and go back to...**

Breakdowns

French	German
You should take a red warning triangle with you in case of any breakdowns or accidents.	You should take a red warning triangle and a warning light with you in case of any breakdowns or accidents.
Ma voiture est en panne *ma vwah-tŌŌr e toñ pan*	Ich habe eine Autopanne *ikh **hah**-bè ine-è **ow**-tŌ-**pa**-nè*
Ma voiture ne démarre pas *ma vwah-tŌŌr nuh day-mar pa*	Mein Auto springt nicht an *mine **ow**-tŌ shpringt nikht an*
Ma voiture est en panne d'essence *ma vwah-tŌŌr e toñ pan de-soñs*	Ich habe kein Benzin mehr *ikh **hah**-bè kine ben-**tseen** mayr*
Ma voiture est à ... kilomètres d'ici *ma vwah-tŌŌr e ta ... kee-lō-me-truh dee-see*	Mein Auto steht ... Kilometer von hier entfernt *mine **ow**-tŌ shtayt ... ki-lō-**may**-tèr fon heer ent-**fernt***
Est-ce que vous pouvez m'emmener au garage le plus proche? *es-kuh voo poo-vay moñ-muh-nay ō ga-razh luh plŌŌ prosh?*	Können Sie mich zur nächsten Werkstatt bringen? ***kur'n**-èn zee toor **naykh**-stèn **verk**-shtat **bring**-èn?*
Est-ce que vous pouvez me remorquer/me donner un bidon d'essence? *es-kuh voo poo-vay muh ruh-mor-kay/muh do-nay uñ bee-doñ de-soñs?*	Können Sie mich abschleppen/mir einen Kanister Benzin geben? ***kur'n**-èn zee mikh **ap**-shlep-èn/meer **ine**-èn ka-**nis**-ter ben-**tseen** **gay**-bèn?*
Est-ce que vous pouvez envoyer un mécanicien/une dépanneuse? *es-kuh voo poo-vay oñ-vwah-yay uñ may-ka-nee-syañ/ŌŌn day-pa-nuhz?*	Können Sie mir einen Mechaniker/einen Abschleppwagen schicken? ***kur'n**-èn zee meer **ine**-èn mekh-**ah**-ni-kèr/**ine**-èn **ap**-shlep-vah-gèn **shi**-kèn?*
Est-ce que vous pouvez réparer (provisoirement) ma voiture? *es-kuh voo poo-vay ray-pa-ray (pro-vee-zwar-moñ) ma vwah-tŌŌr?*	Können Sie mein Auto (provisorisch) reparieren? ***kur'n**-èn zee mine **ow**-tŌ (pro-vi-**zor**-ish) re-pa-**ree**-rèn?*
Est-ce que vous pouvez remplacer l'essuie-glace? *es-kuh voo poo-vay roñ-pla-say les-wee-glas?*	Können Sie den Scheibenwischer auswechseln? ***kur'n**-èn zee dayn **shye**-bèn-vish-èr **ows**-vekh-sèln?*
Est-ce que vous pouvez le faire aujourd'hui/le faire pendant que j'attends? *es-kuh voo poo-vay luh fer ō-zhoor-dwee/luh fer poñ-doñ kuh zha-toñ?*	Können Sie es noch heute machen?/Kann ich darauf warten? ***kur'n**-èn zee es nokh **hoy**-tè **makh**-èn?/kan ikh da-**rowf** **var**-tèn?*
Mon/ma ... est abimé(e), où est-ce que je peux le/la faire réparer? *moñ/ma ... e ta-bee-may, oo es-kuh zhuh puh luh/la fer ray-pa-ray?*	An meinem Wagen ist der/die/das ... kaputt. Wo kann ich das repariert bekommen? *an **mine**-èm **vah**-gèn ist der/dee/das ... ka-**poot**. vō kan ikh das re-pa-**reert** bè-**kom**-èn?*

Spanish

You should take a red warning triangle with you in case of any breakdowns or accidents.

He tenido una avería ay tay-**nee**-dŏ **oo**-na a-bay-**ree**-a	**My car has broken down**
No me arranca el coche nŏ may a-**rrang**-ka el **ko**-chay	**My car won't start**
Me he quedado sin gasolina may ay kay-**da**-dŏ seen ga-sŏ-**lee**-na	**I have run out of petrol (gas)**
El coche está a ... kilómetros de aquí el **ko**-chay es-**ta** a ... kee-**lo**-may-trŏs day a-**kee**	**My car is ... km from here**
¿Puede llevarme al garaje más próximo? **pway**-day lyay-**bar**-may al ga-**ra**-khay mas **prok**-see-mŏ?	**Can you take me to the nearest garage?**
¿Puede remolcarme/darme una lata de gasolina? **pway**-day ray-mol-**kar**-may/**dar**-may **oo**-na **la**-ta day ga-sŏ-**lee**-na?	**Can you give me a tow/give me a can of petrol (gas)?**
¿Puede mandarme un mecánico/mandarme una grúa? **pway**-day man-**dar**-may oon may-**ka**-nee-kŏ/man-**dar**-may **oo**-na **groo**-a?	**Can you send a mechanic/a breakdown van (tow-truck)?**
¿Puede arreglarme (provisionalmente) el coche? **pway**-day a-rray-**glar**-may (pro-bee-syo-nal-**men**-tay) el **ko**-chay?	**Can you repair my car (for the time being)?**
¿Puede ponerme un limpiaparabrisas nuevo? **pway**-day po-**ner**-may oon leem-pya-pa-ra-**bree**-sas **nway**-bŏ?	**Can you replace the windscreen wiper?**
¿Puede hacerlo hoy mismo/hacerlo mientras espero? **pway**-day a-**ther**-lŏ oy **mees**-mŏ/ a-**ther**-lŏ **myen**-tras es-**pay**-rŏ?	**Can you do it today/do it while I wait?**
Se me ha estropeado ..., ¿dónde pueden arreglármelo? say may a es-tro-pay-**a**-do ..., **don**-day **pway**-den a-rray-**glar**-may-lŏ?	**My ... is damaged, where can I get it repaired?**

Breakdowns

French	German
J'ai besoin d'une nouvelle courroie de ventilateur *zhay buh-zwañ dōōn noo-vel koor-wah duh voñ-tee-la-tuhr*	Ich brauche einen neuen Keilriemen *ikh **brow**-khè **ine**-èn **noy**-èn **kile**-ree-mèn*
Il y a quelque chose qui ne va pas dans le/la . . . *eel ya kel-kuh shōz kee nuh va pa doñ luh/la . . .*	Mit dem/der . . . ist etwas nicht in Ordnung *mit dəym/der . . . ist **et**-vas nikht in **ort**-noong*
J'ai perdu la clé de contact *zhay per-dōō la klay duh koñ-takt*	Ich habe den Zündschlüssel verloren *ikh **hah**-bè dayn **tsōōnt**-shlōō-sel fer-**lō**-rèn*
Il y a quelque chose qui claque à l'arrière/à l'avant *eel ya kel-kuh shōz kee klak a lar-yer/a la-voñ*	Hinten/vorn im Wagen klappert etwas ***hin**-tèn/forn im **vah**-gèn **klap**-èrt **et**-vas*
Il y a quelque chose qui grince sur le côté gauche/sur le côté droit *eel ya kel-kuh shōz kee grañs sōōr luh kō-tay gōsh/sōōr luh kō-tay drwah*	Links/rechts im Wagen quietscht etwas *links/rekhts im **vah**-gèn kveetsht **et**-vas*
Ça le fait de temps en temps/tout le temps *sa luh fay duh toñ zoñ toñ/too luh toñ*	Es tritt ab und zu auf/es ist ständig da *es trit ap oont tsoo owf/es ist **shten**-dikh da*
J'ai crevé/la batterie est à plat *zhay kruh-vay/la ba-trœ e ta pla*	Ich habe einen Platten/die Batterie ist leer *ikh **hah**-bè **ine**-èn **plat**-èn/dee ba-tè-**ree** ist **lay**-èr*
Mon pare-brise est cassé *moñ par-breez e ka-say*	Die Windschutzscheibe ist gesprungen *dee **vint**-shoots-shye-bè ist gè-**shproong**-èn*
Le moteur chauffe *luh mo-tuhr shōf*	Der Motor wird zu heiß *der **mō**-tor virt tsoo hise*
Il y a une fuite dans le radiateur *eel ya ōōn fweet doñ luh rad-ya-tuhr*	Der Kühler ist leck *der **kōō**-lèr ist lek*
C'est un fusible qui est grillé *se tuñ fōō-zee-bluh kee e gree-yay*	Eine Sicherung ist durchgebrannt ***ine**-è **zi**-khè-roong ist **doorkh**-gè-brant*
Le pot d'échappement est tombé *luh pō day-shap-moñ e toñ-bay*	Der Auspuff ist abgebrochen *der **ows**-poof ist **ap**-gè-bro-khèn*
Il y a un mauvais contact *eel ya uñ mō-vay koñ-takt*	Da ist irgendwo ein Wackelkontakt *da ist **ir**-gent-vō ine **va**-kèl-kon-takt*
Qu'est-ce qui ne marche pas? *kes-kee nuh marsh pa?*	Was ist es? *vas ist es?*
Est-ce que c'est grave? *es-kuh say grav?*	Ist es etwas Ernstes? *ist es **et**-vas **ern**-stès?*

Spanish

Necesito una correa de ventilador *nay-thay-**see**-tō **oo**-na ko-**rray**-a day ben-tee-la-**dor***	**I need a new fan belt**
El/la ... no va bien *el/la ... no ba byen*	**Something is wrong with the...**
He perdido la llave de contacto *ay per-**dee**-dō la **lya**-bay day kon-**tak**-tō*	**I have lost the ignition key**
Hay un ruido en la parte de atrás/ adelante *a-ee oon **rwee**-dō en la **par**-tay day a-**tras**/a-day-**lan**-tay*	**There is a rattle coming from the back/front**
Hay un chirrido en el lado izquierdo/en el lado derecho *a-ee oon chee-**rree**-dō en el **la**-dō eeth-**kyer**-dō/en el **la**-dō day-**ray**-chō*	**There is a squeak coming from the left-hand side/right-hand side**
Es intermitente/continuo *es een-ter-mee-**ten**-tay/kon-**tee**-noo-ō*	**It is intermittent/continuous**
Tengo una rueda pinchada/La batería está descargada ***teng**-gō **oo**-na **rway**-da peen-**cha**-da/ la ba-tay-**ree**-a es-**ta** des-kar-**ga**-da*	**I have a flat tire/battery**
El parabrisas estalló en pedazos *el pa-ra-**bree**-sas es-ta-**lyó** en pay-**da**-thōs*	**The windscreen (windshield) has shattered**
El motor se calienta *el mō-**tor** say ka-**lyen**-ta*	**The engine's overheating**
El radiador pierde agua *el ra-dya-**dor** **pyer**-day **a**-gwa*	**There's a leak in the radiator**
Se ha fundido un fusible *say a foon-**dee**-dō oon foo-**see**-blay*	**I've blown a fuse**
He perdido el tubo de escape *ay per-**dee**-dō el **too**-bō day es-**ka**-pay*	**The exhaust has fallen off**
Hay un cable que hace mal contacto *a-ee oon **ka**-blay kay **a**-thay mal kon-**tak**-tō*	**There's a bad connection**
¿Que le pasa? *kay lay **pa**-sa?*	**What is wrong with it?**
¿Es muy seria la avería? *es mwee **se**-rya la a-bay-**ree**-a?*	**Is it serious?**

Breakdowns

French	German
Vous pouvez le réparer quand? *voo poo-vay luh ray-pa-ray koñ?*	Wie schnell könnten Sie es machen? *vee shnel **kur'n**-tèn zee es **makh**-èn?*
Faites seulement les réparations vraiment nécessaires, s'il vous plaît *fet suhl-moñ lay ray-pa-ras-yoñ vray-moñ nay-se-ser, see voo play*	Bitte machen Sie nur das Nötigste an Reparaturen ***bit*-è **makh**-èn zee noor das **nur'**-tikh-stè an re-pa-ra-**too**-rèn*
Elle sera prête quand? *el suh-ra pret koñ?*	Wann ist es fertig? *van ist es **fer**-tikh?*
Ça coûtera combien? *sa koo-tra koñ-byañ?*	Wieviel kostet es? *vee-**feel** kos-tèt es?*
Est-ce que je peux avoir une facture détaillée pour ma compagnie d'assurance? *es-kuh zhuh puh za-vwar ōōn fak-tōōr day-tye-yay poor ma koñ-pan-yee da-sōō-roñs?*	Kann ich eine detaillierte Aufstellung für meine Versicherung haben? *kan ikh **ine**-è day-ta-**yeer**-tè **owf**-shtel-oong fōōr **mine**-è fer-**zi**-khè-roong **hah**-bèn?*

Things You May Hear

Je ne peux pas vous le faire aujourd'hui *zhuh nuh puh pa voo luh fer ō-zhoor-dwee*	Das kann ich heute nicht mehr machen *das kan ikh **hoy**-tè nikht mayr **makh**-èn*
Je peux vous le faire tout de suite *zhuh puh voo luh fer toot sweet*	Das kann ich gleich machen *das kan ikh glyekh **makh**-èn*
Ça prendra juste quelques instants *sa proñ-dra zhōōst kel-kuh zañ-stoñ*	Das ist in ein paar Minuten gemacht *das ist in ine pahr mi-**noo**-tèn gè-**makht***
Ça prendra deux jours *sa proñ-dra duh zhoor*	Das dauert zwei Tage *das **dow**-èrt tsvye **tah**-gè*
C'est dangereux *se doñ-zhuh-ruh*	So können Sie nicht fahren. Das ist zu gefährlich *zō **kur'n**-èn zee nikht **fah**-rèn. das ist tsoo gè-**fayr**-likh*
Il faut changer le/la... *eel fō shoñ-zhay luh/la...*	Sie brauchen einen neuen/eine neue/ein neues... *zee **brow**-khèn **ine**-èn **noy**-èn/**ine**-è **noy**-è/ine **noy**-ès...*
Il faut faire venir les pièces *eel fō fer vuh-neer lay pyes*	Ich muß die Ersatzteile erst bestellen *ikh moos dee er-**zats**-tye-lè ayrst be-**shtel**-èn*
Ça vous coûtera... *sa voo koo-tra...*	Das kostet... *das **kos**-tèt...*

Breakdowns

¿Cuánto tardará en hacerlo? *kwan-tō tar-da-ra en a-ther-lō?*	**How soon can you do it?**
Arregle sólo lo imprescindible *a-rray-glay sō-lō lō eem-pres-theen-dee-blay*	**Please do only the essential repairs**
¿Cuándo estará listo? *kwan-dō es-ta-ra lees-tō?*	**When will it be ready?**
¿Cuánto costará? *kwan-tō kos-ta-ra?*	**How much will it cost?**
¿Me da una factura completa para la compañía de seguros? *may da oo-na fak-too-ra kom-play-ta pa-ra la kom-pa-nyee-a day say-goo-rōs?*	**Can I have an itemized bill for my insurance company?**

Things You May Hear

No puedo hacerlo hoy *nō pway-dō a-ther-lō oy*	**I can't do it today**
Puedo hacerlo ahora mismo *pway-dō a-ther-lō a-o-ra mees-mō*	**I can do it straight away**
Sólo tardaré unos minutos *sō-lō tar-da-ray oo-nōs mee-noo-tōs*	**It will only take a few minutes**
Tardaremos dos días *tar-da-ray-mōs dōs dee-as*	**It will take two days**
Es peligroso de conducir *es pay-lee-grō-sō day kon-doo-theer*	**It's not safe to drive**
Necesita un nuevo/una nueva... *nay-thay-see-ta oon nway-bō/oo-na nway-ba...*	**You need a new...**
Tengo que mandar a pedir las piezas *teng-gō kay man-dar a pay-deer las pyay-thas*	**I have to send away for the parts**
Serán... *se-ran...*	**It will cost...**

35

Parts of the Car

French	German	Spanish	
l'accélérateur *lak-say-lay-ra-tuhr*	das Gaspedal *das **gahs**-pe-dahl*	el acelerador *el a-thay-lay-ra-**dor***	**accelerator**
le filtre à air *luh feel-tra er*	das Luftfilter *das **looft**-fil-tèr*	el filtro de aire *el **feel**-trŏ day **a**-ee-ray*	**air filter**
l'alternateur *lal-ter-na-tuhr*	die Lichtma- schine *dee **likht**-ma-shee-nè*	el alternador *el al-ter-na-**dor***	**alternator**
la transmission automatique *la troñz-mee-syoñ ŏ-tŏ-ma-teek*	die Automatik *dee ow-tŏ-**mah**-tik*	la transmisión automática *la trans-mee-**syon** ow-tŏ-**ma**-tee-ka*	**automatic trans- mission**
la batterie *la ba-tree*	die Batterie *dee ba-tè-**ree***	la batería *la ba-te-**ree**-a*	**battery**
la tête de bielle *la tet duh byel*	der Pleuelfuß *der **ploy**-èl-foos*	la cabeza de biela *la ka-**bay**-tha day **byay**-la*	**big end**
le capot *luh ka-pŏ*	die Motorhaube *dee **mŏ**-tor-how-bè*	el capó *el ka-**pŏ***	**bonnet (hood)**
le câble de frein *luh kah-bluh duh frañ*	das Bremsseil *das **brems**-zile*	el cable de freno *el **ka**-blay day **fray**-nŏ*	**brake cable**
le carter de frein *luh kar-ter duh frañ*	der Bremssattel *der **brems**-zat-èl*	el cárter de freno *el **kar**-ter day **fray**-nŏ*	**brake caliper**
le liquide de frein *luh lee-keed duh frañ*	die Bremsflüs- sigkeit *dee **brems**-flŏŏs-ikh-kite*	el líquido de frenos *el **lee**-kee-do day **fray**-nŏs*	**brake fluid**
le flexible de frein *luh flek-see-bluh duh frañ*	die Bremsleitung *dee **brems**-lye-toong*	la tubería de freno *la too-be-**ree**-a day **fray**-nŏ*	**brake hose**
le stop *luh stop*	das Bremslicht *das **brems**-likht*	la luz de freno *la looth day **fray**-nŏ*	**brake light**
la garniture de frein *la gar-nee-tŏŏr de frañ*	der Bremsbelag *der **brems**-bè-lahk*	el forro de freno *el **fo**-rrŏ day **fray**-nŏ*	**brake lining**
le patin de frein *luh pa-tañ duh frañ*	der Bremsklotz *der **brems**-klots*	la zapata de freno *la tha-**pa**-ta day **fray**-nŏ*	**brake pad**
l'arbre à cames *lar-bruh a kam*	die Nockenwelle *dee **nok**-èn-vel-è*	el eje de levas *el **e**-khay day **lay**-bas*	**cam(shaft)**

Parts of the Car

French	German	Spanish	
le carburateur *luh kar-bōō-ra-tuhr*	der Vergaser *der fer-**gah**-zèr*	el carburador *el kar-boo-ra-**dor***	**carburetor**
le starter *luh star-ter*	der Choke *der chōk*	el aire *el **a**-ee-ray*	**choke**
l'embrayage *loñ-bre-yazh*	die Kupplung *dee **koop**-loong*	el embrague *el em-**bra**-gay*	**clutch**
le disque d'embrayage *luh deesk doñ-bre-yazh*	die Kupplungslamelle *dee **koop**-loongs-la-me-lè*	el disco de embrague *el **dees**-kō day em-**bra**-gay*	**clutch plate**
le condensateur *luh koñ-doñ-sa-tuhr*	der Kondensator *der kon-den-**sah**-tor*	el condensador *el kon-den-sa-**dor***	**condenser**
le vilebrequin *luh veel-bruh-kañ*	die Kurbelwelle *dee **koor**-bèl-vel-è*	el eje del cigüeñal *el **e**-khay del thee-gway-**nyal***	**crankshaft**
le pneu à structure diagonale/ radiale *luh pnuh a strōōk-tōōr dya-go-nal/ ra-dyal*	der Diagonal-/ Gürtelreifen *der dee-a-go-**nahl**-/gōōr-tèl-rye-fèn*	el neumático en diagonal/radial *el nay-oo-**ma**-tee-kō en dee-a-go-**nal**/ra-**dyal***	**cross-ply/ radial tyre (tire)**
la culasse *la kōō-las*	der Zylinderkopf *der tsōō-**lin**-dèr-kopf*	la culata de cilindros *la koo-**la**-ta day thee-**leen**-drōs*	**cylinder head**
le frein à disque/ à tambour *luh frañ a deesk/a toñ-boor*	die Scheiben-/ Trommelbremse *dee **shye**-bèn-/**trom**-èl-brem-sè*	el freno de disco/de tambor *el **fray**-nō day **dees**-kō/day tam-**bor***	**disc/drum brake**
le delco *luh del-kō*	der Verteiler *der fer-**tye**-lèr*	el distribuidor *el dees-tree-bwee-**dor***	**distributor**
la tête de delco *la tet duh del-kō*	die Verteilerkappe *dee fer-**tye**-lèr-ka-pè*	la tapa del distribuidor *la **ta**-pa del dees-tree-bwee-**dor***	**distributor cap**
l'arbre de commande *lar-bruh duh kō-moñd*	die Antriebswelle *dee **an**-treeps-vel-è*	el eje propulsor *el **e**-khay pro-pool-**sor***	**drive shaft**
la dynamo *la dee-na-mō*	die Lichtmaschine *dee **likht**-ma-shee-nè*	la dínamo *la **dee**-na-mō*	**dynamo**

Parts of the Car

French	German	Spanish	
la prise du circuit électrique de caravane *la preez dōō seer-kwee tay-lek-treek duh ka-ra-van*	der siebenpolige Stecker *der zee-bèn-pō-li-gè shtek-èr*	la clavija de siete polos *la kla-bee-kha day syay-tay po-lōs*	**electric connection for towing**
le moteur *luh mō-tuhr*	der Motor *der mō-tor*	el motor *el mo-tor*	**engine**
le tuyau d'échappement *luh twee-yō day-shap-moñ*	das Auspuffrohr *das ows-poof-rōr*	el tubo de escape *el too-bō day es-ka-pay*	**exhaust pipe**
la courroie de ventilateur *la koor-wah duh voñ-tee-la-tuhr*	der Keilriemen *der kile-ree-mèn*	la correa del ventilador *la ko-rray-a del ben-tee-la-dor*	**fan belt**
le pont avant/arrière *luh poñ ta-voñ/tar-yer*	die Vorder-/Hinterachse *dee for-dèr-/hin-tèr-ak-sè*	el eje delantero/trasero *el e-khay day-lan-tay-rō/tra-say-rō*	**front/rear axle**
la canalisation de carburant *la ka-na-lee-zas-yoñ duh kar-bōō-roñ*	die Benzin-(zufuhr)-leitung *dee ben-tseen-(-tsoo-foo-èr)-lye-toong*	el tubo de gasolina *el too-bō day ga-so-lee-na*	**fuel pipe**
la pompe pour l'essence *la poñp poor le-soñs*	die Benzinpumpe *dee ben-tseen-poom-pè*	la bomba de la gasolina *la bom-ba day la ga-so-lee-na*	**fuel pump**
le réservoir de carburant *luh ray-zerv-wahr duh kar-bōō-roñ*	der (Benzin)tank *der (ben-tseen-)tank*	el depósito de gasolina *el day-po-see-tō day ga-so-lee-na*	**fuel tank**
le fusible *luh fōō-zee-bluh*	die Sicherung *dee zikh-è-roong*	el fusible *el foo-see-blay*	**fuse**
le joint *luh zhwañ*	die Dichtung *dee dikh-toong*	la junta *la khoon-ta*	**gasket**
la boîte de vitesses *la bwaht duh vee-tes*	der Getriebe-kasten *der ge-tree-bè-kas-tèn*	la caja de cambios *la ka-kha day kam-byōs*	**gearbox**
le levier de vitesses *luh luh-vyay duh vee-tes*	der Schalthebel *der shalt-hay-bèl*	la palanca de cambios *la pa-lang-ka day kam-byōs*	**gear lever (shift)**
le frein à main *luh frañ a mañ*	die Handbremse *dee hant-brem-zè*	el freno de mano *el fray-nō day ma-nō*	**handbrake**

French	German	Spanish	
les phares *lay far*	die Scheinwerfer *dee **shine**-ver-fèr*	los faros *lōs **fa**-rōs*	**headlights**
le chauffage *luh shō-fazh*	die Heizung *dee **hye**-tsoong*	la calefacción *la ka-lay-fak-**thyon***	**heater**
le klaxon *luh klak-soñ*	die Hupe *dee **hoo**-pè*	el claxon *el **klak**-son*	**horn**
la durite *la dōō-reet*	der Schlauch *der shlowkh*	la manguera *la mang-**gay**-ra*	**hose**
l'allumage *la-lōō-mazh*	die Zündung *dee **tsōōn**-doong*	el encendido *el en-then-**dee**-dō*	**ignition**
le clignotant *luh kleen-yo-toñ*	der Blinker *der **bling**-kèr*	el intermitente *el een-ter-mee-**ten**-tay*	**indicator** **(turn** **indicator)**
le cric *luh kreek*	der Wagenheber *der **vah**-gèn-hay-bèr*	el gato *el **ga**-tō*	**jack**
la roue jockey *la roo zho-ke*	das Stützrad *das **shtōōts**-raht*	la rueda de maniobras *la **rway**-da day ma-**nyo**-bras*	**jockey wheel**
			muffler = **silencer**
le filtre à huile *luh feel-tra weel*	das Ölfilter *das **ur'l**-fil-tèr*	el filtro de aceite *el **feel**-trō day a-**the**-ee-tay*	**oil filter**
le manomètre d'huile *luh ma-nō-me-truh dweel*	der Öldruck- messer *der **ur'l**-drook- me-sèr*	el manómetro de aceite *el ma-**no**-may-trō day a-**the**-ee-tay*	**oil pressure** **gauge**
la pompe à huile *la poñp à weel*	die Ölpumpe *dee **ur'l**-poom-pè*	la bomba de aceite *la **bom**-ba day a-**the**-ee-tay*	**oil pump**
la bague d'étanchéité *la bag day-toñ- shay-ee-tay*	der Simmerring *der **zim**-èr-ring*	la junta de aceite *la **khoon**-ta day a-**the**-ee-tay*	**oil seal**
le piston *luh pees-toñ*	der Kolben *der **kol**-bèn*	el pistón *el pees-**ton***	**piston**
la tige de piston *la teezh duh pees-toñ*	die Kolbenstange *dee **kol**-bèn- shtang-è*	la barra del pistón *la **ba**-rra del pees-**ton***	**piston rod**
les vis platinées *lay vees pla-tee-nay*	die Unter- brecher- kontakte *dee **oon**-tèr- brekh-èr-kon- **tak**-tè*	los platinos *lōs pla-**tee**-nōs*	**points**

Parts of the Car

French	German	Spanish	
le radiateur *luh rad-ya-tuhr*	der Kühler *der **kōō**-lèr*	el radiador *el ra-dya-**dor***	**radiator**
le phare de recul *luh far duh ruh-kōōl*	der Rückfahr-scheinwerfer *der **rōōk**-fahr-shine-**ver**-fèr*	la luz de marcha atrás *la looth day **mar**-cha a-**tras***	**reversing light (back-up light)**
le rotor de delco *luh ro-tor duh del-kō*	der Verteiler-finger *der fer-**tye**-lèr-fing-èr*	el rotor del distribuidor *el ro-**tor** del dees-tree-bwee-**dor***	**rotor arm**
le tournevis *luh toor-nuh-vees*	der Schrau-benzieher *der **shrow**-bèn-tsee-èr*	el destornillador *el des-tor-nee-lya-**dor***	**screwdriver**
l'amortisseur *la-mor-tee-suhr*	der Stoßdämpfer *der **shtōs**-demp-fèr*	el amortiguador *el a-mor-tee-gwa-**dor***	**shock absorber**
le silencieux *luh see-loñs-yuh*	der Auspufftopf *der **ows**-poof-topf*	el silenciador *el see-len-thya-**dor***	**silencer (muffler)**
la roue de secours *la roo duh suh-koor*	der Reservereifen *der ray-**zer**-vè-rye-fèn*	la rueda de recambio *la **rway**-da day ray-**kam**-byo*	**spare wheel**
la bougie *la boo-zhee*	die Zündkerze *dee **tsōō**nt-ker-tsè*	la bujía *la boo-**khee**-a*	**spark plug**
le compteur *luh koñ-tuhr*	der Tachometer *der takh-ō-**may**-tèr*	el cuentakiló-metros *el kwen-ta-kee-**lo**-may-trōs*	**speedometer**
le stabilisateur *luh sta-bee-lee-za-tuhr*	der Stabilisator *der shta-bee-lee-**zah**-tor*	el estabilizador *el es-ta-bee-lee-tha-**dor***	**stabilizer**
le démarreur *luh day-ma-ruhr*	der Anlasser *der **an**-las-èr*	el motor de arranque *el mo-**tor** day a-**rrang**-kay*	**starter motor**
la direction *la dee-rek-syoñ*	die Lenkung *dee **leng**-koong*	la dirección *la dee-rek-**thyon***	**steering**
la suspension *la sōōs-poñs-yoñ*	die Aufhängung *dee **owf**-heng-oong*	la suspensión *la soos-pen-**syon***	**suspension**
la lanterne arrière *la loñ-tern ar-yer*	das Rücklicht *das **rōōk**-likht*	la luz trasera *la looth tra-**say**-ra*	**tail light**

French	German	Spanish	
la barre de remorque *la bar duh ruh-mork*	die Anhänger-kupplung *dee **an**-heng-èr-**koop**-loong*	la barra de remolque *la **ba**-rra day ray-**mol**-kay*	**towbar**
la boule pour le remorquage *la bool poor luh ruh-mor-kazh*	der Anhänger-zughaken *der **an**-heng-èr-tsook-**hah**-kèn*	la bola del remolcador *la **bo**-la del ray-mol-ka-**dor***	**towing ball**
l'armature pour le remorquage *lar-ma-tōōr poor luh ruh-mor-kazh*	die Anhänger-zuggabel *dee **an**-heng-èr-tsook-**gah**-bèl*	el soporte del remolcador *el so-**por**-tay del ray-mol-ka-**dor***	**towing bracket**
la remorque *la ruh-mork*	der Anhänger *der **an**-heng-èr*	el remolque *el ray-**mol**-kay*	**trailer**
la transmission *la troñs-mees-yoñ*	das Getriebe *das gè-**tree**-bè*	la transmisión *la trans-mee-**syon***	**transmission**
			turn indicator = indicator
la soupape *la soo-pap*	das Ventil *das ven-**teel***	la válvula *la **bal**-boo-la*	**valve**
le poussoir (de soupape) *luh poo-swar (duh soo-pap)*	der Stößel *der **shtur'**-sèl*	el alza-válvulas *el **al**-tha-**bal**-boo-las*	**valve adjuster**
la pompe à eau *la poñp a ō*	die Wasser-pumpe *dee **vas**-èr-poom-pè*	la bomba de agua *la **bom**-ba day a-gwa*	**water pump**
le pare-brise *luh par-breez*	die Wind-schutzscheibe *dee **vint**-shoots-shye-bè*	el parabrisas *el pa-ra-**bree**-zas*	**windscreen (windshield)**
le lave-glace *luh lav-glas*	die Scheiben-waschanlage *dee **shye**-bèn-vash-**an**-lah-gè*	el lavaparabrisas *el la-ba-pa-ra-**bree**-sas*	**windscreen washer**
les essuie-glace *lay zes-wee-glas*	die Scheiben-wischer *dee **shye**-ben-vish-èr*	los limpiapara-brisas *lōs leem-pya-pa-ra-**bree**-sas*	**windscreen wipers**
			windshield = windscreen
la clé à molette *la klay a mo-let*	der Schrauben-schlüssel *der **shrow**-bèn-shlōō-sèl*	la llave inglesa *la **lya**-bay eeng-**glay**-sa*	**wrench**

Accidents & the Police

French	German
Je suis désolé, Monsieur *zhuh swee day-zo-lay, muh-syuh*	Es tut mir sehr leid *es toot meer zayr lite*
Je n'ai pas vu le panneau *zhuh nay pa vōō luh pa-nō*	Ich habe das Signal nicht gesehen *ikh **hah**-bè das zig-**nahl** nikht gè-**zay**-èn*
Je ne connaissais pas ce règlement *zhuh nuh ko-ne-say pa suh reg-luh-moñ*	Ich wußte nichts von dieser Verkehrsregel *ikh **voo**-stè nikhts fon **dee**-zer fer-**kayrs**-ray-gèl*
Je n'ai pas compris le panneau *zhuh nay pa koñ-pree luh pa-nō*	Ich wußte nicht, was das Schild bedeutet *ikh **voo**-stè nikht, vas das shilt bè-**doy**-tèt*
Voilà mon permis *vwah-la moñ per-mee*	Hier ist mein Führerschein *heer ist mine **fōō**-rèr-shine*
Voilà ma carte verte *vwah-la ma kart vert*	Hier ist meine grüne Versicherungskarte *heer ist **mine**-è **grōō**-nè fer-**zikh**-è-roongs-kar-tè*
La contravention est de combien? *la koñ-tra-voñs-yoñ ay duh koñ-byañ?*	Wie hoch ist das Bußgeld? *vee hōkh ist das **boos**-gelt?*
Je n'ai pas assez. Est-ce que je peux payer au poste de police? *zhuh nay pa zas-ay. es-kuh zhuh puh pe-yay ō post duh po-lees?*	Ich habe soviel nicht bei mir. Kann ich auf dem Polizeirevier bezahlen? *ikh **hah**-bè zō-**feel** nikht bye meer. kan ikh owf daym po-li-**tsye**-re-veer bè-**tsah**-lèn?*
Je roulais à quatre-vingts kilomètres à l'heure *zhuh roo-le za kat-ruh-vañ kee-lō-met-ra luhr*	Ich bin mit achtzig Stundenkilometern gefahren *ikh bin mit **akh**-tsikh **shtoon**-dèn- kee-lō-**may**-tèrn gè-**fah**-rèn*
Il me suivait de trop près *eel muh swee-ve duh trō pre*	Er ist zu dicht aufgefahren *er ist tsoo dikht **owf**-gè-fah-rèn*
Je ne l'ai pas vu *zhuh nuh lay pa vōō*	Ich habe ihn nicht gesehen *ikh **hah**-bè een nikht gè-**zay**-èn*
Il conduisait trop vite *eel koñ-dwee-zay trō veet*	Er ist zu schnell gefahren *er ist tsoo shnel gè-**fah**-rèn*
Il ne s'est pas arrêté *eel nuh say pa za-re-tay*	Er hat nicht angehalten *er hat nikht **an**-gè-hal-tèn*
Il n'a pas respecté la priorité *eel na pa res-pek-tay la pree-o-ree-tay*	Er hat die Vorfahrt mißachtet *er hat dee **fōr**-fart mis-**akh**-tèt*
Il s'est arrêté brusquement *eel se ta-re-tay brōōsk-moñ*	Er hat plötzlich gebremst *er hat **plur'ts**-likh gè-**bremst***
Il a donné un coup de volant *eel a do-nay uñ koo duh vo-loñ*	Er ist ausgeschert *er ist **ows**-gè-shayrt*

Spanish

Lo siento mucho, agente *lō syen-tō moo-chō, a-khen-tay*	**I'm very sorry officer**
No ví la señal *nō bee la say-nyal*	**I did not see the signal**
No conocía esa norma *nō ko-nō-thee-a e-sa nor-ma*	**I did not know about that regulation**
No entendí el letrero *nō en-ten-dee el lay-tray-rō*	**I did not understand the sign**
Aquí está mi permiso de conducir *a-kee es-ta mee per-mee-sō day kon-doo-theer*	**Here is my driving license**
Aquí está mi carta verde *a-kee es-ta mee kar-ta ber-day*	**Here is my green card**
¿Cuánto es la multa? *kwan-tō es la mool-ta?*	**How much is the fine?**
No tengo suficiente. ¿Puedo pagar en la comisaría de policía? *nō teng-gō soo-fee-thyen-tay. pway-dō pa-gar en la ko-mee-sa-ree-a day po-lee-thee-a?*	**I haven't got that much. Can I pay at the police station?**
Iba a ochenta kilómetros por hora *ee-ba a o-chen-ta kee-lo-may-trōs por ō-ra*	**I was driving at 80 kmh**
Él estaba demasiado cerca *el es-ta-ba day-ma-sya-dō ther-ka*	**He was too close**
No le ví *nō lay bee*	**I did not see him**
Él iba demasiado rápido *el ee-ba day-ma-sya-dō ra-pee-dō*	**He was driving too fast**
Él no paró *el nō pa-rō*	**He did not stop**
No cedió el paso *no thay-dyō el pa-sō*	**He did not give way (yield)**
Se paró de repente *say pa-rō day ray-pen-tay*	**He stopped very suddenly**
Dió un volantazo *dyō oon bo-lan-ta-thō*	**He swerved**

Accidents & the Police

French	German
La voiture a tourné sans clignoter *la vwah-tōōr a toor-nay soñ* *kleen-yō-tay*	Das Auto hat gewendet, ohne Zeichen zu geben *das **ow**-tō hat gè-**ven**-dèt, **ō**-nè* ***tsye**-khèn tsoo **gay**-bèn*
Il m'est rentré dedans *eel may roñ-tray duh-doñ*	Er ist mir hineingefahren *er ist meer hin-**ine**-gè-fah-rèn*
Il m'a dépassé dans le virage *eel ma day-pa-say doñ luh vee-razh*	Er hat in einer Kurve überholt *er hat in **ine**-èr **koor**-vè ōō-bèr-**hōlt***
Il a brûlé un feu rouge *eel a brōō-lay uñ fuh roozh*	Er ist über die rote Ampel gefahren *er ist ōō-bèr dee **rō**-tè **am**-pèl* *gè-**fah**-rèn*
Le numéro de la voiture était ... *luh nōō-may-rō duh la vwah-tōōr* *ay-tay ...*	Seine Autonummer war ... ***zine**-è **ow**-tō-noo-mèr var ...*
La route était mouillée *la root ay-tay moo-yay*	Die Straße war naß *dee **shtrah**-sè var nas*
J'ai dérapé *zhay day-ra-pay*	Ich bin ins Schleudern gekommen *ikh bin ins **shloy**-dèrn gè-**ko**-mèn*
Mes freins ont lâché *may frañ oñ la-shay*	Meine Bremsen haben versagt ***mine**-è **brem**-zèn **hah**-bèn fer-**zahgt***
Un pneu a éclaté *uñ pnuh a ay-kla-tay*	Ich hatte eine Reifenpanne *ikh **ha**-tè **ine**-è **rye**-fèn-pa-nè*
Je n'ai pas pu m'arrêter à temps *zhuh nay pa pōō ma-re-tay a toñ*	Ich konnte nicht mehr rechtzeitig anhalten *ikh **kon**-tè nikht mayr **rekht**-tsye-tikh* ***an**-hal-tèn*
Quel est votre nom et votre adresse? *kel ay vot-ruh noñ ay vot-ra-dres?*	Geben Sie mir bitte Ihren Namen und Ihre Adresse ***gay**-bèn zee meer **bit**-è **ee**-rèn* ***nah**-mèn oont **ee**-rè a-**dres**-è*
Quel est le nom et l'adresse de votre compagnie d'assurances? *kel ay luh noñ ay la-dres duh vot-ruh* *koñ-pa-nyee da-sōō-roñs?*	Können Sie mir Namen und Adresse Ihrer Versicherung geben? ***kur'**-nèn zee meer **nah**-mèn oont* *a-**dres**-è **ee**-rèr fer-**zikh**-èr-oong* ***gay**-bèn?*
Nous devrions appeler la police *noo duh-vree-yoñ zap-lay la po-lees*	Wir sollten die Polizei rufen *veer **zol**-tèn dee po-li-**tsye** **roo**-fèn*

Accidents & the Police

El coche giró sin indicación *el **ko**-chay khee-**rō** seen* *een-dee-ka-**thyon***	**The car turned without signalling**
Se me echó encima *say may ay-**chō** en-**thee**-ma*	**He ran into me**
Adelantó en una curva *a-day-lan-**tō** en **oo**-na **koor**-ba*	**He overtook on a bend (passed on a curve)**
Se saltó un semáforo en rojo *say sal-**tō** oon say-**ma**-fō-rō en **rō**-khō*	**He went through a red light**
Su matrícula era ... *soo ma-**tree**-koo-la e-ra ...*	**His car number (license number) was ...**
La carretera estaba mojada *la ka-rray-**tay**-ra es-**ta**-ba mo-**kha**-da*	**The road was wet**
Patiné *pa-tee-**nay***	**I skidded**
Me fallaron los frenos *may fa-**lya**-ron lōs **fray**-nōs*	**My brakes failed**
Se me reventó una rueda *say may ray-ben-**tō** oo-na **rway**-da*	**I had a blow-out**
No pude parar a tiempo *no **poo**-day pa-**rar** a **tyem**-pō*	**I could not stop in time**
Su nombre y dirección por favor? *soo **nom**-bray ee dee-rek-**thyon** por fa-**bor**?*	**What is your name and address?**
Deme el nombre y dirección de su compañía de seguros ***day**-may el **nom**-bray ee dee-rek-**thyon** day soo kom-pa-**nyee**-a day say-**goo**-ros*	**What is the name and address of your insurance company?**
Deberíamos llamar a la policía *day-bay-**ree**-a-mōs lya-**mar** a la po-lee-**thee**-a*	**We should call the police**

Camping

French	German

Camping in France is a very sophisticated activity, and there is an enormous number of campsites, many with excellent facilities. The local syndicat d'initiative may be able to help if you can't find a site. Off-site camping is allowed (except in the South because of the danger of fire), provided permission has been obtained from the relevant authority (land-owner, police, etc). An International Camping Carnet is useful as proof of identity as well as providing third party insurance. It is necessary at certain sites; at others, reductions may be given to Carnet holders.

There are numerous campsites throughout Germany, Austria and Switzerland, many with excellent facilities. If you have difficulty in finding a site the local Fremdenverkehrsamt may be able to help. Off-site camping is allowed, provided permission has been obtained from the landowner or local police. An International Camping Carnet provides proof of identity, as well as third-party insurance.

Est-ce que nous pouvons camper quelque part dans les environs? *es-kuh noo poo-voñ koñ-pay kel-kuh par doñ lay zoñ-vee-roñ?*	Können wir irgendwo hier in der Nähe zelten? ***kur'n**-èn veer **ir**-gènt-võ heer in der **nay**-è **tselt**-èn?*
Est-ce que nous pouvons camper ici cette nuit? *es-kuh noo poo-voñ koñ-pay ee-see set nwee?*	Können wir heute nacht hier zelten? ***kur'n**-èn veer **hoy**-tè nakht heer **tselt**-èn?*
Est-ce qu'il y a des douches? *es-keel ya day doosh?*	Haben Sie Duschen? ***hah**-bèn zee **doosh**-èn?*
Est-ce qu'il faut payer l'eau chaude/les douches en plus? *es-keel fõ pe-yay lõ shõd/lay doosh oñ plõõs?*	Müssen wir für heißes Wasser/für das Duschen extra bezahlen? ***mõõs**-èn veer fõõr **hye**-sès **vas**-èr/fõõr das **doosh**-èn **eks**-tra bè-**tsah**-lèn?*
Est-ce que je vous règle maintenant ou en partant? *es-kuh zhuh voo reg-luh mañ-tuh-noñ oo oñ par-toñ?*	Muß ich jetzt bezahlen, oder erst bei der Abreise? *moos ikh yetst bè-**tsah**-lèn **õ**-dèr erst bye der **ap**-rye-zè?*
Où est-ce que nous pouvons mettre notre tente/caravane? *õõ es-kuh noo poo-voñ met-ruh not-ruh toñt/ka-ra-van?*	Wo können wir unser Zelt aufschlagen/unseren Wohnwagen abstellen? *võ **kur'n**-èn veer **oon**-zèr tselt **owf**-shlah-gèn/**oon**-zèr-èn **võn**-vah-gèn **ab**-shtel-èn?*
Est-ce que je peux mettre la voiture juste à côté de la tente? *es-kuh zhuh puh met-ruh la vwah-tõõr zhõõst a kõ-tay duh la toñt?*	Kann ich meinen Wagen neben dem Zelt abstellen? *kan ikh **mine**-èn **vah**-gèn **nay**-bèn daym tselt **ab**-shtel-èn?*
Est-ce qu'il y a des installations pour branchements électriques? *es-keel ya day zan-sta-la-syoñ poor broñsh-moñ ay-lek-treek?*	Kann man hier seinen Wohnwagen ans Netz anschließen? *kan man heer **sine**-èn **võn**-vah-gèn ans nets **an**-shlee-sèn?*
Nous souhaitons rester trois nuits/jusqu'à mercredi/jusqu'à la semaine prochaine *noo swe-toñ res-tay trwah nwee/zhõõs-ka mer-kruh-dee/zhõõs-ka la smen pro-shen*	Wir wollen drei Nächte/bis Mittwoch/bis irgendwann nächste Woche bleiben *veer **vol**-èn drye **nekh**-tè/bis **mit**-vokh/bis **ir**-gènt-van **naykh**-stè **vo**-khe **blye**-bèn*

Camping

There are numerous campsites on the Costa Brava and elsewhere on the Spanish coast; there are not many inland. These are classified according to the service and facilities which they provide, and this classification and prices should be on display near the entrance or reception office. The local Oficina de Información y Turismo should be able to help if you can't find a site. Off-site camping is allowed with the permission of local authorities or the landowner; however, there is a number of regulations governing where camping is or is not allowed, so check with the authorities first. An International Camping Carnet provides proof of identity, as well as third-party insurance.

¿Hay algún sitio para acampar cerca de aquí? *a-ee al-**goon** see-tyŏ **pa**-ra a-kam-**par ther**-ka day a-**kee**?*	**Is there anywhere for us to camp near here?**
¿Podemos acampar aquí esta noche? *po-**day**-mos a-kam-**par** a-**kee es**-ta **no**-chay?*	**Can we camp here tonight?**
¿Hay duchas? *a-ee **doo**-chas?*	**Are there showers?**
¿Hay que pagar extra por el agua caliente/las duchas? *a-ee kay pa-**gar ek**-stra por el **a**-gwa ka-**lyen**-tay/las **doo**-chas?*	**Do we pay extra for hot water/showers?**
¿Tengo que pagar ahora o al marcharme? *teng-gŏ kay pa-**gar** a-**ŏ**-ra ŏ al mar-**char**-may?*	**Do I pay now or when I leave?**
¿Dónde podemos poner la tienda/la caravana? *don-day po-**day**-mos po-**ner** la **tyen**-da/la ka-ra-**ba**-na?*	**Where can we put our tent/trailer?**
¿Puedo aparcar el coche al lado de la tienda? ***pway**-dŏ a-par-**kar** el **ko**-chay al **la**-dŏ day la **tyen**-da?*	**Can I park the car next to the tent?**
¿Se puede conectar con el circuito eléctrico? *say **pway**-day ko-nek-**tar** con el theer-**kwee**-tŏ ay-**lek**-tree-kŏ?*	**Are there hook-up facilities?**
Queremos estar tres noches/hasta el miércoles/hasta la semana que viene *kay-**ray**-mos es-**tar** tres **no**-chays/**as**-ta el **myer**-ko-lays/**as**-ta la say-**ma**-na kay **byay**-nay*	**We want to stay three nights/until Wednesday/until sometime next week**

Camping

French	German

Nous avons une tente pliante sur
remorque et une voiture
*noo za-voñ zōōn toñt plee-oñt
sōōr ruh-mork ay ōōn
vwah-tōōr*

Wir haben ein Anhängerzelt und ein
Auto
*veer **hah**-bèn ine **an**-heng-èr-tselt
oont ine **ow**-tō*

Nous avons une voiture et une caravane
*noo za-voñ zōōn vwah-tōōr
ay ōōn ka-ra-van*

Wir haben ein Auto und einen
Wohnwagen
*veer **hah**-bèn ine **ow**-tō oont **ine**-èn
vōn-vah-gèn*

Il y a deux adultes et deux enfants
eel ya duh za-dōōlt ay duh zoñ-foñ

Wir sind zwei Erwachsene und zwei
Kinder
*veer zint tsvye er-**vak**-sè-nè oont tsvye
kin-dèr*

Le bureau ouvre/ferme à quelle heure?
luh bōō-rō oo-vruh/ferm a kel uhr?

Wann macht das Büro auf/zu?
*van makht das bōō-**rō** owf/tsoo?*

Où sont les magasins les plus proches?
oo soñ lay ma-ga-zañ lay plōō prosh?

Wo sind die nächsten Geschäfte?
*vō zint dee **naykh**-stèn gè-**shef**-tè?*

Est-ce qu'il y a un magasin pour le
matériel de camping en ville?
*es-keel ya uñ ma-ga-zañ poor luh
ma-tay-ree-el duh koñ-peeng oñ veel?*

Gibt es in der Stadt ein
Campingfachgeschäft?
*gipt es in der shtat ine
kem-ping-fakh-gè-**sheft**?*

Un jeton pour les douches, s'il vous
plaît
*uñ zhuh-toñ poor lay doosh, see voo
play*

Kann ich bitte eine Duschmarke
haben?
*kan ikh **bit**-è **ine**-è **doosh**-mar-kè
hah-bèn?*

Où peut-on faire la vaisselle/la
lessive/mettre les ordures?
*oo puh-toñ fer la ve-sel/la
le-seev/met-ruh lay zor-dōōr?*

Wo können wir Geschirr spülen/Wä-
sche waschen/den Abfall hinbringen?
*vō **kur'n**-èn veer gè-**shir** shpōōl-èn/
vesh-è **vash**-èn/dayn **ap**-fal
hin-bring-èn?*

Est-ce qu'il y a un endroit pour faire
sécher les vêtements/nos sacs de
couchage?
*es-keel ya uñ noñ-drwah poor fer
say-shay lay vet-moñ/nō sak-duh
koo-shazh?*

Können wir hier irgendwo unsere
Kleider/Schlafsäcke trocknen?
***kur'n**-èn veer heer **ir**-gènt-vō
oon-zè-rè **klye**-dèr/**shlaf**-sek-è
trok-nèn?*

Le robinet/la douche ne marche pas
luh ro-bee-nay/la doosh nuh marsh pa

Der Wasserhahn/die Dusche
funktioniert nicht
*der **vas**-èr-hahn/dee **doo**-shè
foonk-tsi-ō-**neert** nikht*

Les toilettes sont bouchées
lay twah-let soñ boo-shay

Die Toilette ist verstopft
*dee tō-a-**le**-tè ist fer-**shtopft***

Quel est le voltage?
kel e luh vol-tazh?

Wieviel Volt sind das?
*vee-**feel** volt zint das?*

Spanish

Tenemos un remolque y un coche *tay-**nay**-mos oon ray-**mol**-kay ee oon **ko**-chay*	**We have a trailer-tent and a car**
Tenemos un coche y una caravana *tay-**nay**-mos oon **ko**-chay ee **oo**-na ka-ra-**ba**-na*	**We have a car and trailer**
Somos dos adultos y dos niños *s**ō**-mōs dōs a-**dool**-tōs ee dōs **nee**-nyōs*	**There are two adults and two children**
¿A qué hora abre/cierra la oficina? *a kay **ō**-ra **a**-bray/**thye**-rra la o-fee-**thee**-na?*	**What time does the office open/close?**
¿Dónde están las tiendas más próximas? ***don**-day es-**tan** las **tyen**-das mas **prok**-see-mas?*	**Where are the nearest shops?**
¿Hay alguna tienda de artículos de camping en la ciudad? *a-ee al-**goo**-na **tyen**-da day ar-**tee**-koo-lōs day **kam**-peen en la thyoo-**dad**?*	**Is there a camping shop in the town?**
¿Puede darme una ficha para la ducha, por favor? ***pway**-day **dar**-may **oo**-na **fee**-cha **pa**-ra la **doo**-cha, por fa-**bor**?*	**Can I have a token for the shower please?**
¿Dónde podemos lavar los platos/la ropa/tirar la basura? ***don**-day po-**day**-mos la-**bar** los **pla**-tōs/la **rō**-pa/tee-**rar** la ba-**soo**-ra?*	**Where can we wash our dishes/wash clothes/put the rubbish?**
¿Hay algún sitio para secar la ropa/los sacos de dormir? *a-ee al-**goon** **see**-tyō **pa**-ra say-**kar** la **rō**-pa/ los **sa**-kōs day dor-**meer**?*	**Is there somewhere to dry our clothes/sleeping bags?**
El grifo/la ducha no funciona *el **gree**-fō/la **doo**-cha nō foon-**thyo**-na*	**The tap/shower doesn't work**
El wáter está atascado *el **ba**-ter es-**ta** a-tas-**ka**-dō*	**The toilet is blocked**
¿Que voltaje hay aquí? *kay bol-**ta**-khay **a**-ee a-**kee**?*	**What is the voltage?**

Camping

French	*German*
Pouvez-vous m'aider s'il vous plaît? Je n'arrive pas à monter ma tente *poo-vay voo me-day, see voo play?* *zhuh na-reev pa za moñ-tay ma toñt*	Können Sie mir bitte helfen, ich kann mein Zelt nicht aufbauen *kur'n-èn zee meer bit-è helf-en, ikh kan mine tselt nikht owf-bow-èn*
Pouvez-vous me prêter ..., s'il vous plaît? *poo-vay voo muh pre-tay ..., see voo play?*	Können Sie mir ... leihen? *kur'n-èn zee meer ... lye-èn?*
Pouvons-nous allumer un feu? *poo-voñ noo za-lōō-may uñ fuh?*	Dürfen wir ein Feuer machen? *dōōrf-èn veer ine foy-èr makh-èn?*
Pouvons-nous nager/pêcher dans le lac/la rivière? *poo-voñ noo na-zhay/pe-shay doñ luh lak/la ree-vyer?*	Darf man im See/Fluß schwimmen/angeln? *darf man im zay/floos schvim-èn/ang-èln?*
Quelle est la meilleure plage près d'ici? *kel e la mye-yuhr plahzh pre dee-see?*	Wo ist hier in der Nähe der beste Strand? *vō ist heer in der nay-è der best-è shtrant?*
Est-ce que je peux vous payer maintenant? Nous partirons tôt demain matin *es-kuh zhuh puh voo pe-yay mañ-tuh-noñ? noo par-tee-roñ tō duh-mañ ma-tañ*	Kann ich jetzt bezahlen? Wir wollen morgen sehr früh abfahren *kan ikh yetst bè-tsah-lèn? veer vol-èn mor-gèn zayr frōō ap-fah-rèn*
Nous partons tout de suite, je voudrais vous payer *noo par-toñ toot sweet, zhuh voo-dre voo pe-yay*	Wir fahren ab, ich möchte gern bezahlen *veer fah-rèn ap, ikh mur'kh-tè gern bè-tsah-lèn*
Nous sommes arrivés lundi/mardi dernier/hier *noo som za-ree-vay luñ-dee/mar-dee der-nyay/yer*	Wir sind am Montag/am letzten Dienstag/gestern angekommen *veer zint am mōn-tahk/am let-stèn deens-tahk/ges-tèrn an-gè-kom-èn*
Est-ce que la note est exacte? Nous sommes restés ici deux nuits seulement *es-kuh la not e teg-zakt? noo som res-tay ee-see duh nwee suhl-moñ*	Stimmt die Rechnung? Wir waren nur zwei Nächte hier *shtimmt dee rekh-noong? veer vah-rèn noor tsvye nekh-tè heer*
Je voudrais mon carnet de camping/passeport, s'il vous plaît *zhuh voo-dray moñ kar-nay duh koñ-peeng/pas-por, see voo play*	Kann ich bitte meinen Camping-Paß/meinen Paß zurückhaben? *kan ikh bit-è mine-èn kem-ping-pas/mine-èn pas tzoo-rōōk-hah-bèn?*
Merci, nous avons passé un agréable séjour. Au revoir *mer-see, noo za-voñ pa-say uñ na-gray-a-bluh say-zhoor. ō ruh-vwahr*	Vielen Dank, es hat uns gut gefallen. Auf Wiedersehen *feel-èn dank, es hat oons goot gè-fal-èn. owf vee-dèr-zay-èn*

Spanish

¿Puede ayudarme, por favor? no puedo armar la tienda **pway**-day a-yoo-**dar**-may, por fa-**bor**? nõ **pway**-dõ ar-**mar** la **tyen**-da	**Can you help me please, I can't put my tent up**
¿Puede prestarme . . . , por favor? **pway**-day pres-**tar**-may . . . , por fa-**bor**?	**Can you lend me ... please?**
¿Podemos encender un fuego? po-**day**-mõs en-then-**der** oon **fway**-gõ?	**May we light a fire?**
¿Se puede nadar/pescar en el lago/río? say **pway**-day na-**dar**/pes-**kar** en el **la**-gõ/**ree**-õ?	**Can we swim/fish in the lake/river?**
¿Cuál es la mejor playa de por aquí? kwal es la may-**khor pla**-ya day por a-**kee**?	**Which is the best beach near here?**
¿Puedo pagarle ahora? Nos marchamos mañana temprano **pway**-dõ pa-**gar**-lay a-**õ**-ra? nos mar-**cha**-mos ma-**nya**-na tem-**pra**-nõ	**Can I pay you now? We shall be leaving early in the morning**
Nos marchamos ahora mismo, quisiera pagarle nos mar-**cha**-mos a-**õ**-ra **mees**-mõ, kee-**syay**-ra pa-**gar**-lay	**We are leaving now, I would like to pay**
Llegamos el lunes/el martes pasado/ayer lyay-**ga**-mos el **loo**-nays/el **mar**-tays pa-**sa**-dõ/a-**yer**	**We came on Monday/last Tuesday/yesterday**
¿Puede revisar la cuenta, por favor? Sólo hemos estado aquí dos noches **pway**-day ray-bee-**sar** la **kwen**-ta, por fa-**bor**? **sõ**-lõ **ay**-mos es-**ta**-dõ a-**kee** dõs **no**-chays	**Is the bill correct? We've only been here two nights**
Puede devolverme el carnet de camping/pasaporte, por favor? **pway**-day day-bol-**ber**-may el **kar**-nay day **kam**-peen/pa-sa-**por**-tay, por fa-**bor**?	**Can I have my camping permit/passport back please?**
Gracias, ha sido una estancia muy agradable. Adiós. **gra**-thyas, a **see**-dõ **oo**-na es-**tan**-thya mwee a-gra-**da**-blay. a-**dyõs**	**Thank you, we have enjoyed our stay. Goodbye**

Camping
Things You May Hear

French	German
Vous désirez rester combien de temps? *voo day-zee-ray res-tay koñ-byañ duh toñ?*	Wie lange wollen Sie bleiben? *vee **lang**-è **vol**-èn zee **blye**-bèn?*
Est-ce que vous avez une tente ou une caravane? *es-kuh voo za-vay zōōn toñt oo ōōn ka-ra-van?*	Haben Sie ein Zelt oder einen Wohnwagen? ***hah**-bèn zee ine tselt **ō**-dèr **ine**-èn **vōn**-vah-gèn?*
Vous êtes combien dans votre groupe? *voo zet koñ-byañ doñ vot-ruh groop?*	Wieviele Personen sind Sie? *vee-**feel**-è per-**zōn**-èn zint zee?*
(Est-ce que vous pouvez me donner) votre nom et votre adresse, s'il vous plaît? *(es-kuh voo poo-vay muh do-nay) vot-ruh noñ ay vot-ra-dres, see voo play?*	Kann ich bitte Ihren Namen und Ihre Adresse haben? *kan ikh **bit**-è **eer**-èn **nah**-mèn oont **eer**-è a-**dres**-è **hah**-bèn?*
Quel est le numéro d'immatriculation de votre voiture? *kel ay luh nōō-may-rō dee-ma-tree-kōō-la-syoñ duh vot-ruh vwah-tōōr?*	Was ist Ihr Kraftfahrzeugkennzeichen (Kfz-Kennzeichen)? *vas ist eer **kraft**-fahr-tsoyg-**ken**-tsye-khèn (ka-ef-**tset**-ken-tsye-khèn)?*
Est-ce que je peux voir votre passeport, s'il vous plaît? *es-kuh zhuh puh vwahr vot-ruh pas-por, see voo play?*	Kann ich bitte Ihren Paß sehen? *kan ikh **bit**-è **eer**-èn pas **zay**-èn?*
Avez-vous un carnet de camping? *a-vay voo zuñ kar-nay duh koñ-peeng?*	Haben Sie einen Camping-Paß? ***hah**-bèn zee **ine**-èn **kem**-ping-pas?*
Nous demandons des arrhes *noo duh-moñ-doñ day zar*	Sie müssen eine Kaution hinterlegen *zee **mōōs**-èn **ine**-è kow-tsi-**ōn** **hin**-tèr-lay-gèn*
Veuillez remplir cette fiche, s'il vous plaît *vye-yay roñ-pleer set feesh, see voo play*	Bitte füllen Sie dieses Formular aus ***bit**-è **fōōl**-èn zee **dee**-zès for-moo-**lahr** ows*
Plantez votre tente/mettez votre caravane entre les piquets qui délimitent chaque emplacement *ploñ-tay vot-ruh toñt/me-tay vot-ruh ka-ra-van oñ-truh lay pee-kay kee day-lee-meet shak oñ-plas-moñ*	Bauen Sie Ihr Zelt zwischen den Markierungen auf/Stellen Sie Ihren Wohnwagen zwischen die Markierungen ***bow**-èn zee eer tselt **tsvish**-èn dayn mar-**keer**-oong-èn owf/**shtel**-èn zee **eer**-èn **vōn**-vah-gèn **tsvish**-èn dee mar-**keer**-oong-èn*
Je suis désolé mais le camping est plein *zhuh swee day-zo-lay may luh koñ-peeng ay plañ*	Wir sind leider voll besetzt *veer zint **lye**-dèr fol bè-**zetst***
Combien de nuits avez-vous passé ici? *koñ-byañ duh nwee a-vay voo pa-say ee-see?*	Wieviele Nächte waren Sie hier? *vee-**feel**-è **nekh**-tè **vah**-rèn zee heer?*

Spanish

¿Cuánto tiempo quieren quedarse? **kwan**-tŏ **tyem**-pŏ **kyay**-ren kay-**dar**-say?	How long do you want to stay?
¿Tienen tienda o caravana? **tyay**-nen **tyen**-da ŏ ka-ra-**ba**-na?	Do you have a tent or a trailer?
¿Cuántos son ustedes? **kwan**-tŏs son oos-**tay**-days?	How many are there in your party?
¿Puede darme su nombre y dirección, por favor? **pway**-day **dar**-may soo **nom**-bray ee dee-rek-**thyon**, por fa-**bor**?	Can I have your name and address please?
¿Cuál es su número de matrícula? kwal es soo **noo**-may-rŏ day ma-**tree**-koo-la?	What is your car registration number?
El pasaporte, por favor el pa-sa-**por**-tay, por fa-**bor**	Can I see your passport please?
¿Tiene carnet de camping? **tyay**-nay **kar**-nay day **kam**-peen?	Do you have a camping permit?
Debe dejar un depósito **day**-bay day-**khar** oon day-**po**-see-tŏ	You must leave a deposit
Rellene esta hoja, por favor ray-**lyay**-nay **es**-ta ŏ-kha, por fa-**bor**	Please fill in this form
Ponga su tienda/caravana entre los indicadores **pong**-ga soo **tyen**-da/ka-ra-**ba**-na **en**-tray lŏs een-dee-ka-**do**-rays	Pitch your tent/put your trailer between the markers
Lo siento, está todo lleno lŏ **syen**-tŏ, es-**ta** tŏ-dŏ **lyay**-nŏ	I'm sorry, we're full
Cuántas noches han estado aquí? **kwan**-tas **no**-chays an es-**ta**-dŏ a-**kee**?	How many nights have you been here?

Camping Signs

French	German	Spanish	
Eau potable	Trinkwasser	Agua potable	Drinking water
Hommes/ Messieurs	Herren	Caballeros/ Señores	Gentlemen
Alimentation	Lebensmittel	Alimentación	Grocer's
Eau chaude	Warmwasser	Agua caliente	Hot water
Dames	Damen	Damas/Señoras	Ladies
(Eau) Non potable	Kein Trinkwasser	(Agua) No potable	Not drinking water
Bureau	Büro	Oficina	Office
Douches et Lavabos	Duschen und Waschbecken	Duchas y Lavabos	Showers & Washbasins
Toilettes	Toiletten	Aseos/Retrete/ Servicios	Toilets

Some more useful words:

French	German	Spanish	
le matelas pneumatique *luh mat-la pnuh-ma-teek*	die Luftmatratze *dee **looft**-ma-trat-sè*	el colchón hinchable *el kol-**chon** een-**cha**-blay*	**air bed** or **mattress**
le gonfleur *luh goñ-fluhr*	die Luftpumpe *dee **looft**-poom-pè*	la bomba de aire *la **bom**-ba day a-ee-ray*	**air pump**
le barbecue *luh bar-buh-kyoo*	der Grill *der gril*	la barbacoa *la bar-ba-**kō**-a*	**barbecue**
la pile *la peel*	die Batterie *dee ba-tè-**ree***	la pila *la **pee**-la*	**battery** (*torch etc*)
la couverture *la koo-ver-tōōr*	die Decke *dee **de**-kè*	la manta *la **man**-ta*	**blanket**
l'ouvre-bouteilles *loo-vruh-boo-tye*	der Flaschen-öffner *der **flash**-èn-ur'f-nèr*	el abrebotellas *el a-bray-bo-**te**-lyas*	**bottle opener**
le bol *luh bol*	die Schüssel *dee **shōō**-sèl*	el tazón *el ta-**thon***	**bowl**
la boîte *la bwaht*	die Kiste *dee **kis**-tè*	la caja *la **ka**-kha*	**box**
la brosse *la bros*	der Besen *der **bay**-zèn*	el cepillo *el thay-**pee**-lyō*	**brush**
le seau *luh sō*	der Eimer *der **eye**-mèr*	el cubo *el **koo**-bō*	**bucket**
le butane *luh bōō-tan*	das Butan *da boo-**tahn***	el butano *el boo-**ta**-nō*	**butane**
le lit de camp *luh lee duh koñ*	die Campingliege *dee **kem**-ping-lee-gè*	la cama de camping *la **ka**-ma day **kam**-peen*	**camp bed**

French	German	Spanish	
la chaise de camping *la shez duh koñ-peeng*	der Camping-stuhl *der **kem**-ping-shtool*	la silla de camping *la **see**-lya day **kam**-peen*	**camp chair**
le Camping Gaz *luh koñ-peeng gaz*	das Camping-Gas *das **kem**-ping-gahz*	el Camping Gaz *el **kam**-peen gas*	**Camping Gas**
la cuisine du camping *la kwee-zeen dōō koñ-peeng*	die Küche auf dem Camping-platz *dee **kōō**-khè owf daym **kem**-ping-plats*	la cocina de camping *la ko-**thee**-na day **kam**-peen*	**camp kitchen**
l'ouvre-boîtes *loo-vruh-bwaht*	der Dosenöffner *der **dō**-zèn-ur'f-nèr*	el abrelatas *el a-bray-**la**-tas*	**can opener**
la caravane *la ka-ra-van*	der Wohnwagen *der **vōn**-vah-gèn*	la caravana *la ka-ra-**ba**-na*	**caravan (trailer)**
la cartouche *la kar-toosh*	die Patrone *dee pa-**trō**-nè*	el cartucho de gas *el kar-**too**-chō day gas*	**cartridge (gas)**
le charbon de bois *luh shar-boñ duh bwah*	die Holzkohle *dee **holts**-kō-lè*	el carbón vegetal *el kar-**bon** bay-khay-**tal***	**charcoal**
la cuve chimique *la kōōv shee-meek*	die chemische Abfallbeseiti-gungsanlage *dee **khay**-mish-è **ap**-fal-bè-**zye**-ti-goongs-**an**-lah-gè*	el lugar para vaciar el wáter portátil *el loo-**gar** pa-ra ba-**thyar** el **ba**-ter por-**ta**-teel*	**chemical disposal point**
les toilettes chimiques *lay twah-let shee-meek*	die chemische Toilette *dee-**khay**-mish-è to-a-**le**-tè*	el wáter portátil *el **ba**-ter por-**ta**-teel*	**chemical toilet**
le fil à linge *luh feel a lañzh*	die Wäscheleine *dee **vesh**-è-lye-nè*	la cuerda para tender la ropa *la **kwer**-da **pa**-ra ten-**der** la **ro**-pa*	**clothes line**
les pinces à linge *lay pañs a lañzh*	die Wäscheklam-mern *dee **vesh**-è-klam-èrn*	las pinzas *las **peen**-thas*	**clothes pegs**
le tire-bouchon *luh teer-boo-shoñ*	der Korkenzieher *der **kor**-kèn-tsee-èr*	el sacacorchos *el sa-ka-**kor**-chōs*	**corkscrew**
la tasse *la tas*	die Tasse *dee **tas**-è*	la taza *la **ta**-tha*	**cup**

Camping

French	German	Spanish	
la lavette *la la-vet*	der Spüllappen *der **shpool**-lap- èn*	el paño de cocina *el **pa**-nyō day ko-**thee**-na*	**dishcloth**
les facilités pour faire sécher le linge *lay fa-see-lee-tay poor fer say- shay luh lañzh*	die Trocken- räume *dee **trok**-èn- roy-mè*	el secadero de ropa *el say-ka-**day**-rō day ro-pa*	**drying facilities**
les prises d'alimentation électrique pour les caravanes *lay preez da-lee- moñ-ta-syoñ ay-lek-treek poor lay ka-ra-van*	die Elektroan- schlüsse für Wohnwagen *dee ay-**lek**-trō- an-shlōō-sè **fōōr vōn**-vah- gèn*	las conexiones eléctricas para caravanas *las ko-nek-**syo**- nays ay-**lek**-tree- kas **pa**-ra ka-ra- **ba**-nas*	**electric points for trailers**
le feu *luh fuh*	das Feuer *das **foy**-èr*	el fuego *el **fway**-gō*	**fire**
la trousse de premiers secours *la troos duh pruhm-yay suh-koor*	die Erste-Hilfe- Ausrüstung *dee **ayr**-stè-**hil**- fè-**ows**-rōōs- toong*	el botiquín *el bo-tee-**keen***	**first aid kit**
			flashlight = torch
la moustiquaire *la moos-tee-ker*	der Insekten- schutz *der in-**zek**-tèn- shoots*	el mosquitero *el mos-kee-**tay**-rō*	**flyscreen**
le double toit *luh doo-bluh twah*	das Überzelt *das **ōō**-bèr-**tselt***	el doble techo *el **do**-blay **te**-chō*	**flysheet**
la table pliante *la ta-bluh plee-oñt*	der Klapptisch *der **klap**-tish*	la mesa plegable *la **may**-sa play- **ga**-blay*	**folding table**
la fourchette *la foor-shet*	die Gabel *dee **gah**-bèl*	el tenedor *el tay-nay-**dor***	**fork**
la tente à armature *la toñt a ar-ma-tōōr*	das Steilwandzelt *das **shtile**-vant- tselt*	la tienda de armazón *la **tyen**-da day ar-ma-**thon***	**frame tent**
la poêle *la pwahl*	die Bratpfanne *dee **braht**-pfan-è*	el sartén *el sar-**ten***	**frying pan**
le fusible *luh fōō-zee-bluh*	die Sicherung *dee **zikh**-èr-oong*	el plomo *el **plo**-mō*	**fuse**
la bouteille de gaz *la boo-tye duh gaz*	die Gasflasche *dee **gahs**-flash-è*	la botella de gas *la bo-**te**-lya day gas*	**gas bottle**

French	German	Spanish	
le verre *luh ver*	das Glas *das glahs*	el vaso *el **ba**-sō*	**glass**
le tapis de sol *luh ta-pee duh sol*	die Bodenplane *dee **bō**-dèn-plah-nè*	la tela impermeable la **tay**-la eem-per-may-**a**-blay	**groundsheet**
la ficelle *la fee-sel*	die Zeltschnur *dee **tselt**-shnoor*	la cuerda la **kwer**-da	**guy (line** or **rope)**
le séchoir à cheveux *luh say-shwar a shuh-vuh*	der Haartrockner *der **hahr**-trok-nèr*	el secador de pelo *el say-ka-**dor** day **pay**-lō*	**hair dryer**
la hachette *la a-shet*	das Beil *das bile*	el hacha *el **a**-cha*	**hatchet**
l'eau chaude *lō shōd*	das warme Wasser *das **varm**-è **vas**-èr*	el agua caliente *el **a**-gwa ca-**lyen**-tay*	**hot water**
la glacière *la glas-yer*	die Eisbox *dee **ise**-boks*	la nevera *la nay-**bay**-ra*	**ice-box**
le sac de glace *luh sak duh glas*	die Kühlpatrone *dee **kool**-pa-trō-nè*	la bolsa de hielo *la **bol**-sa day **yay**-lō*	**ice pack**
la cruche *la krōōsh*	der Krug *der krook*	la jarra *la **kha**-rra*	**jug**
le couteau *luh koo-tō*	das Messer *das **mes**-èr*	el cuchillo *el koo-**chee**-lyō*	**knife**
la lampe *la loñp*	die Lampe *dee **lamp**-è*	la lámpara *la **lam**-pa-ra*	**lamp**
les facilités pour faire la lessive *lay fa-see-lee-tay poor fer la le-seev*	die Möglichkeit, Wäsche zu waschen *dee **mur'g**-likh-kite, **vesh**-è tsoo **vash**-èn*	los lavaderos *lōs la-ba-**day**-rōs*	**laundry facilities**
le maillet *luh mye-yay*	der Holzhammer *der **holts**-ham-èr*	el mazo *el **ma**-thō*	**mallet**
le manchon *luh moñ-shoñ*	der Glühstrumpf *der **glōō**-shtroompf*	el manguito incandescente *el mang-**gee**-tō een-kan-des-**then**-tay*	**mantle**
les allumettes *lay za-lōō-met*	die Streichhölzer *dee **shtryekh**-hur'l-tsèr*	las cerillas *las thay-**ree**-lyas*	**matches**
le réchaud à alcool *luh ray-shō a al-kol*	der Spiritus- kocher *der **shpee**-ri-toos-kokh-èr*	la estufa de alcohol *la es-**too**-fa day al-**kol***	**meths stove**

Camping

French	German	Spanish	
l'alcool à brûler *lal-kol a brōō-lay*	der Brennspiritus *der **bren**-shpee-ri-toos*	el alcohol metilado *el al-**kol** may-tee-**la**-dō*	**methylated spirits**
le miroir *luh meer-war*	der Spiegel *der **shpee**-gèl*	el espejo *el es-**pay**-khō*	**mirror**
la moto *la mō-tō*	das Motorrad *das **mō**-tor-raht*	la motocicleta *la mō-tō-thee-**klay**-ta*	**motorcycle**
la casserole *la kas-rol*	die Pfanne *dee **pfan**-è*	la cazuela *la ka-**thway**-la*	**pan**
le pétrole *luh pay-trol*	das Paraffin *das pa-ra-**feen***	el petróleo *el pay-**tro**-lay-ō*	**paraffin**
le poêle à pétrole *luh pwahl a pay-trol*	der Paraffin-kocher *der pa-ra-**feen**-kokh-èr*	la estufa de petróleo *la es-**too**-fa day pay-**tro**-lay-ō*	**paraffin stove**
le canif *luh ka-neef*	das Taschen-messer *das **tash**-èn-mes-èr*	la navaja *la na-**ba**-kha*	**pen-knife**
l'oreiller *lo-rye-yay*	das Kissen *das **kis**-èn*	la almohada *la al-mo-**a**-da*	**pillow**
le sac en plastique *luh sak oñ plas-teek*	die Plastiktüte *dee **plas**-tik-tōō-tè*	la bolsa de plástico *la **bol**-sa day **plas**-tee-kō*	**plastic bag**
l'assiette *las-yet*	der Teller *der **te**-lèr*	el plato *el **pla**-tō*	**plate**
la pince plate *la pañs plat*	die Kombizange *dee **kom**-bi-tsang-è*	las tenazas *las tay-**na**-thas*	**pliers**
la prise (de courant) *la preez (duh koo-roñ)*	der Stecker *der **shte**-kèr*	el enchufe *el en-**choo**-fay*	**plug**
le réchaud de camping (à pétrole) *luh ray-shō duh koñ-peeng (a pay-trol)*	der Primus-kocher *der **pree**-moos-kokh-èr*	la cocinilla de camping *la ko-thee-**nee**-lya day **kam**-peen*	**primus stove**
les poubelles *lay poo-bel*	die Müllecke *dee **mōōl**-ek-è*	el basurero *el ba-soo-**ray**-rō*	**refuse area**
le restaurant *luh res-tō-roñ*	das Restaurant *das res-tō-**roñ***	el restaurante *el res-tow-**ran**-tay*	**restaurant**
la tente *la toñt*	das Firstzelt *das **first**-tselt*	la tienda triangular *la **tyen**-da tree-ang-goo-**lar***	**ridge tent**

French	German	Spanish	
la corde *la kord*	das Seil *das zile*	la cuerda *la **kwer**-da*	**rope**
les caoutchoucs *lay ka-oo-choo*	die Gummiringe *dee **goo**-mi-ring-è*	las gomas *las **go**-mas*	**rubbers** *(for pegs)*
le sac à dos *luh sak a dō*	der Rucksack *der **rook**-zak*	la mochila *la mo-**chee**-la*	**rucksack**
les ciseaux *lay see-zō*	die Schere *dee **shay**-rè*	las tijeras *las tee-**khay**-ras*	**scissors**
le tournevis *luh toor-nuh-vees*	der Schrauben-zieher *der **shrow**-bèn-tsee-èr*	el destornillador *el des-tor-nee-lya-**dor***	**screwdriver**
la prise pour rasoirs *la preez poor ra-zwar*	die Steckdose für Rasierapparate *dee **shtek**-dō-zè fōōr ra-**zeer**-a-pa-rah-tè*	el enchufe de la máquina de afeitar *el en-**choo**-fay day la **ma**-kee-na day a-fe-ee-**tar***	**shaver socket**
l'évier *lay-vyay*	der Spülstein *der **shpōōl**-shtine*	el fregadero *el fray-ga-**day**-rō*	**sink**
l'emplacement *loñ-plas-moñ*	der Platz *der plats*	el sitio *el **see**-tyō*	**site** *(individual)*
le sac de couchage *luh sak duh koo-shazh*	der Schlafsack *der **shlaf**-zak*	el saco de dormir *el **sa**-kō day dor-**meer***	**sleeping bag**
la cuiller *la kwee-yer*	der Löffel *der **lur'**-fèl*	la cuchara *la koo-**cha**-ra*	**spoon**
l'attache à ressort *la-tash a ruh-sor*	der Sprengring *der **shpreng**-ring*	la grapa de muelle *la **gra**-pa day **mwe**-lyay*	**spring clip**
les pattes de stabilisation *lay pat duh sta-bee-lee-zas-yoñ*	die Stützen *dee **stōōt**-sèn*	los soportes *lōs so-**por**-tays*	**steadies**
le piquet en métal *luh pee-kay oñ may-tal*	der Stahlhering *der **shtahl**-hay-ring*	la estaca de acero *la es-**ta**-ka day a-**thay**-rō*	**steel peg**
le marchepied *luh mar-shuh-pyay*	die Treppe *dee **trep**-è*	el estribo *el es-**tree**-bō*	**step** *(trailer)*
le tabouret *luh ta-boo-ray*	der Hocker *der **hok**-èr*	el taburete *el ta-boo-**ray**-tay*	**stool**
le réchaud *luh ray-shō*	der Kocher *der **kokh**-èr*	la cocina *la ko-**thee**-na*	**stove**
la ficelle *la fee-sel*	die Schnur *dee shnoor*	la cuerda *la **kwer**-da*	**string**
le fauteuil relax *luh fō-tye ruh-laks*	das Sonnenbett *das **zon**-èn-bet*	la tumbona *la toom-**bo**-na*	**sun lounger**

Camping

French	German	Spanish	
le robinet *luh ro-bee-nay*	der Wasserhahn *der **vas**-èr-hahn*	el grifo *el **gree**-fō*	**tap**
la bande *la boñd*	das Band *das bant*	la cinta *la **theen**-ta*	**tape** *(on canvas)*
la théière *la tay-yer*	die Teekanne *dee **tay**-kan-è*	la tetera *la tay-**tay**-ra*	**teapot**
la petite cuiller *la puh-teet kwee-yer*	der Teelöffel *der **tay**-lur'-fèl*	la cucharilla *la koo-cha-**ree**-lya*	**teaspoon**
le torchon (à vaisselle) *luh tor-shoñ (a ve-sel)*	das Geschirrtuch *das gè-**shir**-tookh*	el paño de cocina *el **pa**-nyō day ko-**thee**-na*	**teatowel**
le téléphone *luh tay-lay-fon*	das Telefon *das tay-lay-**fōn***	el teléfono *el tay-**lay**-fo-nō*	**telephone**
la tente *la toñt*	das Zelt *das tselt*	la tienda *la **tyen**-da*	**tent**
le piquet de tente *luh pee-kay duh toñt*	der Hering *der **hay**-ring*	la clavija *la kla-**bee**-kha*	**tent peg**
le mât de tente *luh mah duh toñt*	die Zeltstange *dee **tselt**-shtang-è*	el mástil *el **mas**-teel*	**tent pole**
la thermos *la ter-mōs*	die Thermos-flasche *dee **ter**-mōs-flash-è*	el termo *el **ter**-mō*	**Thermos flask**
les toilettes *lay twah-let*	die Toiletten (-einheit) *dee tō-a-**le**-tèn (-**ine**-hite)*	los lavabos *lōs la-**ba**-bōs*	**toilet block**
le papier hygiénique *luh pa-pyay ee-zhyay-neek*	das Toiletten-papier *das tō-a-**le**-tèn-pa-peer*	el papel higiénico *el pa-**pel** ee-**khye**-nee-kō*	**toilet paper**
la tente avec les sanitaires *la toñt a-vek lay sa-nee-ter*	das Toilettenzelt *das tō-a-**le**-tèn-tselt*	la tienda del wáter *la **tyen**-da del **ba**-ter*	**toilet tent**
le jeton *luh zhuh-toñ*	die Marke *dee **mar**-kè*	la ficha *la **fee**-cha*	**token**
la lampe de poche *la loñp duh posh*	die Taschen-lampe *dee **tash**-èn-lamp-è*	la linterna *la leen-**ter**-na*	**torch (flashlight)**
la serviette *la ser-vyet*	das Handtuch *das **hant**-tookh*	la toalla *la tō-**a**-lya*	**towel**

French	German	Spanish	
la remorque *la ruh-mork*	der Anhänger *der **an**-heng-èr*	el remolque *el ray-**mol**-kay*	**trailer**
			trailer *(US)* = **caravan**
le caravaning *luh ka-ra-va-neeng*	der Camping- platz für Wohnwagen *der **kem**-ping- plats f$\overline{oo}$r **v$\overline{o}$n**-vah-gèn*	el camping *el **kam**-peen*	**trailer site**
la tente pliante sur remorque *la to$\tilde{n}$t plee-o$\tilde{n}$t s$\overline{oo}$r ruh-mork*	das Anhängerzelt *das **an**-heng-èr- tselt*	la tienda de remolque *la **tyen**-da day ray-**mol**-kay*	**trailer tent**
le produit à vaisselle *luh pro-dwee a ve-sel*	das Spülmittel *das **shp$\overline{oo}$l**- mit-èl*	el detergente de fregar *el day-ter-**khen**- tay day fray-**gar***	**washing-up liquid**
le jerrycan à eau *luh zhe-ree-kan a $\overline{o}$*	der Wasserbeutel *der **vas**-èr-boy- tèl*	el recipiente de agua *el ray-thee-**pyen**- tay day **a**-gwa*	**water carrier** *or* **container**
la pompe à eau *la po$\tilde{n}$p a $\overline{o}$*	die Wasser- pumpe *dee **vas**-èr- poom-pè*	la bomba de agua *la **bom**-ba day **a**-gwa*	**water pump**
les pastilles pour purifier l'eau *lay pas-tee poor p$\overline{oo}$-ree-fyay l$\overline{o}$*	die Wasserrei- nigungsta- bletten *dee **vas**-èr-rye- ni-goongs-tab- **le**-tèn*	las pastillas para purificar el agua *las pas-**tee**-lyas **pa**-ra poo-ree- fee-**kar** el **a**-gwa*	**water purifying tablets**
le robinet d'eau *luh ro-bee-nay d$\overline{o}$*	der Wasserhahn *der **vas**-èr-hahn*	el grifo *el **gree**-f$\overline{o}$*	**water tap**
le pare-vent *luh par-vo$\tilde{n}$*	der Windschutz *der **vint**-shoots*	el parabrisas *el pa-ra-**bree**-sas*	**windshield**
la fermeture éclair *la fer-muh-t$\overline{oo}$r ay-kler*	der Reiß- verschluß *der **rise**-fer- shloos*	la cremallera *la kray-ma-**lyay**-ra*	**zip**

Hotels

French	German
Hotels are grouped into categories of 1, 2, 3 or 4 stars and further graded as A, B or C. You can also stay at one of the relais routiers (primarily for lorry drivers, but of a good standard) or, in country areas, in a logis de France.	Hotels are officially grouped into categories of 1, 2, 3 or 4 stars. You can also stay at one of the Raststätten (primarily for lorry drivers, but of a good standard) or, especially in country areas, in a Pension, Hotel Garni, Gasthof or Gasthaus.
J'ai besoin d'une chambre pour une personne/pour deux personnes (avec salle de bains/avec douche) *zhay buh-zwañ dōōn shoñ-bruh poor ōōn per-son/poor duh per-son (a-vek sal duh bañ/a-vek doosh)*	Ich hätte gerne ein Einzelzimmer/ein Doppelzimmer (mit Bad/Dusche) *ikh **het**-è **gern**-è ine-tsèl-tsim-èr/ ine **dop**-èl-tsim-èr (mit bat/**doosh**-è)*
La chambre fait combien pour une nuit? *la shoñ-bruh fe koñ-byañ poor ōōn nwee?*	Wieviel kostet das Zimmer pro Nacht? *vee-**feel kos**-tèt das **tsim**-èr prō nakht?*
Toutes taxes comprises? *toot taks koñ-preez?*	Ist dabei alles inbegriffen? *ist da-**bye al**-ès **in**-bè-grif-èn?*
Petit déjeuner compris? *puh-tee day-zhuh-nay koñ-pree?*	Ist das mit Frühstück? *ist das mit **frōō**-shtōōk?*
Est-ce que vous avez un petit lit pour le bébé? *es-kuh voo za-vay uñ puh-tee lee poor luh bay-bay?*	Haben Sie ein Kinderbett für das Baby? ***hah**-bèn zee ine **kin**-dèr-bet fōōr das **bay**-bee?*
Est-ce que mon fils peut partager notre chambre? *es-kuh moñ fees puh par-ta-zhay not-ruh shoñ-bruh?*	Kann mein Sohn bei uns im Zimmer schlafen? *kan mine zōn bye oons im **tsim**-èr **shlah**-fèn?*
Je désire rester une nuit/deux nuits *zhuh day-zeer res-tay ōōn nwee/duh nwee*	Ich möchte eine Nacht/zwei Nächte bleiben *ikh **mur'kh**-tè **ine**-è nakht/tsvye **nekh**-tè **blye**-bèn*
Est-ce que vous servez des repas? *es-kuh voo ser-vay day ruh-pa?*	Kann man hier auch essen? *kan man heer owkh **es**-èn?*
Est-ce que vous pouvez recommander un restaurant? *es-kuh voo poovay ruh-ko-moñ-day uñ res-tō-roñ?*	Können Sie mir ein Restaurant empfehlen? ***kur'n**-èn zee meer ine res-tō-**roñ** emp-**fayl**-èn?*
À quelle heure servez-vous le petit déjeuner/le déjeuner/le dîner? *a kel uhr ser-vay-voo luh puh-tee day-zhuh-nay/luh day-zhuh-nay/luh dee-nay?*	Wann gibt es hier Frühstück/ Mittagessen/Abendessen? *van gipt es heer **frōō**-shtōōk/ **mi**-tag-es-èn/**ah**-bènt-es-èn?*
Réveillez-moi à huit heures, s'il vous plaît *ray-vye-yay-mwah a wee tuhr, see voo play*	Bitte wecken Sie mich um acht Uhr ***bit**-è **vek**-èn zee mikh oom akht **oo**-èr*

Hotels

Hotels are grouped into categories of 1, 2, 3, 4 or 5 stars and boarding houses (pensiones and hostales) are graded as 1, 2 or 3 stars. You can also stay in paradores nacionales, often converted historical buildings in recognised beauty spots, and albergues de carretera, set at strategic points on main roads and motorways.

Necesito una habitación individual/doble (con baño/ducha) *nay-thay-**see**-tō **oo**-na a-bee-ta-**thyon** een-dee-bee-**dwal**/**do**-blay (kon **ba**-nyō/**doo**-cha)*	**I need a single/double room (with bath/shower)**
¿Cuánto es la habitación por noche? ***kwan**-tō es la a-bee-ta-**thyon** por **no**-chay?*	**How much is the room per night?**
¿Todo incluido? ***tō**-dō een-kloo-**ee**-dō?*	**Is that inclusive?**
¿Está incluido el desayuno? *es-**ta** een-kloo-**ee**-dō el des-a-**yoo**-nō?*	**Is breakfast included?**
¿Tienen una cuna para el niño? ***tyay**-nen **oo**-na **koo**-na **pa**-ra el **nee**-nyō?*	**Do you have a cot (crib) for the baby?**
¿Puede dormir mi hijo en nuestra habitación? ***pway**-day dor-**meer** mee **ee**-khō en **nues**-tra a-bee-ta-**thyon**?*	**Can my son sleep in our room?**
Quiero quedarme una noche/dos noches ***kyay**-rō kay-**dar**-may **oo**-na **no**-chay/**dōs no**-chays*	**I want to stay for one night/two nights**
¿Sirven comidas? ***seer**-ben ko-**mee**-das?*	**Do you serve meals?**
¿Puede recomendarme un restaurante? ***pway**-day ray-ko-men-**dar**-may oon res-tow-**ran**-tay?*	**Can you recommend a restaurant?**
¿A qué hora se sirve el desayuno/la comida/la cena? *a kay **ō**-ra say **seer**-bay el de-sa-**yoo**-nō/la ko-**mee**-da/la **thay**-na?*	**At what time do you serve breakfast/lunch/dinner?**
Despiérteme a las ocho, por favor *des-**pyer**-tay-may a las **o**-chō, por fa-**bor***	**Please call me at eight o'clock**

Hotels

French	German
Est-ce que l'eau du robinet est potable? *es-kuh lõ dõõ ro-bee-nay e po-ta-bluh?*	Kann man das Leitungswasser trinken? *kan man das **lye**-toongs-vas-èr **tring**-kèn?*
Est-ce que le voltage est du 220 ou du 110? *es-kuh luh vol-tazh e dõõ duh soñ vañ oo dõõ soñ dees?*	Ist die Spannung hier zweihundert-zwanzig oder einhundertzehn Volt? *ist dee **shpan**-oong heer **tsvye**-hoon-dèrt-**tsvan**-tsikh õ-dèr **ine**-hoon-dèrt-**tsayn** volt?*
Où est la salle de bains? *oo e la sal duh bañ?*	Wo ist das Badezimmer? *võ ist das **bah**-dè-tsim-èr?*
Il n'y a pas de papier hygiénique/de serviette *eel nya pa duh pa-pyay eezh-yay-neek/duh ser-vyet*	Es ist kein Toilettenpapier/kein Handtuch da *es ist kine tõ-a-**le**-tèn-pa-peer/kine **hant**-tookh dah*
Est-ce que je peux avoir ma clé/un cendrier/une autre couverture? *es-kuh zhuh puh za-vwar ma klay/uñ soñ-dree-ay/õõn õ-truh koo-ver-tõõr?*	Kann ich bitte meinen Schlüssel/einen Aschenbecher/noch eine Decke haben? *kan ikh **bit**-è **mine**-èn **shlõõ**-sèl/**ine**-èn **ash**-èn-be-khèr/nokh **ine**-è **de**-kè **hah**-bèn?*
La lumière/l'air conditionné/le chauffage ne marche pas *la lõõm-yer/ler koñ-dee-syo-nay/luh shõ-fazh nuh marsh pa*	Das Licht/die Klimaanlage/die Heizung geht nicht *das likht/dee **klee**-ma-an-lah-gè/dee **hye**-tsoong gayt nikht*
Il n'y a pas d'eau chaude *eel nya pa dõ shõd*	Es ist kein heißes Wasser da *es ist kine **hye**-sès **vas**-èr dah*
Le lavabo est sale *luh la-va-bõ e sal*	Das Waschbecken ist schmutzig *das **vash**-be-kèn ist **shmoot**-tsikh*
Il n'y a pas de bouchon dans le lavabo *eel nya pa duh boo-shoñ doñ luh la-va-bõ*	Der Stöpsel für das Waschbecken fehlt *der **shtur'p**-zèl fõõr das **vash**-be-kèn faylt*
Je voudrais rester une nuit supplémentaire *zhuh voo-dray res-tay õõn nwee sõõ-play-moñ-ter*	Ich möchte noch eine Nacht bleiben *ikh **mur'kh**-tè nokh **ine**-è nahkht **blye**-bèn*
Nous partirons demain matin à neuf heures *noo par-tee-roñ duh-mañ ma-tañ a nuh vuhr*	Wir reisen morgen um neun Uhr ab *veer **rye**-zèn **mor**-gèn oom noyn **oo**-èr ap*
La note, s'il vous plaît *la not, see voo play*	Die Rechnung, bitte *dee **rekh**-noong, **bit**-è*
Est-ce que vous acceptez les chèques de voyage? *es-kuh voo zak-sep-tay lay shek duh vwah-yazh?*	Nehmen Sie Reiseschecks an? *nay-mèn zee **rye**-zè-sheks an?*

Spanish

¿Se puede beber el agua del grifo? *say pway-day bay-ber el a-gwa del gree-fŏ?*	**Can I drink the tap-water?**
¿La corriente está a doscientos veinte o a ciento diez? *la ko-rryen-tay es-ta a dŏs-thyen-tŏs be-een-tay ŏ a thyen-tŏ dyeth?*	**Is the voltage 220 or 110?**
¿Dónde está el cuarto de baño? *don-day es-ta el kwar-tŏ day ba-nyŏ?*	**Where is the bathroom?**
No hay papel higiénico/toalla *nŏ a-ee pa-pel ee-khye-nee-kŏ/to-a-lya*	**There is no toilet paper/towel**
¿Puede darme la llave/un cenicero/otra manta, por favor? *pway-day dar-may la lya-bay/oon thay-nee-thay-rŏ/ŏ-tra man-ta, por fa-bor?*	**Can I have my key/an ashtray/another blanket please?**
La luz/el aire acondicionado/la calefacción no funciona *la looth/el a-ee-ray a-con-dee-thyo-na-dŏ/la ka-lay-fak-thyon nŏ foon-thyo-na*	**The light/air-conditioning/heating is not working**
No hay agua caliente *nŏ a-ee a-gwa ka-lyen-tay*	**There is no hot water**
El lavabo está sucio *el la-ba-bŏ es-ta soo-thyŏ*	**The washbasin is dirty**
No hay tapón en el lavabo *no a-ee ta-pon en el la-ba-bŏ*	**There is no plug in the washbasin**
Quiero quedarme otra noche *kyay-rŏ kay-dar-may ŏ-tra no-chay*	**I want to stay an extra night**
Nos marchamos mañana a las nueve *nŏs mar-cha-mŏs ma-nya-na a las nway-bay*	**We will be leaving tomorrow at 9 o'clock**
La factura, por favor *la fak-too-ra, por fa-bor*	**I would like the bill please**
Aceptan cheques de viaje? *a-thep-tan che-kays day bya-khay?*	**Do you accept traveller's cheques?**

Travelling with a Family

French	German
Nous sommes quatre *noo som kat-ruh*	Wir sind zu viert *veer zint tsoo feert*
ma femme *ma fam*	meine Frau **mine**-è *frow*
mon mari *moñ ma-ree*	mein Mann *mine man*
ma fille *ma fee*	meine Tochter **mine**-è **tokh**-*tèr*
mon fils *moñ fees*	mein Sohn *mine zōn*
Quel âge ont vos enfants? *kel azh oñ vō zoñ-foñ?*	Wie alt sind Ihre Kinder? *vee alt zint **ee**-rè **kin**-dèr?*
Le garçon a neuf ans *luh gar-soñ a nuh voñ*	Der Junge ist neun Jahre alt *der **yoong**-è ist noyn **yah**-rè alt*
La fille a quinze mois *la fee a kañz mwah*	Das Mädchen ist fünfzehn Monate alt *das **mayt**-khèn ist **fōōnf**-tsayn **mō**-na-tè alt*
J'ai besoin de couches à jeter *zhay buh-zwañ duh koosh a zhuh-tay*	Ich brauche Papierwindeln *ikh **brow**-khè pa-**peer**-vin-dèln*
Est-ce que vous avez une chaise de bébé? *es-kuh voo za-vay zōōn shez duh bay-bay?*	Haben Sie einen Kinderstuhl? **hah**-bèn zee **ine**-èn **kin**-dèr-shtool?
Est-ce qu'il y a des activités organisées pour les enfants? *es-keel ya day zak-tee-vec-tay or-ga-nee-zay poor lay zoñ-foñ?*	Gibt es irgendwelche Freizeitveranstaltungen für Kinder? *gipt es **ir**-gènt-vel-khè **frye**-tsite-fer-**an**-shtal-toong-èn fōōr **kin**-dèr?*
Est-ce qu'il y a un petit bassin pour les enfants? *es-keel ya uñ puh-tee ba-sañ poor lay zoñ-foñ?*	Gibt es hier ein Planschbecken? *gipt es heer ine **plansh**-be-kèn?*
Est-ce qu'il y a un parc d'attractions? *es-keel ya uñ par da-trax-yoñ?*	Gibt es hier einen Vergnügungspark? *gipt es heer **ine**-èn fer-**gnōō**-goongs-park?*
Est-ce qu'il y a un zoo dans les environs? *es-keel ya uñ zō doñ lay zoñ-vee-roñ?*	Gibt es hier in der Nähe einen Zoo? *gipt es heer in der **nay**-è **ine**-èn tsō?*
Mon fils s'est blessé *moñ fees say ble-say*	Mein Sohn hat sich weh getan *mine zōn hat zikh vay gè-**tahn***
Ma fille est malade *ma fee ay ma-lad*	Meine Tochter ist krank **mine**-è **tokh**-tèr ist krank
Pardon, madame (etc), il/elle n'aurait pas dû faire ça *par-doñ ma-dam, eel/el nō-re pa dōō fer sa*	Es tut mir leid – das war sehr ungezogen von ihm/ihr *es toot meer lite – das var zayr **oon**-gè-tsō-gèn fon eem/eer*

Spanish

Somos cuatro *sō-mōs kwa-trō*	**There are four of us**
mi mujer *mee moo-kher*	**my wife**
mi marido *mee ma-ree-dō*	**my husband**
mi hija *mee ee-kha*	**my daughter**
mi hijo *mee ee-khō*	**my son**
¿Qué edad tienen sus niños? *kay ay-dad tyay-nen soos nee-nyōs?*	**How old are your children?**
El niño tiene nueve años *el nee-nyō tyay-nay nway-bay a-nyōs*	**The boy is 9 years old**
La niña tiene quince meses *la nee-nya tyay-nay keen-thay may-says*	**The girl is 15 months**
Necesito pañales de tirar *nay-thay-see-tō pa-nya-lays day tee-rar*	**I need some disposable nappies (diapers)**
¿Tiene una silla alta de niño? *tyay-nay oo-na see-lya al-ta day nee-nyō?*	**Have you got a high chair?**
¿Hay actividades organizadas para los niños? *a-ee ak-tee-bee-da-days or-ga-nee-tha-das pa-ra lōs nee-nyōs?*	**Are there any organized activities for the children?**
¿Hay un estanque de juegos? *a-ee oon es-tan-kay day khway-gōs?*	**Is there a wading pool?**
¿Hay parque de atracciones? *a-ee par-kay day a-trak-thyo-nays?*	**Is there an amusement park?**
¿Hay algún zoológico cerca? *a-ee al-goon tho-o-lo-khee-kō ther-ka?*	**Is there a zoo nearby?**
Mi hijo se ha hecho daño *mee ee-khō say a ay-chō da-nyō*	**My son has hurt himself**
Mi hija está enferma *mee ee-kha es-ta en-fer-ma*	**My daughter is ill**
Lo siento mucho. Es terrible que haya hecho eso *lō syen-tō moo-chō. es tay-rree-blay kay a-ya ay-chō e-sō*	**I'm very sorry. That was very naughty of him/her**

Sightseeing

French	German
Qu'est-ce qu'il y a à voir ici? *kes-keel ya a vwahr ee-see?*	Was gibt es hier zu sehen? *vas gipt es heer tsoo zay-èn?*
Qu'est-ce que c'est, ce bâtiment? *kes-kuh se, suh ba-tee-moñ?*	Was für ein Gebäude ist das? *vas fōōr ine gè-boy-dè ist das?*
Est-ce qu'il est ouvert au public? *es-keel e too-ver tō pōō-bleek?*	Kann man es besichtigen? *kan man es bè-zikh-ti-gèn?*
Est-ce qu'il y a des visites guidées? *es-keel ya day vee-zeet gee-day?*	Gibt es hier Besichtigungsfahrten/(in town) Stadtrundfahrten? *gipt es heer bè-zikh-ti-goongs-fahr-tèn/shtat-roont-fahr-tèn?*
Est-ce qu'il y a des visites guidées du château/de la cathédrale? *es-keel ya day vee-zeet gee-day dōō sha-tō/duh la ka-tay-dral?*	Gibt es eine Führung durch das Schloß/die Kathedrale? *gipt es ine-è fōō-roong doorkh das shlos/dee ka-tay-drah-lè?*
Combien de temps dure la visite? *koñ-byañ duh toñ dōōr la vee-zeet?*	Wie lange dauert die Führung? *vee lang-è dow-èrt dee fōō-roong?*
Est-ce qu'il y a un guide qui parle anglais? *es-keel ya uñ geed kee parl oñ-glay?*	Gibt es hier einen Fremdenführer, der Englisch spricht? *gipt es heer ine-èn frem-dèn-fōō-rèr, der eng-lish shprikht?*
Est-ce que vous avez un guide en anglais? *es-kuh voo za-vay uñ geed oñ noñ-glay?*	Haben Sie einen englischen Stadtführer? *hah-bèn zee ine-èn eng-lish-èn shtat-fōō-rèr?*
À quelle heure ouvre le musée? *a kel uhr oo-vruh luh mōō-zay?*	Wann macht das Museum auf? *van makht das moo-zay-oom owf?*
C'est combien pour entrer? *se koñ-byañ poor oñ-tray?*	Wieviel kostet der Eintritt? *vee-feel kos-tèt der ine-trit?*
Est-ce que nous pouvons monter jusqu'en haut? *es-kuh noo poo-voñ moñ-tay zhōōs-koñ ō?*	Können wir bis ganz nach oben gehen? *kur'n-èn veer bis gants nakh ō-bèn gay-èn?*
Où est la meilleure vue? *oo e la mye-yuhr vōō?*	Von wo aus hat man die beste Aussicht? *fon vō ows hat man dee bes-tè ows-zikht?*
Est-ce que je peux prendre des photos/utiliser un flash? *es-kuh zhuh puh proñ-druh day fō-tō/ōō-tee-lee-zay uñ flash?*	Kann ich hier fotografieren/Blitzlicht benutzen? *kan ikh heer fō-tō-gra-fee-rèn/blits-likht bè-noots-èn?*
Est-ce que vous voulez bien prendre une photo de nous, s'il vous plaît? *es-kuh voo voo-lay byañ proñ-druh ōōn fō-tō duh noo, see voo play?*	Würden Sie bitte ein Bild von uns machen? *vōōr-dèn zee bit-è ine bilt fon oons makh-èn?*

Sightseeing

¿Qué hay aquí interesante para ver? *kay **a**-ee a-**kee** een-tay-ray-**san**-tay **pa**-ra ber?*	**What is there to see here?**
¿Qué es este edificio? *kay es **es**-tay ay-dee-**fee**-thyō?*	**What is this building?**
¿Está abierto al público? *es-**ta** a-**byer**-tō al **poo**-blee-kō?*	**Is it open to the public?**
¿Hay excursiones turísticas? ***a**-ee ek-skoor-**syo**-nays too-**rees**-tee-kas?*	**Are there any sightseeing tours?**
¿Hay visitas con guía al castillo/a la catedral? ***a**-ee bee-**see**-tas con **gee**-a al kas-**tee**-lyō/a la ka-tay-**dral**?*	**Are there any guided tours of the castle/the cathedral?**
¿Cuánto dura la visita? ***kwan**-tō **doo**-ra la bee-**see**-ta?*	**How long does the tour take?**
¿Hay un guía que hable inglés? ***a**-ee oon **gee**-a kay **a**-blay eeng-**glays**?*	**Is there an English-speaking guide?**
¿Tiene una guía en inglés? ***tyay**-nay **oo**-na **gee**-a en eeng-**glays**?*	**Do you have an English guidebook?**
¿A qué hora abre el museo? *a kay **ō**-ra **a**-bray el moo-**say**-ō?*	**When does the museum open?**
¿Cuánto cuesta la entrada? ***kwan**-tō **kwes**-ta la en-**tra**-da?*	**What is the admission charge?**
¿Podemos subir hasta arriba? *po-**day**-mōs soo-**beer as**-ta a-**rree**-ba?*	**Can we go up to the top?**
¿Desde dónde hay mejor vista? ***des**-day **don**-day **a**-ee may-**khor bees**-ta?*	**Where is the best view?**
¿Puedo hacer fotos/usar el flash? ***pway**-dō a-**ther fō**-tōs/oo-**sar** el flash?*	**Can I take photos/use a flash?**
¿Puede hacernos una foto, por favor? ***pway**-day a-**ther**-nōs **oo**-na **fō**-tō, por fa-**bor**?*	**Would you take a photo of us, please?**

On the Beach

French	German
If you see a red flag flying on the beach, don't go swimming – it's not safe and there's no lifeguard. If the flag's orange, it's still unsafe but there is a lifeguard around. If the flag's green, it's safe to swim.	A red flag flying on a German beach means that it's unsafe to swim and there's no lifeguard. An orange flag means that it's still unsafe, but there is a lifeguard around. If the flag is green, it's safe to swim.
Est-ce qu'il est prudent de nager ici? *es-keel e prōō-doñ duh na-zhay ee-see?*	Kann man hier schwimmen? *kan man heer **shvim**-èn?*
Est-ce une plage privée, ici? *es ōōn plahzh pree-vay, ee-see?*	Ist dies ein Privatstrand? *ist dees ine pree-**vaht**-shtrant?*
Est-ce que vous connaissez une plage tranquille? *es-kuh voo ko-ne-say ōōn plahzh troñ-keel?*	Können Sie mir/uns einen ruhigen Strand empfehlen? ***kur'n**-èn zee meer/oons **ine**-èn **roo**-ikh-èn shtrant emp-**fay**-lèn?*
Où sont les vestiaires? *oo soñ lay vest-yer?*	Wo können wir uns umziehen? *vō **kur'n**-èn veer oons **oom**-tsee-èn?*
Est-ce que je peux louer un transat/un parasol/un voilier/un bateau à moteur? *es-kuh zhuh puh loo-ay uñ troñ-za/uñ pa-ra-sol/uñ vwahl-yay/uñ ba-tō a mō-tuhr?*	Kann ich einen Liegestuhl/einen Sonnenschirm/ein Segelboot/ein Motorboot mieten? *kan ikh **ine**-èn **lee**-gè-shtool/**ine**-èn **zon**-èn-shirm/ine **say**-gèl-bōt/ine **mō**-tor-bōt **mee**-tèn?*
Est-ce qu'il est possible de faire de la voile/du ski nautique/du surf/de la planche à voile? *es-keel e po-see-bluh duh fer duh la vwahl/dōō skee nō-teek/dōō sōōrf/duh la ploñsh a vwahl?*	Kann man hier segeln/Wasserski fahren/surfen/windsurfen? *kan man heer **say**-gèln/**vas**-èr-shee **fah**-rèn/**zoor**-fèn/**vint**-zoor-fèn?*
Ça coûte combien? *sa koot koñ-byañ?*	Wieviel kostet das? *vee-**feel** kos-tèt das?*
Est-ce qu'il y a des courants/des méduses ici? *es-keel ya day koo-roñ/day may-dōōz ee-see?*	Gibt es hier Strömungen/Quallen? *gipt es heer **shtrur'**-moong-èn/**kval**-èn?*
Est-ce que l'eau est chaude? *es-kuh lō ay shōd?*	Ist das Wasser warm? *ist das **vas**-èr varm?*
Où est-ce que je peux acheter des glaces/de la lotion solaire/des lunettes de soleil? *oo es-kuh zhuh puh zash-tay day glas/duh la lō-syoñ so-ler/day lōō-net duh so-lye?*	Wo kann ich Eis/Sonnenöl/eine Sonnenbrille kaufen? *vō kan ikh ise/**zon**-èn-ur'l/**ine**-è **son**-èn-bril-è **kow**-fèn?*
Où est le poste de secours sur la plage? *oo e luh post duh suh-koor sōōr la plahzh?*	Wo ist der Rettungsschwimmer? *vō ist der **ret**-oongs-shvim-èr?*

On the Beach

*A red flag flying on a Spanish beach means that it's
not safe to go swimming. A yellow flag means that
you can swim, but it's not recommended. If the
flag is green, it's safe to swim.*

¿Se puede nadar sin peligro aquí? *say pway-day na-dar seen pay-lee-grŏ a-kee?*	**Is it safe to swim here?**
¿Es privada esta playa? *es pree-ba-da es-ta pla-ya?*	**Is this a private beach?**
¿Puede recomendarme una playa tranquila? *pway-day ray-ko-men-dar-may oo-na pla-ya trang-kee-la?*	**Can you recommend a quiet beach?**
¿Dónde podemos cambiarnos? *don-day po-day-mŏs kam-byar-nŏs?*	**Where can we change?**
¿Puedo alquilar una silla de playa/una sombrilla/un barco de vela/una motora? *pway-dŏ al-kee-lar oo-na see-lya day pla-ya/oo-na som-bree-lya/oon bar-ko day bay-la/oo-na mo-to-ra?*	**Can I rent a deck-chair/a sunshade/a sailing boat/a motor boat?**
¿Se puede navegar a vela/hacer esquí acuático/hacer surfing/hacer surfing a vela? *say pway-day na-bay-gar a bay-la/ a-ther e-skee a-kwa-tee-kŏ/a-ther soor-feeng/a-ther soor-feeng a bay-la?*	**Is it possible to go sailing/ water-skiing/surfing/wind surfing?**
¿Cuánto es? *kwan-tŏ es?*	**How much is it?**
¿Hay corrientes/medusas aquí? *a-ee ko-rryen-tays/may-doo-sas a-kee?*	**Are there any currents/jellyfish here?**
¿Está el agua caliente? *es-ta el a-gwa ka-lyen-tay?*	**Is the water warm?**
¿Dónde puedo comprar helado/aceite bronceador/gafas de sol? *don-day pway-dŏ kom-prar ay-la-dŏ/a-the-ee-tay bron-thay-a-dor/ga-fas day sol?*	**Where can I buy ice-cream/ sun-tan lotion/sunglasses?**
¿Dónde está el vigilante? *don-day es-ta el bee-khee-lan-tay?*	**Where is the lifeguard?**

Outdoors & Nightlife

French	German
Est-ce qu'il y a une piscine/un court de tennis/un terrain de golf? *es-keel ya ōōn pee-seen/uñ koor duh te-nees/uñ te-rañ duh golf?*	Gibt es hier ein Freibad/einen Tennisplatz/einen Golfplatz? *gipt es heer ine **frye**-bat/**ine**-èn te-nis-plats/**ine**-èn **golf**-plats?*
Est-ce qu'il est possible de faire du cheval/d'aller à la pêche? *es-keel ay po-see-bluh duh fer dōō shuh-val/da-lay a la pesh?*	Kann man hier reiten/angeln gehen? *kan man heer **rye**-tèn/**ang**-èln **gay**-èn?*
Est-ce que je peux louer le matériel? *es-kuh zhuh puh loo-ay luh ma-tay-ree-el?*	Kann ich die Ausrüstung leihen? *kan ikh dee **ows**-rōōs-toong **lye**-èn?*
Est-ce que vous connaissez des promenades intéressantes à faire? *es-kuh voo ko-ne-say day prom-nad añ-tay-re-soñt a fer?*	Kennen Sie irgendwelche interessanten Spaziergänge? ***ken**-èn zee **ir**-gent-vel-khè in-tè-re-**san**-tèn shpa-**tseer**-geng-è?*
Est-ce qu'il y a des fêtes dans la région en ce moment? *es-keel ya day fet doñ la ray-zhyoñ oñ suh mo-moñ?*	Sind zur Zeit irgendwelche Festivals? *zint tsoor tsite **ir**-gènt-vel-khè **fes**-ti-vèls?*
Est-ce qu'il y a des films en anglais? *es-keel ya day feelm oñ noñ-glay?*	Laufen hier Filme in englischer Sprache? ***low**-fèn heer **fil**-mè in **eng**-lish-èr **shprah**-khè?*
Est-ce qu'il y a un concert? *es-keel ya uñ koñ-ser?*	Gibt es ein Konzert? *gipt es ine kon-**tsert**?*
Est-ce que je peux réserver à l'avance? *es-kuh zhuh puh ray-zer-vay a la-voñs?*	Kann ich im voraus buchen? *kan ikh im **fōr**-ows **bookh**-èn?*
Deux balcons, s'il vous plaît *duh bal-koñ, see voo play*	Zweimal erster Rang, bitte ***tsvye**-mal **erst**-èr rang, **bit**-è*
Deux orchestres, s'il vous plaît *duh zor-kes-truh, see voo play*	Zweimal Sperrsitz, bitte ***tsvye**-mal **shper**-zits, **bit**-è*
Est-ce qu'il y a de bonnes boîtes de nuit? *es-keel ya duh bon bwaht duh nwee?*	Gibt es hier gute Nachtclubs? *gipt es heer **goo**-tè **nakht**-kloops?*
Est-ce qu'il y a une discothèque? *es-keel ya ōōn dees-kō-tek?*	Gibt es hier eine Diskothek? *gipt es heer **ine**-è dis-kō-**tayk**?*

Spanish

Hay piscina/pista de tenis/campo de golf? *a-ee pees-**thee**-na/**pees**-ta day e-nees/**kam**-pō day golf?*	**Is there a swimming pool/tennis court/golf course?**
Se puede montar a caballo/ir a pescar? *say **pway**-day mon-**tar** a ka-**ba**-lyō/eer a pes-**kar**?*	**Is it possible to go riding/fishing?**
Puedo alquilar el equipo? ***pway**-dō al-kee-**lar** el ay-**kee**-pō?*	**Can I hire the equipment?**
Sabe de alguna ruta interesante para caminar? *sa-bay day al-**goo**-na **roo**-ta en-tay-ray-**san**-tay **pa**-ra ka-mee-**nar**?*	**Do you know any interesting walks?**
Se celebra alguna fiesta por estas fechas? *ay thay-**lay**-bra al-**goo**-na **fyes**-ta por **es**-tas **fe**-chas?*	**Are there any local festivals on just now?**
Hay alguna película en inglés? *a-ee al-**goo**-na pay-**lee**-koo-la en eng-**glays**?*	**Are there any films in English?**
Hay concierto? *a-ee kon-**thyer**-tō?*	**Is there a concert?**
Puedo reservar las entradas? ***pway**-dō ray-ser-**bar** las en-**tra**-das?*	**Can I book in advance?**
Dos entradas de palco, por favor *dōs en-**tra**-das day **pal**-kō, por fa-**bor***	**2 balcony seats please**
Dos entradas de butaca, por favor *dōs en-**tra**-das day boo-**ta**-ka, por a-**bor***	**2 stalls (orchestra) tickets please**
Hay algún club nocturno bueno? *a-ee al-**goon** kloob nok-**toor**-nō **bway**-nō?*	**Are there any good night-clubs?**
Hay discoteca? *a-ee dees-kō-**tay**-ka?*	**Is there a disco?**

Restaurants

French	German
A trip to France is an invitation to good eating, whether in 4-star restaurants or more modest establishments. Set price menus are often good value, but beware of menus touristiques in places obviously catering for tourists, where standards are not likely to be high for customers who are only passing through. The best recommendation is the presence of the French themselves. The menu-reader on page 80 will help you decide what to eat.	Eating out in Germany can be a memorable experience. In cities you will find international-style restaurants but most Germans prefer the traditional Wirtshaus and Gasthof, where you will find authentic local cooking. Try to avoid places obviously catering for tourists, where standards are not likely to be high for customers who are only passing through. The best recommendation is the presence of the Germans themselves. The menu-reader on page 84 will help you decide what to eat.
Est-ce que nous pouvons avoir une table pour deux? *es-kuh noo poo-voñ za-vwar ōōn ta-bluh poor duh?*	Können wir einen Tisch für zwei Personen haben? **kur'n**-èn veer **ine**-èn tish fōōr tsvye per-**zō**-nèn **hah**-bèn?
Est-ce que je peux réserver une table pour quatre à huit heures? *es-kuh zhuh puh ray-zer-vay ōōn ta-bluh poor ka-truh a weet uhr?*	Kann ich für acht Uhr einen Tisch für vier Personen bestellen? *kan ikh fōōr akht* **oo**-èr **ine**-èn tish fōōr feer per-**zō**-nèn bè-**shtel**-èn?
Nous voudrions une table près de la fenêtre/sur la terrasse *noo voo-dree-oñ zōōn ta-bluh pre duh la fne-truh/sōōr la te-ras*	Wir hätten gerne einen Tisch am Fenster/auf der Terrasse *veer* **he**-tèn **gern**-è **ine**-èn tish am **fen**-stèr/owf der te-**ras**-è
La carte, s'il vous plaît *la kart, see voo play*	Die Speisekarte, bitte *dee* **shpye**-zè-kar-tè, **bit**-è
Nous prendrons le menu à trente-cinq francs *noo proñ-droñ luh muh-nōō a troñt-sañk froñ*	Wir hätten gerne das Menü zu fünfzehn Mark *veer* **he**-tèn **gern**-è das mè-**nōō** tsoo **fōōnf**-tsayn mark
Est-ce que vous avez une spécialité locale? *es-kuh voo za-vay ōōn spays-yal-ee-tay lō-kal?*	Haben Sie eine Spezialität aus dieser Gegend? **hah**-bèn zee **ine**-è shpay-tsee-a-li-**tayt** ows **dee**-zèr **gay**-gènt?
Je prendrai cela *zhuh proñ-dray sla*	Ich nehme das *ikh* **nay**-mè das
Nous commencerons par une soupe à l'oignon *noo ko-moñs-roñ par ōōn soop a lo-nyoñ*	Als Vorspeise hätten wir gerne Zwiebelsuppe *als* **fōr**-shpye-zè **he**-tèn veer **gern**-è **tsvee**-bèl-zoo-pè
Je prendrai un steak-frites *zhuh proñ-dray uñ stayk-freet*	Ich hätte gerne ein Steak und Pommes frites *ikh* **he**-tè **gerne**-è ine shtayk oont por frit
Je le voudrais bleu/saignant/à point/bien cuit *zhuh luh voo-dray bluh/sen-yoñ/a pwañ/byañ kwee*	Ich hätte es gerne blutig/rot/halbgebraten/durchgebraten *ikh* **he**-tè es **gern**-è **bloo**-tikh/rōt/**halp**-gè-brah-tèn/**doorkh**-gè-brah-tè

Spanish

Spain has much to offer lovers of good food. You can have memorable meals all over the country, in elegant city restaurants or in local inns (fondas). Set price menus are usually good value, but beware of *menús turísticos* in places obviously catering for tourists, where standards are not likely to be high or customers who are only passing through. The best recommendation is the presence of the Spanish themselves. The menu-reader on page 88 will help you to decide what to eat.

Una mesa para dos, por favor **oo**-na **may**-sa **pa**-ra dōs, por fa-**bor**	**Can we have a table for two?**
Puedo reservar una mesa para cuatro a las ocho? **way**-dō ray-ser-**bar oo**-na **may**-sa **pa**-ra **kwa**-trō a las **o**-chō?	**Can I book a table for four at 8 o'clock?**
Querríamos una mesa junto a la ventana/en la terraza kay-**rree**-a-mōs **oo**-na **may**-sa **hoon**-tō a la ben-**ta**-na/en la **te-rra**-tha	**We'd like a table by the window/on the terrace**
La carta, por favor la **kar**-ta, por fa-**bor**	**The menu please**
Tráiganos el plato del día de quinientas pesetas **tra**-ee-ga-nōs el **pla**-tō del **dee**-a day kee-**nyen**-tas pay-**say**-tas	**We will take the menu at 35 francs/15 Deutschmarks/500 pesetas**
Tiene alguna especialidad local? **tyay**-nay al-**goo**-na es-pe-thya-lee-**dad** lō-**kal**?	**Do you have a local speciality?**
Tráigame eso **tra**-ee-ga-may e-**sō**	**I'll take that**
Empezaremos con sopa de cebolla em-pay-tha-**ray**-mōs kon **sō**-pa day thay-**bo**-lya	**We'll begin with onion soup**
Tráigame un filete con patatas fritas **tra**-ee-ga-may oon fee-**lay**-tay con pa-**ta**-tas **free**-tas	**I'll have steak and chips (French fries)**
Me gusta muy poco pasado/poco pasado/medianamente pasado/bien asado may **goos**-ta mwee **pō**-kō pa-**sa**-dō/**pō**-kō pa-**sa**-dō/may-dya-na-**men**-ty pa-**sa**-dō/byen pa-**sa**-dō	**I like it very rare/rare/medium rare/well done**

Restaurants

French	German
Est-ce que les légumes sont compris? *es-kuh lay lay-gōōm soñ koñ-pree?*	Ist das Gemüse dabei? *ist das gè-mōō-zè da-bye?*
C'est pour moi *say poor mwah*	Das ist für mich *das ist fōōr mikh*
Ce n'est pas ce que j'ai commandé *snay pa suh kuh zhay ko-moñ-day*	Das habe ich nicht bestellt *das hah-bè ikh nikht bè-shtelt*
On mange ça comment? *on moñzh sa ko-moñ?*	Wie ißt man das? *vee ist man das?*
Du pain, s'il vous plaît *dōō pañ, see voo play*	Könnten wir bitte noch Brot haben? *kur'n-tèn veer bit-è nokh brōt hah-bèn?*
Du beurre, s'il vous plaît *dōō buhr, see voo play*	Kann ich bitte Butter haben? *kan ikh bit-è boo-tèr hah-bèn?*
Ça s'appelle comment? *sa sa-pel ko-moñ?*	Wie heißt das? *vee hyest das?*
Un autre verre, s'il vous plaît *uñ nō-truh ver, see voo play*	Würden Sie bitte noch ein Glas bringen? *vōōr-dèn zee bit-è nokh ine glas bring-èn?*
Ceci est très salé *suh-see ay tray sa-lay*	Das ist sehr salzig *das ist zayr zal-tsikh*
Je voulais du fromage *zhuh voo-lay dōō fro-mazh*	Ich hatte Käse bestellt *ikh ha-tè kay-zè bè-shtelt*
Est-ce que vous avez oublié la soupe? *es-kuh voo za-vay zoo-blee-ay la soop?*	Haben Sie die Suppe vergessen? *hah-bèn zee dee zoo-pè ver-ges-èn?*
Ceci est froid *suh-see ay frwah*	Das ist kalt *das ist kalt*
Ceci est très bon *suh-see ay tray boñ*	Es schmeckt sehr gut *es shmekt zayr goot*
Je prendrai un dessert, s'il vous plaît *zhuh proñ-dray uñ de-ser, see voo play*	Ich hätte gerne ein Dessert *ikh he-tè gern-è ine de-ser*
La carte des vins, s'il vous plaît *la kart day vañ, see voo play*	Die Getränkekarte, bitte *dee gè-treng-kè-kar-tè, bit-è*
Quel vin me conseillez-vous? *kel vañ muh koñ-se-yay-voo?*	Welchen Wein können Sie mir empfehlen? *vel-khèn vine kur'n-èn zee meer em-pfay-lèn?*
Est-ce que le vin du pays est bon? *es-kuh luh vañ dōō pay-ee ay boñ?*	Ist der Wein aus dieser Gegend gut? *ist der vine ows dee-zèr gay-gènt goot?*
Une bouteille de ..., s'il vous plaît *ōōn boo-tye duh ..., see voo play*	Eine Flasche ..., bitte *ine-è flash-è ..., bit-è*

Restaurants

¿Incluye verduras? een-**kloo**-yay ber-**doo**-ras?	**Are vegetables included?**
Eso es para mí e-sō es **pa**-ra mee	**That is for me**
Eso no es lo que pedí e-sō nō es lō kay pay-**dee**	**That is not what I ordered**
¿Cómo se come esto? **kō**-mō say **kō**-may es-tō?	**How do I eat this?**
¿Nos puede traer más pan, por favor? nos **pway**-day tra-**er** mas pan, por fa-**bor**?	**Could we have some more bread, please?**
¿Me puede traer mantequilla? may **pway**-day tra-**er** man-tay-**kee**-lya?	**Could I have some butter?**
¿Cómo se llama esto? **kō**-mō say **lya**-ma es-tō?	**What is this called?**
¿Puede traernos otro vaso, por favor? **pway**-day tra-**er**-nōs ō-trō **ba**-sō, por fa-**bor**?	**Would you bring another glass please?**
Esto está muy salado es-tō es-**ta** mwee sa-**la**-dō	**This is very salty**
Quería queso kay-**ree**-a **kay**-sō	**I wanted cheese**
¿Se ha olvidado de la sopa? say a ol-bee-**da**-dō day la **sō**-pa?	**Have you forgotten the soup?**
Esto está frío es-tō es-**ta free**-ō	**This is cold**
Esto está muy bueno es-tō es-**ta** mwee **bway**-nō	**This is very good**
Voy a tomar postre, por favor boy a tō-**mar pos**-tray, por fa-**bor**	**I'll have a dessert please**
La carta de vinos, por favor la **kar**-ta day **bee**-nōs, por fa-**bor**	**The wine list please**
¿Qué vino recomienda usted? kay **bee**-nō ray-ko-**myen**-da oos-**ted**?	**Which wine do you recommend?**
¿Es bueno el vino del país? es **bway**-nō el **bee**-nō del pa-**ees**?	**Is the local wine good?**
Una botella de ..., por favor **oo**-na bo-**te**-lya day ..., por fa-**bor**	**A bottle of ..., please**

Restaurants

French	German
Une carafe de rouge *ōōn ka-raf duh roozh*	Eine Karaffe Rotwein *ine-è ka-raf-è rōt-vine*
Une bouteille/une demi-bouteille de blanc *ōōn boo-tye/ōōn duh-mee boo-tye duh bloñ*	Eine Flasche/eine halbe Flasche Weißwein *ine-è flash-è/ine-è hal-bè flash-è vise-vine*
Une autre bouteille, s'il vous plaît *ōōn ō-truh boo-tye, see voo play*	Noch eine Flasche, bitte *nokh ine-è flash-è, bit-è*
Une bière, s'il vous plaît *ōōn byer, see voo play*	Ein Bier, bitte *ine beer, bit-è*
Un café, s'il vous plaît *uñ ka-fay, see voo play*	Einen schwarzen Kaffee, bitte *ine-èn shvar-tsèn ka-fay, bit-è*
Un café-crème, s'il vous plaît *uñ ka-fay-krem, see voo play*	Einen Kaffee mit Milch, bitte *ine-èn ka-fay mit milkh, bit-è*
L'addition, s'il vous plaît *la-dee-syoñ, see voo play*	Die Rechnung, bitte *dee rekh-noong, bit-è*
Est-ce que le service est compris? *es-kuh luh ser-vees ay koñ-pree?*	Ist Bedienung inbegriffen? *ist bè-dee-noong in-bè-grif-èn?*
Il y a une erreur ici *eel ya ōōn e-ruhr ee-see*	Ich glaube, Sie haben hier einen Fehler gemacht *ikh glow-bè, zee hah-bèn heer ine-èn fay-lèr gè-makht*
Le repas était excellent *luh ruh-pa ay-te tek-se-loñ*	Das Essen war ausgezeichnet *das es-èn var ows-gè-tsyekh-nèt*

Spanish

Una jarra de vino tinto *oo-*na **kha**-rra day **bee**-nō **teen**-tō	**A carafe of red wine**
Una botella/media botella de vino blanco *oo-*na bo-**te**-lya/**may**-dya bo-**te**-lya day **bee**-nō **blang**-kō	**A bottle/half bottle of white wine**
Otra botella, por favor *ō*-tra bo-**te**-lya, por fa-**bor**	**Another bottle please**
Una cerveza, por favor *oo-*na ther-**bay**-tha, por fa-**bor**	**A beer please**
Un café solo, por favor *oon ka-**fay** s**ō**-lō, por fa-**bor**	**Black coffee please**
Un café con leche, por favor *oon ka-**fay** kon **lay**-chay, por fa-**bor**	**Coffee with milk please**
La cuenta, por favor *la **kwen**-ta, por fa-**bor**	**The bill please**
¿Está incluido el servicio? *es-ta een-kloo-**ee**-dō el ser-**bee**-thyō?	**Is service included?**
Hay un error aquí *a-ee oon e-**rror** a-**kee**	**There's a mistake here**
Ha sido una comida excelente *a **see**-dō **oo**-na ko-**mee**-da eks-thay-**len**-tay	**The meal was excellent**

Menu Reader
France

Andouille
Tripe sausage

Aubergines farcies
Stuffed aubergines (eggplants)

Bifteck
see *Steak*

Blanquette de veau
Stewed veal in a white sauce

Bœuf bourguignon
Beef stew with red wine

Bœuf en daube
Beef casserole

Boudin
Black (blood) pudding

Bouillabaisse
A speciality of Marseille, a
soup/stew made with fish and
shellfish

Caille sur canapé
Quail on toast

Canard à l'orange
Roast duck stuffed with orange and
served with an orange and wine
sauce

Canard rôti
Roast duck

Carottes Vichy
Slightly caramelized carrots cooked
in sugar and butter

Cassoulet
A stew of beans with pork or mutton

Cervelles
Brains

Champignons à la crème
Mushrooms with cream sauce

Champignons à la grecque
Mushrooms served in oil, wine and
herbs

Chapirons
Small octopus

Choucroûte garni
Sauerkraut garnished with assorted
pork meats and boiled potatoes

Confit d'oie
Goose cooked and preserved in its
own fat

Consommé
Clear soup

Coq au vin
Chicken cooked in red wine

Coquilles Saint-Jacques
Scallops served in their shells

Côtelettes de veau
Veal cutlets

Crudités
Assorted raw vegetables (grated
carrots, sliced tomatoes etc) served
as an hors d'œuvre

Dinde truffée
Truffled turkey

Entrecôte grillé
Grilled rib steak

Épaule d'agneau
Shoulder of lamb

Escalopes de veau à la crème
Veal escalopes in a cream sauce

Escargots à la bourguignonne
Snails in garlic butter sauce

Faisan rôti
Roast pheasant

Filet de sole meunière
Sole cooked in butter and served
with lemon

Filets de sole normande
Sole in white wine with mushrooms,
oysters and shrimps

Frites
Chips (French fries)

Gigot d'agneau rôti
Roast leg of lamb

Gratin dauphinois
Baked sliced potatoes with cheese and cream

Hachis parmentier
A sort of shepherd's pie – minced beef mixed into mashed potatoes, then baked

Homard à l'armoricaine
Lobster sautéed with shallots, tomatoes and white wine; brandy is sometimes added

Jambon de Bayonne
Raw, cured ham from the Pays Basque

Lapin chasseur
Rabbit cooked with white wine and herbs

Lapin de Garenne aux pruneaux
Wild rabbit marinated in a red wine and herb mixture, then casseroled with prunes

Lotte farcie
Stuffed turbot

Macédoine de légumes
Mixture of diced vegetables

Maquereaux au vin blanc
Mackerel in white wine

Morue Provençale
Cooked salt cod with tomatoes, onions, olives, capers and garlic and dressed in olive oil

Moules marinières
Mussels in white wine

Omelette
Omelette:
   aux champignons – mushroom
   aux fines herbes – mixed herb
   au fromage – cheese
   au jambon – ham
   nature – plain

Paupiettes de veau
Thin rolls of veal with a forcemeat filling

Perdreau/pigeon rôti
Roast partridge/pigeon

Pipérade
Cooked tomatoes and pimentos with an omelette mixture added

Pommes (de terre) allumettes
Matchstick potatoes

Pommes (de terre) à l'anglaise
Boiled potatoes

Pommes dauphine
Potato balls covered in choux pastry and deep fried

Pommes frites
Chips (French fries)

Pommes rissolées
Small round potatoes cooked in deep fat

Pommes vapeur
Steamed potatoes

Potée
Vegetable soup

Pot au feu
A very thick soup made from beef and vegetables

Poule au riz
Boiled chicken and rice

Poulet Basquaise
Chicken pieces cooked with tomatoes, peppers, mushrooms, diced ham and white wine

Poulet à la crème
Fried chicken with mushrooms and cream

Poulet rôti
Roast chicken

Quiche lorraine
Pastry flan filled with bacon, eggs and cream

Râble de lièvre
Roast saddle of hare

Ragoût de veau
Stewed veal

Menu Reader
France

Raie au beurre noir
Skate in black butter

Ratatouille Niçoise
Onions, green peppers, courgettes
(zucchini), aubergine (eggplant),
garlic and tomatoes stewed together.
Served hot or cold

Ris de veau au beurre noir
Sweetbreads in brown butter sauce

Rognons sautés madère
Sautéed kidneys in madeira sauce

Rôti de bœuf
Roast beef

Rôti de porc
Roast pork

Rôti de veau
Roast veal

Salade Niçoise
There are many variations of this
salad. The basic ingredients are
green beans, anchovies, black olives
and green peppers

Salade de tomates
Sliced tomatoes in a vinaigrette
sauce

Soufflé
Soufflé: the savoury varieties are the
same as for omelettes

Soupe à l'oignon
Onion soup

Soupe de poissons
Fish soup

Steak au poivre
Steak with crushed peppercorns

Steak tartare
Minced raw steak mixed with raw
egg, chopped onion, tartare or
Worcester sauce, parsley and capers

Tomates farcies
Stuffed tomatoes

Tomates à la provençale
Grilled tomatoes steeped in garlic

Tournedos Rossini
Tournedos steak on fried bread with
foie gras and truffles on top

Tripes à la mode de Caen
Tripe with vegetables, herbs, cider
and calvados

Truite à la crème
Trout with cream

Truite aux amandes
Trout with almonds

Veau sauté Marengo
Veal casseroled with white wine,
garlic and mushrooms

Cheeses

*The cheese course normally comes
straight after the main course, while
the wine is still on the table.*

Bleu de Bresse
One of the milder blue-veined
cheeses with a soft mottled texture

Brie
Soft and creamy, one of the
best-known French cheeses

Camembert
Soft and well flavoured, pungent
when fully ripened

Cantal
Semi-hard, fairly strong-flavoured
cheese

Carré de l'est
Mild-tasting cheese with a flowery
rind, best eaten between November
and May

Chèvre
Goat's milk cheese: it comes in
many varieties and shapes

Comté
A hard cheese from Jura with a
tangy taste

Coulommiers
Similar to *Brie*, soft and creamy

Emmenthal
From Switzerland, but also made in
France, a hard cheese with large
holes, often used in cooking

Gruyère
A hard Swiss cheese with a delicate
flavour

Livarot
Strong-flavoured soft cheese

Petit Suisse
Small pots of rich creamy soft
cheese, usually eaten with sugar

Pont-l'évêque
Softish, mature, square-shaped
cheese

Reblochon
Soft, mild cheese of buttery
consistency

Roquefort
Blue-veined cheese made from ewe's
milk. Rich and pungent with a
crumbly texture

Saint Paulin
Large round cheese made from rich
cow's milk

Tomme aux raisins
Semi-soft cheese covered with grape
pips

Desserts

Baba au rhum
Sweet yeast sponge soaked in a
rum-flavoured syrup

Beignets de pommes
Apple fritters

Clafoutis
Pastry or batter pudding filled with
black cherries

Crème caramel
Caramel custard

Crème renversée
Caramelized custard

Crêpes
Pancakes

Gauffres
Waffles

Glace
Ice-cream:
    au café – coffee
    au chocolat – chocolate
    au praliné – almonds and burnt
    sugar crushed up when cold
    à la vanille – vanilla

Millefeuille
Layers of wafer-thin puff pastry
filled with cream and raspberry jam

Mousse au chocolat
Chocolate mousse

Pêche Melba
Vanilla ice-cream with peaches,
raspberry sauce and whipped cream

Sorbet
Water ice or sherbet

Soufflé
Soufflé:
    au chocolat – chocolate
    au Grand Marnier – orange
    liqueur

Tarte aux fraises
Strawberry flan

Tarte aux pommes
Apple flan

Yaourt
Yoghourt

Menu Reader
Germany, Austria & Switzerland

Aal Grün mit Dillsauce
Fresh eel with dill sauce

Aufgebackene Spätzli
Fried dumplings served with an egg
sauce (Switzerland)

Bauernfrühstück
Omelette with bacon and cooked
potatoes

Bauernschmaus
Assortment of roast and smoked
pork; sausages, sauerkraut and
dumplings (Austria)

Bayerisches Kraut
Shredded cabbage cooked with
sliced apples, wine and sugar

Biersuppe
Beer soup flavoured with cinnamon
and lemon

Bismarckheringe
Herring fillets marinated in a
vinegary sauce

Bohnensuppe
Thick brown bean soup with pieces
of smoked bacon (esp. Austria)

Bouillon
Clear soup

Brathähnchen
Roast chicken

Bratheringe
Fresh fried herring marinated in a
vinegar, herb and onion dressing

Bündnerfleisch
Raw beef, smoked and dried, served
thinly sliced (Switzerland)

Dampfnudel
Yeast dumpling

**Deutsche Beefsteaks/Bouletten/
Frikadellen**
Fried, flat minced meat balls

Eierkuchen
Pancakes

Eisbein
Pickled knuckle of pork

Erdäpfelknödel
Potato and semolina dumplings
(Austria)

Erdäpfelnudeln
Fried, boiled potato balls tossed in
fried breadcrumbs (Austria)

Falscher Hase
Baked minced meat loaf

Fischauflauf
Fish pudding (Austria)

Fleischbrühe
see *Bouillon*

Forelle blau
Trout

Forelle Steiermark
Small filleted trout, larded with
bacon strips and served with a white
sauce (Austria)

Gebratene Ente/Gans
Roast duck/goose

Gebackenes Goldbarschfilet
Fried golden perch fillet in egg and
breadcrumbs

Gefüllte Kalbsbrust
Roast stuffed breast of veal

Gemüseplatte
Assorted vegetables

Geräucherter Aal
Smoked eel

Geschnetzeltes Kalbfleisch
Thinly sliced veal with a thick
cream sauce (Switzerland)

Gitziprägel
Baked rabbit in batter (Switzerland)

Grießklößchen
Semolina dumplings

Grießnockerlnsuppe
Beef broth with chives, served with
semolina dumplings (Austria)

Grüner Salat
Lettuce mixed with a vinegar and oil
dressing

Güggeli
Roast chicken with onions and
mushrooms in a white wine sauce
(Switzerland)

Gulasch
Highly seasoned stew, flavoured
with paprika

Gulaschsuppe
Thick, spicy meat soup, flavoured
with paprika

Hasenpfeffer
Jugged hare

Hühnerfrikassée
Chicken fricassee

Huhn mit Käsesauce
Boiled chicken with cheese sauce
(Switzerland)

Jägergulasch
Venison stew with bacon, ham,
juniper berries and sour cream,
flavoured with paprika (Austria)

Jura Omelette
Emmentaler cheese, bacon, tomato,
onion and potato omelette
(Switzerland)

Junges Gemüse
Young vegetables

Kaiserfleisch
Boiled smoked pork (Austria)

Kalbsnierenbraten
Roast loin of veal including the
kidneys

Karpfen in Bier
Carp poached in beer, red wine and
onion, flavoured with bay leaf,
lemon peel and peppercorns
(Austria)

Kartoffelklöße
Potato dumplings

Kartoffelpfluten
Potato dumplings served with fried
onion rings (Switzerland)

Kartoffelpitte
Baked potatoes, dried pears, milk
and diced bacon (Switzerland)

Kartoffelpüree/Kartoffelbrei
Mashed potatoes

Käsefondue
Cheese fondue, usually made with a
mixture of *Gruyère* and *Emmentaler*
cheese, melted with white wine and
Kirsch. Bits of bread are dipped into
the hot cheese mixture (Switzerland)

Käsesuppe
Cheese soup (Switzerland)

Kasseler Rippenspeer
Pickled smoked saddle of pork

Kloß
Dumpling

Knödel
Dumpling (Austria)

Kohlroulade
Cabbage stuffed with a minced meat
mixture and baked in the oven
(Austria)

Königsberger Kloß
Meatballs served in a thick white
sauce with capers in it

Kopfsalat
see *Grüner Salat*

Krautsalat
Cabbage salad flavoured with
caraway seeds

Kümmelbraten
Caraway-flavoured roast beef
(Austria)

Leberknödel/Leberspätzle
Liver dumplings

Leipziger Allerlei
A mixture of green peas, carrots,
cauliflower and cabbage

Menu Reader
Germany, Austria & Switzerland

Maluns
Sliced and grated potato mixture
fried in lard (Switzerland)

Markklößchen
Small beef-marrow dumplings

Matjesfilets
Soused herring fillets in a thick
sauce

Maultasche
Small ravioli-like pasta bags filled
with a pork, veal and spinach
mixture

Mistchratzerli
see *Güggeli*

Nockerl
Small dumplings (Austria)

Nudeln
Noodles

Omelette mit Pilzen
Mushroom omelette

Ochsenschwanzsuppe
Oxtail soup

Paprikahähnchen
Chicken stewed with onions and
flavoured with paprika

Pfannkuchen
Pancakes

Pommes frites
Chips (French fries)

Räucherlachs
Smoked salmon

Rehrücken
Roast saddle of venison

Rind(er)braten
Roast beef

Rippchen mit Sauerkraut
Pickled pork ribs with *sauerkraut*

Rösti
Fried diced potatoes mixed with
small fried bacon cubes

Rührei
Scrambled egg

Salatplatte
Selection of salads

Sauerbraten
Marinated roast beef

Sauerkraut
Shredded, salted and fermented
white cabbage

Schlachtplatte
A mixture of cold sausages and
meats

Schweinebraten
Roast pork

Schweinekotelett
Pork chop dipped in egg and
breadcrumbs and fried

Spätzle
Home-made noodles served with
breadcrumbs and browned butter

Spiegelei
Fried egg

Strammer Max
Fried egg with raw ham and rye
bread

Tiroler Eierspeise
Hard-boiled eggs, potatoes, cream
and anchovies, topped with
breadcrumbs and baked (Austria)

Topfenknödel
Curd cheese dumplings sprinkled
with fried breadcrumbs (Austria)

Urner Kraut mit Reis
Cooked cabbage strips mixed with
cheese and cooked rice, with fried
onion

Weckklöße
Bread dumplings

Wiener Schnitzel
Veal escalope fried in breadcrumbs

Wiener Fischfilets
Fish fillets baked with soured cream, gherkins and capers

Wildgulasch
Game stew

Wildbraten
Roast venison

Cheeses

Achleitner
Sharp, appetizing cheese (Austria)

Edamer
A German version of the Dutch cheese. Mild flavour

Emmentaler
Hard, whole-milk cheese with fairly large holes (Switzerland)

Limburger
Strong cheese flavoured with herbs

Liptauer
Cream cheese with paprika and herbs (Austria)

Münster
Strong cheese with caraway seeds

Quark
Curd cheese

Schweizer Käse
see *Emmentaler*

Tilsiter
Savoury, straw-coloured cheese; smooth, with a slightly sour and sharpish taste

Desserts

Apfelkompott
Stewed apple

Apfelrösti
Cooked apple slices fried in butter together with bread slices (Switzerland)

Auflauf
Soufflé

Eis(creme)
Ice-cream

Eisbecher
Ice-cream sundae

Kaiserschmarren
Pieces of chopped-up batter with raisins, sugar and cinnamon

Obstsalat
Fruit salad

Palatschinken
Pancakes filled with curd cheese mixture, or with apricot jam

Rote Grütze
Raspberry, redcurrant and wine jelly served with fresh cream

Salzburger Nockerl
Foamy soufflé omelette with a light centre and a puffed and golden outside (Austria)

Zwetschkenknödel
Boiled plum dumplings fried in breadcrumbs, sprinkled with sugar, and served hot (Austria)

Menu Reader
Spain

Ajo de las manos (Patatas bravas)
Sliced, boiled potatoes mixed with a
garlic, oil and vinegar dressing, and
flavoured with red peppers

Albóndigas
Meat-ball rissoles

Almejas marinera
Steamed mussels/clams with a
parsley, olive oil and garlic sauce

Angulas en cazuelita
Garlic flavoured, fried baby eels
seasoned with hot pepper

Arroz a la levantina
Rice with shellfish, onions,
artichokes, peas, tomatoes and
saffron

Arroz a la valenciana
The Valencian version of *paella*. For
this dish eel is usually added

Arroz a la zamorana
Rice with pork and peppers,
flavoured with garlic (León)

Bacalao al ajo arriero
Dried cod fried with garlic to which
vinegar, paprika and chopped
parsley are added (Navarre)

Bacalao a la vizcaína
Fried dried cod with tomato,
pepper, onion and garlic purée

Bacalao con patatas
Dried cod baked with potatoes,
peppers, tomatoes, onions, olives
and bayleaves (Cádiz)

Berenjenas rellenas
Stuffed aubergines

Berenjenas salteadas
Aubergines sautéed with tomatoes
and onions

Boquerones fritos
Fried anchovies (Málaga)

Buñuelos
A brandy or rum flavoured batter
filled with ham, mussel and prawn
mixture, then deep fried

Butifarra con judías
Pork sausage with beans

Cachelos
Chopped boiled potatoes, boiled
cabbage and garlic, red pepper and
fried bacon. Often served with
chorizo sausage and ham

Calabacines rellenos
Stuffed baby marrows

Calamares fritos
Fried squid or cuttlefish

Calamares a la romana
Squid fried in batter

Calamares en su tinta
Squid cooked in their ink

Caldeirada
Fish soup (Galicia)

Caldo
Clear soup or broth

Caldo de pescado
Fish soup

Cebollas rellenas
Stuffed onions

Cerdo asado
Roast pork

Cocido
Boiled chicken, meat and vegetable
stew. There are many different
regional variations of this dish and it
is worth trying the local *cocido*
wherever you are staying

Codornices asadas
Roast quail

Consomé de gallina
Chicken consommé

Cordero asado
Roast lamb

Croquetas de camarones
Shrimp croquettes

Empanadas de carne
Small meat and vegetable pies which can be eaten hot or cold

Ensaladilla
Cold cooked vegetables mixed with mayonnaise

Escabeche de pescado
Fish marinated in oil and served cold

Escalopes de ternera
Veal escalopes

Escudilla de pages
Dry white bean, sausage, ham and pork soup (Catalonia)

Fabada
Pork, ham, black pudding, beans and sausage stew. *Fabada* also can vary from region to region

Faisán trufado
Truffled pheasant

Fiambre
Cold meat

Filetes de lenguado
Rolled sole baked with wine, mushrooms and butter (Madrid)

Gambas a la plancha
Grilled prawns

Gazpacho
The traditional cold soup of Spain. There are many variations, but basically it is water, tomatoes, onions, cucumber, green pepper, breadcrumbs, vinegar, oil and seasoning, served with garnishes from the above ingredients

Gazpacho extremeña
Gazpacho made with finely chopped green peppers and onions, with these also served separately with the soup (Extremadura)

Hígado con cebolla
Fried calf's liver with onions

Huevos a la española
Stuffed eggs with a cheese sauce

Huevos a la flamenca
Baked eggs with tomatoes, peas, peppers, asparagus and sausage (Seville)

Huevos al plato
Eggs baked in butter

Huevos revueltos con carne
Scrambled eggs with minced beef

Jamón de jabugo
An Andalucian ham

Jamón serrano
Aromatic, dark red smoked ham

Judías verdes a la castellana/española
Boiled green beans mixed with fried parsley, garlic and pimentos (Castile)

Lacón con grelos
Shoulder of salted pork with young turnip tops and white cabbage hearts (León)

Lenguados fritos
Fried fillets of sole, often served on a bed of mixed sautéed vegetables

Lenguados rellenos
Fillets of sole stuffed with shrimps or prawns

Liebre estofada
Stewed hare (Castile)

Liebre estofada con judías
Hare stew with French beans

Menestra de legumbres
Braised spring vegetables

Menestra de legumbres frescas
Vegetable stew decorated with poached eggs and boiled asparagus (Murcia)

Merluza con sidra
Hake baked with clams, onions and cider

Menu Reader
Spain

Moros y cristianos
Boiled rice, black beans and onions
served with garlic sausage

Olla podrida
Ham, vegetable and chick pea stew

Paella
Paella varies from region to region
but usually consists of rice, chicken,
shellfish, vegetables, garlic and
saffron

Patatas bravas
see *Ajo de las manos*

Patatas fritas
Chips (French fries)

Pato a la sevillana
Joints of wild duck cooked with
sherry, onion and tomatoes and
flavoured with herbs and garlic, and
served with oranges and olives in the
sauce (Seville)

Pavo relleno
Stuffed turkey

Pepitoria de pavo/pollo
Turkey/chicken casserole (Córdoba)

Perdices de capellán
Rolled slices of fried veal, filled with
ham and sausage (Balearic Islands)

Pimientos morrones
Pimento hors d'œuvre

Pinchos morunos
Meat grilled on a skewer

Pisto
A mixture of sautéed peppers,
onions, aubergines, tomatoes, garlic
and parsley. Served cold

Pollo asado
Roast chicken

Pollo a la chilindrón
Chicken cooked with onion, ham,
garlic, red peppers and tomatoes
(Aragón)

Pollo a la pepitoria
Breaded chicken pieces fried, then
casseroled with herbs, almonds,
garlic and sherry

Pollo estofado
Chicken stewed with potatoes,
button mushrooms, shallots, bayleaf
and brandy

Pollo relleno
Stuffed chicken

Potaje madrileño
Vegetable soup (Madrid)

Puré de garbanzos
Thick chick pea soup

Quinad
Green vegetable stew with wild
white peas and silver beet. A Good
Friday speciality eaten in Ibiza

Rustido a la catalana
Veal roasted with rum, herbs and
white wine and flavoured with
cinnamon and cloves (Catalonia)

Salmorejo
A type of *gazpacho* (Córdoba)

Sesos fritos
Fried brains

Sopa de cebolla
Onion soup

Sopa de mariscos
Shellfish soup

Sopa de pescado
Fish soup

Sopa de rape
Soup made with the Mediterranean
angler-fish, tomatoes, onions and
nuts

**Ternera asada con tomates
rellenos**
Roast veal with onion and sherry,
served garnished with small stuffed
tomatoes

Ternera fiambre
Veal pâté

Ternera fría
Cold veal usually served in a sauce

Tortilla a la española
Traditional Spanish omelette made with potato, onion, garlic, tomato, peppers and seasoning

Tortilla con espárragos
Asparagus omelette

Tortilla de habas
Broad bean omelette (Alicante)

Tortilla de patatas
Potato omelette

Trucha a la navarra
Trout stuffed with ham slices (Navarre)

Trucha con jamón
Trout baked with ham and wine and served with a rasher of crisp fried bacon on each trout (Costa del Sol)

Zarzuela de mariscos
Seafood casserole

Zarzuela de pescado
Fish stew

Cheeses

Queso de bola
Cow's milk cheese similar to Dutch cheese

Queso de Burgos
Soft cheese from Castile

Queso de cabra
Goat's milk cheese

Queso fresco
Curd cheese

Queso manchego
Sheep's cheese from La Mancha

Queso de oveja
Sheep's cheese

Queso del país
Local cheese

Desserts

Bizcocho borracho de Guadalajara
Sponge ring filled with brandy or rum and flavoured whipped cream, and decorated with strawberries or glacé cherries

Cabello de ángel
Sugared pumpkin

Crema catalana
Rich cinnamon and lemon flavoured custard, topped with caramelized sugar (Catalonia)

Flan (crema de caramelo)
Caramel cream

Helado
Ice-cream

Leche frita
Very thick custard dipped into an egg and breadcrumb mixture, fried and served hot in squares

Leche merengada
Milk and egg sorbet

Tocino de cielo
A rich caramel cream

Tortilla al ron
Sweet rum omelette

Tortilla soufflé
Sweet omelette soufflé

Tortitas
Pancakes

Yemas
Beaten egg yolk and sugar dessert

Wine Lists

France

These are only a few of the names that are to be found on any wine list. Le vin en carafe – the house wine – is likely to be worth trying, as is the local wine, le vin de pays. If the names on the list mean nothing to you, ask the waiter what he recommends, or describe what you want:

vin rouge *vañ roozh*	– **red wine**	doux *doo*	– **sweet**
vin blanc *vañ bloñ*	– **white wine**	sec *sek*	– **dry**
vin rosé *vañ ro-zay*	– **rosé wine**	demi-sec *duh-mee sek*	– **medium-dry**

Barsac
Very good sweet white wines

Beaujolais
Light and fruity red or white wines

Bourgogne
Burgundy (full-bodied, red or white)

Bourgueil
Light, fruity, deep red Loire wine

Chablis
Dry white Burgundy

Champagne
Better-quality white sparkling wine

Châteauneuf du Pape
Full-bodied red Rhône wines

Côtes du Rhône
Good-bodied Rhône wines, usually red

Mâcon
Good ordinary red or white Burgundy

Monbazillac
Sweet white wine from the Dordogne

Muscadet
Very dry white Loire wine

Pouilly-Fuissé
Light, dry white Burgundy

Pouilly-Fumé
Flinty, spicy, dry white Loire wine

Rosé d'Anjou
Rosé wine from the Loire valley

Sancerre
Dry, stony, delicate white Loire wine

Sauternes
A good sweet white wine

Vouvray
Fine white Loire wine, medium-dry to medium-sweet

Germany, Austria & Switzerland

These are only some of the names that are likely to be on any wine list. An ordinary wine is called a Tafelwein; higher-quality wines will be described as Qualitätswein, Kabinett or mit Prädikat. If the names on the list mean nothing to you, ask the waiter what he recommends, or describe what you want:

Rotwein *rōt-vine*	– **red wine**	süß *zōōs*	– **sweet**
Weißwein *vise-vine*	– **white wine**	trocken *tro-kèn*	– **dry**
Roséwein *rō-zay-vine*	– **rosé wine**		

Bernkasteler
A light, flowery white Moselle wine

Burgunder
A full-bodied red wine

Gewürztraminer
A spicy white wine from Alsace

Gutedel
A very dry white wine

Johannisberg
A light, dry white wine

Kalterer See
A soft red wine from the Southern Tyrol

Liebfraumilch
A medium-dry to sweet white Rheinhessen wine

Niersteiner
A light, dry white Rheinhessen wine

Oppenheimer
One of the best light, dry Rheinhessen wines

Riesling
A light, dry, fruity white wine

Rüdesheimer
One of the best full-bodied, dry white Rheingau wines

Ruländer
A heavy-bodied white wine

Schaumwein
Sparkling wine

Sekt
Better-quality sparkling wine

Spätburgunder Rotwein
An excellent light red wine

Sylvaner
A strong dry white wine

Spain

These are only some of the names that are to be found on any wine list. Vino de la casa – the house wine – is likely to be worth trying, as is the local wine, vino del país. If the names on the list mean nothing to you, ask the waiter what he recommends, or describe what you want:

vino tinto	– **red wine**	dulce	– **sweet**
*bee-nō teen-*tō		*dool-thay*	
vino blanco	– **white wine**	seco	– **dry**
bee-nō blang-kō		*say-kō*	
vino rosado	– **rosé wine**		
bee-nō ro-sa-dō			

Amontillado
A medium sherry

Castellblanch
A fruity, sweet, sparkling wine

Fino
A light, dry sherry

Jerez
Sherry – fortified wine from Jerez de la Frontera in Andalucia

Málaga
Sweet, dark dessert wine from Málaga, sometimes fortified

Manzanilla
Pale, extra-dry sherry

Montilla
Strong, sherry-like unfortified wine

Oloroso
Dark, sweetish sherry

Ribeiro
Fresh, slightly sparkling red or white wines

Rioja
Good, plain dry red or white table wines

San Sadurní de Noya
Sparkling wine from Panades

Sangría
Iced fruit punch

Tarragona
Sweet red dessert wine, sometimes fortified

Valdepeñas
Lightish red and white wines from La Mancha

Bars & Cafés
France

The French café is a cross between a café and a bar – sit on the terrace and watch the world go by while you have breakfast, a leisurely glass of wine or an after-dinner coffee. Many sell snacks and some serve complete meals. You can telephone from a café (phrases page 120) and, if there's a red diamond-shaped *TABAC* sign outside, you can also buy cigarettes and stamps. You usually pay for your drinks when you leave, not when they arrive, and remember to check whether service is included.

un verre de rouge *uñ ver duh roozh*	a glass of red wine	**un verre de blanc** *uñ ver duh bloñ*	a glass of white wine
une bière en bouteille *ōōn byer oñ boo-tye*	a bottle of beer	**un demi** *uñ duh-mee*	a glass of beer
		un whisky *uñ wee-skee*	a whisky
un cognac *uñ kon-yak*	a brandy	**un martini** *uñ mar-tee-nee*	a martini

You may prefer to try something more characteristically French, such as

un pastis an aniseed drink, taken with water and ice
uñ pas-tees

or one of the bitter herb aperitifs, like

un Ambassadeur
uñ noñ-ba-sa-duhr

un Dubonnet
uñ dōō-bo-nay

un Byrrh
uñ beer

un Saint Raphael
uñ sañ ra-fa-el

and after dinner you could try a special brandy:

un marc
uñ mar

un armagnac
uñ nar-ma-nyak

or a fruit brandy:

un calvados (from apples)
uñ kal-va-dōs

une mirabelle (from plums)
ōōn mee-ra-bel

You may want something hot like

un café *uñ ka-fay*	black coffee	**un café-crème** *uñ ka-fay-krem*	coffee with mil
un thé au lait *uñ tay ō lay*	tea with milk	**un thé au citron** *uñ tay ō see-troñ*	tea with lemon
un chocolat chaud *uñ sho-ko-la shō*	hot chocolate		

If you want a soft drink for yourself or the children, you can ask for:

un jus d'orange
uñ zhōō do-roñzh
an orange juice

un jus de pamplemousse
uñ zhōō duh poñ-pluh-moos
a grapefruit juice

un jus d'ananas
uñ zhōō da-na-na
a pineapple juice

un citron pressé
uñ see-troñ pre-say
a fresh lemon juice

un Orangina
uñ no-roñ-zhee-na
an orangeade drink

un Perrier
uñ pe-ree-yay
a sparkling mineral water

une fraise
ōōn frez
a strawberry cordial

une menthe
ōōn moñt
a mint cordial

In the morning, ask for a croissant (*uñ krwah-soñ*) with your coffee; if you're hungry later in the day you may be able to get snacks such as:

un sandwich ... au fromage
uñ soñ-dweech ... ō fro-mazh
a cheese sandwich

...au jambon
... ō zhoñ-boñ
a ham sandwich

...au pâté
... ō pa-tay
a pâté sandwich

...au saucisson
... ō sō-see-soñ
a salami sandwich

des chips
day sheep
potato crisps (chips)

un œuf dur
uñ nuhf dōōr
a hard-boiled egg

un œuf jambon
uñ nuhf zhoñ-boñ
ham and egg

une crêpe
ōōn krep
a pancake

une omelette
ōōn om-let
an omelette (*see page 81 for varieties*)

un croque-monsieur
uñ krok-muh-syuh
a toasted cheese sandwich with ham

un croque-madame
uñ krok-ma-dam
a toasted cheese sandwich with ham and egg

Bars & Cafés
Germany, Austria & Switzerland

Germans do not have separate places for eating and drinking: at a *Wirtshaus* you can have a good meal or a snack, or just sit and have a drink at any time of day. You will be served at your table, and you pay for your drinks when you leave rather than when they arrive. Don't sit at a table with the sign "*Stammtisch*" on it as it is reserved for the regulars.

ein Viertel Rot-wein ine **fir**-tèl **rōt**-vine	a large glass of red wine	**ein Achtel Rot-wein** ine **akh**-tèl **rōt**-vine	a small glass of red wine
ein Viertel Weiß-wein ine **fir**-tèl **vise**-vine	a large glass of white wine	**ein Achtel Weiß-wein** ine **akh**-tèl **vise**-vine	a small glass of white wine
ein kleines Bier ine **kline**-ès beer	a small beer	**ein großes Bier** ine **grō**-sès beer	a large beer
ein kleines Helles ine **kline**-ès **hel**-ès	a small lager	**ein großes Helles** ine **grō**-sès **hel**-ès	a large lager
einen Cognac **ine**-èn **kon**-yak	a French brandy	**einen Weinbrand** **ine**-èn **vine**-brant	a German brandy

You might prefer to try something more typically German:

einen Schnaps **ine**-èn shnaps	corn brandy	**ein Kirschwasser** ine **kirsh**-vas-èr	kirsch
einen Doornkaat **ine**-èn **dorn**-kaht	strong juniper gin	**einen Kümmel** **ine**-èn **kōō**-mèl	caraway liqueur
einen Himbeer-geist **ine**-èn **him**-bay-èr-gyest	raspberry brandy	**einen Steinhäger** **ine**-èn **shtine**-hay-gèr	juniper brandy
einen Glühwein **ine**-èn **glōō**-vine	warmed, spiced wine		

If you want a soft drink for yourself or the children:

eine Cola **ine**-è **kō**-la	Coke	**einen Orangen-saft** **ine**-èn o-**ran**-zhèn-zaft	orange juice
einen Apfelsaft **ine**-èn **ap**-fèl-zaft	apple juice	**einen Trauben-saft** **ine**-èn **trow**-bèn-zaft	grape juice
ein Mineral-wasser ine mi-nè-**rahl**-vas-èr	mineral water	**eine Limonade** **ine**-è lee-mo-**nah**-dè	fizzy drink

Another institution is the *Konditorei, Café* or *Kaffeehaus,* as it is known in Austria. This is a café and confectionery shop where you go for *Kaffee und Kuchen* (coffee and cakes), although you can have something stronger if you prefer.

einen Kaffee *ine-èn ka-fay*	coffee		**eine Tasse Schokolade** *ine-è tas-è sho-ko-lah-de*	hot chocolate
einen Kaffee Hag *ine-èn ka-fay hahg*	decaffeinated coffee			
einen Tee mit Milch *ine-èn tay mit milkh*	tea with milk		**einen Tee mit Zitrone** *ine-èn tay mit tsi-trō-nè*	tea with lemon
einen Milchkaffee *ine-èn milkh-ka-fay*	coffee with milk			

You can simply point to one of the cakes on display and say "Geben Sie mir bitte das da" (*gay-bèn zee meer bit-è das dah*), but it's worth knowing the names of some of the best-known:

Berliner (Pfannkuchen) *ber-lee-nèr (pfan-koo-khèn)*	doughnuts with jam
Blätterteigstricken *ble-tèr-tike-shtrik-èn*	Danish pastry
Gugelhupf *goo-gèl-hoopf*	ring-shaped yeast cake with fruit
Käsekuchen *kay-zè-koo-khèn*	cheesecake
Linzertorte *lin-tsèr-tor-tè*	cake with layers of almond-flavoured pastry and jam
Sachertorte *za-khèr-tor-tè*	chocolate sponge cake with chocolate icing and apricot filling

You can sometimes get savoury snacks, but there is not usually a great selection. You might find some of these:

ein belegtes Brot *ine bè-layg-tès brōt*	open sandwich
ein belegtes Brötchen *ine bè-layg-tès brur't-khèn*	filled roll
Königinpastete *kur'-ni-gin-pas-tay-tè*	chicken vol-au-vent
Ochsenschwanzsuppe *ok-sèn-shvants-zoo-pè*	oxtail soup
serbische Bohnensuppe *zer-bi-shè bō-nèn-zoo-pè*	bean soup

Bars & Cafés
Spain

Bars and cafés are an essential part of Spanish life, places where you can have breakfast, an apéritif, after-dinner coffee, or just relax over a drink at any time of day. Many serve snacks, meals and *tapas* (hors d'oeuvres). Most sell cigarettes and have a public telephone (for phrases see pages 121 and 127). You usually pay for your drinks when you leave, not when they arrive, and remember to check whether service is included.

un tinto oon **teen**-tõ	a glass of red wine	**un blanco** oon **blang**-kõ	a glass of white wine
una caña **oo**-na **ka**-nya	a glass of beer (draught)	**una cerveza** **oo**-na ther-**bay**-tha	a glass of beer (bottled)
un coñac oon ko-**nyak**	a brandy	**una ginebra** **oo**-na khee-**nay**-bra	a gin
una vodka **oo**-na **bod**-ka	a vodka	**un ron** oon ron	a rum
un whisky oon **wees**-kee	a whisky		

You may prefer to try something more typically Spanish:

un jerez oon khe-**reth**	sherry	**un vermut** oon ber-**moot**	vermouth
un espumoso oon es-poo-**mo**-sõ	sparkling wine	**un mosto** oon **mos**-tõ	grape juice
una montilla **oo**-na mon-**tee**-lya	strong, sherry-like wine	**una Cuba libre** **oo**-na **koo**-ba **lee**-bray	rum and Coke

and after dinner:

un anís oon a-**nees**	anise liqueur	**un sol y sombra** oon sol ee **som**-bra	brandy with anís

If you want a hot drink:

un café solo oon ka-**fay** so-lõ	black coffee	**un café con leche** oon ka-**fay** kon **lay**-chay	coffee with milk
un té con limón oon tay kon lee-**mon**	tea with lemon	**un té con leche** oon tay kon **lay**-chay	tea with milk
un chocolate oon cho-ko-**la**-tay	hot chocolate		

Two chilled drinks are very common:

una horchata de almendra **oo**-na or-**cha**-ta day al-**men**-dra	a milky drink made from almonds	**un granizado de limón** oon gra-nee-**tha**-dõ day lee-**mon**	a lemon drink with crushed ice

Other soft drinks for yourself or the children:

una gaseosa *oo-na ga-say-ō-sa*	lemonade
una limonada *oo-na lee-mo-na-da*	fizzy lemon drink
una naranjada *oo-na na-rang-kha-da*	orangeade
un zumo de naranja *oon thoo-mō day na-rang-kha*	fresh orange juice
un zumo de limón *oon thoo-mō day lee-mon*	fresh lemon juice

If you're hungry you may be able to get some of the following:

un bocadillo ... de jamón *oon bo-ka-dee-lyō ... day kha-mon*	a ham sandwich
... de queso *... day kay-sō*	a cheese sandwich
... de salchichón *... day sal-chee-chon*	a salami sandwich
un sandwich de jamón *oon sang-gweech day kha-mon*	a toasted ham sandwich
patatas fritas *pa-ta-tas free-tas*	potato crisps (chips)
un huevo duro *oon way-bō doo-rō*	a hard-boiled egg
huevos con jamón *way-bōs kon kha-mon*	ham and eggs
tortilla de patata *tor-tee-lya day pa-ta-ta*	potato omelette
empanadillas *em-pa-na-dee-lyas*	small filled pastries
banderillas *ban-day-ree-lyas*	hors d'oeuvres on a stick

Wherever you go you can ask for una ración de tapas (*oo-na ra-thyon day ta-pas*) – a portion of hors d'oeuvres – with your drinks.

aceitunas *a-the-ee-too-nas*	olives	**champiñones** *cham-pee-nyo-nays*	mushrooms
boquerones *bo-kay-ro-nays*	anchovies	**gambas** *gam-bas*	prawns
calamares *ka-la-ma-rays*	squid	**mejillones** *me-khee-lyo-nays*	mussels

Shop Names

French	German	Spanish	
Boulangerie	Bäckerei	Panadería	**Baker**
Banque	Bank	Banco	**Bank**
Coiffeur	(Herren)friseur	Peluquería Barbería	**Barber**
Librairie	Buchhandlung	Librería	**Bookshop**
Boucherie	Fleischerei Metzgerei Schlachterei	Carnicería	**Butcher**
Café(-Restaurant)	Café	Café	**Café**
Pâtisserie	Konditorei	Pastelería	**Cake Shop**
Pharmacie	Apotheke (*drugs etc*) Drogerie (*toiletries etc*)	Farmacia (*drugs etc*) Droguería (*toiletries etc*)	**Chemist**
Café Cafétéria	Café	Café Cafetería	**Coffee bar**
Confiserie (-Pâtisserie)	Süßwarenladen	Bombonería Confitería Repostería	**Confectioner**
Crémerie Laiterie	Milchgeschäft	Lechería	**Dairy**
Épicerie fine	Delikatessen-geschäft Feinkostgeschäft	Mantequería	**Delicatessen**
Teinturerie Pressing	Reinigung	Limpieza en seco Tintorería	**Dry cleaner**
Poissonnerie	Fischgeschäft	Pescadería	**Fishmonger**
Bureau de change	Wechselbüro	Oficina de cambio	**Foreign exchange office**
Fourreur	Kürschnerei	Peletería	**Furrier**
Garage	(Reparatur-)werkstatt	Garaje	**Garage**
Fruiterie Marchand de légumes	Obst- und Gemüsehand-lung	Frutería Verdulería	**Greengrocer**
Épicerie	Lebensmittel-geschäft	Alimentación Comestibles Ultramarinos Abacería	**Grocer**
Pension	(Fremden-)pension	Casa de huespedes Pensión	**Guest house, Boarding house**
Salon de coiffure	Friseur(salon)	Peluquería	**Hairdresser**

Shop Names

French	German	Spanish	
Quincaillerie	Eisen- und Haushalts-warenhand-lung	Ferretería Quincallería	**Hardware store**
Hôtel	Hotel	Hotel	**Hotel**
Auberge Hôtellerie	Gasthaus Gasthof	Albergue Fonda Hostería Mesón Posada	**Inn**
Bijouterie Joaillerie	Juweliergeschäft	Joyería	**Jeweller**
Maroquinerie	Lederwaren-handlung	Artículos de piel Cuero Curtidos	**Leather goods shop**
Marchand de journaux	Zeitungshand-lung	Tienda de periódicos	**Newsagent**
Parfumerie	Parfümerie	Perfumería	**Perfume shop**
Magasin de photo	Fotoartikel	Fotografía Material fotográfico	**Photographic shop**
Charcuterie	Schweinemetz-gerei	Salchichería	**Pork butcher**
Postes Télécom-munications	Post(amt)	(Casa or Oficina de) Correos	**Post office**
Bar Bistro(t) Brasserie Café(-Bar) Pub	Bar Gaststätte Lokal Wirtschaft Wirtshaus	Bar Café Taberna	**Pub, Bar**
Station-service	Tankstelle	Estación de servicio	**Service station**
Restaurant	Gasthof Gaststätte Lokal Restaurant	Casa de comidas Fonda Merendero Restaurante	**Restaurant**
Cordonnerie Réparation de chaussures	(Flick)schusterei	Salón de limpiabotas Zapatero remendón	**Shoe repairer**
Magasin de chaussures	Schuhgeschäft	Calzados Zapatería	**Shoe shop**
Papeterie	Schreibwaren-handlung	Papelería	**Stationer**
Tabac	Tabak(waren)-laden	Estanco Tabacalera	**Tobacconist**

Other Signs

French	German	Spanish	
Prudence	Achtung Vorsicht	Precaución	**Caution**
Fermé	Geschlossen	Cerrado	**Closed**
Fròid	Kalt	Frío	**Cold**
Douane	Zoll	Aduana	**Customs**
Danger Attention	(Lebens)gefahr	Peligro	**Danger**
Caisse	Kasse	Caja	**Desk** (*in banks etc*)
Ne pas toucher	Nicht berühren	No tocar No toquen, por favor	**Do not touch**
Sortie de secoùrs	Notausgang	Salida de emergencia	**Emergency exit**
Occupé	Besetzt	Ocupado	**Engaged**
Entrée	Eingang	Entrada	**Entrance**
Sortie	Ausgang	Salida	**Exit**
Pompiers	Feuerwehr	Bomberos	**Fire Brigade**
Défense de …	… verboten	Prohibido/-a … Se prohibe …	**…forbidden**
À louer	Zu vermieten	Se alquila	**For hire**
À vendre	Zu verkaufen	Se vende Venta	**For sale**
Complet	Voll Ausverkauft Ausgebucht	Completo	**Full**
Messieurs	Herren	Caballeros Señores	**Gentlemen**
Hôpital	Krankenhaus	Hospital	**Hospital**
Chaud	Heiß	Caliente	**Hot**
Renseignements	Auskunft	Información	**Information**
Défense de marcher sur les pelouses	Betreten des Rasens verboten	Prohibido pisar la hierba *or* el césped	**Keep off the grass**
Dames	Damen	Damas Señoras	**Ladies**
Ascenseur	Aufzug	Ascensor	**Lift (Elevator)**
Objets trouvés	Fundbüro	Objetos perdidos	**Lost property office**
Entrée libre	Eintritt frei	Entrada libre	**No admission charge**
Baignade interdite	Baden verboten	Prohibido bañarse	**No bathing**
Défense d'entrée Entrée interdite	Kein Zutritt	Prohibido el paso Prohibida la entrada	**No entrance**
Entrée gratuite *or* libre	Kein Kaufzwang	Entrada libre	**No obligation to buy**

Other Signs

French	German	Spanish	
Défense de fumer	Nichtraucher Rauchen verboten	Prohibido fumar	**No smoking**
Passage interdit	Kein Durchgang	Prohibido el paso	**No thoroughfare**
Entrée interdite Propriété privée	Für Unbefugte verboten	Prohibido el paso	**No trespassing**
Ouvert	Geöffnet	Abierto	**Open**
En panne	Außer Betrieb	No funciona	**Out of order**
Caisse	Kasse	Caja	**Pay here** (*in shops*)
Piétons	Fußgänger	Peatones	**Pedestrians**
Police (*in towns*) Gendarmerie (*in the country*)	Polizei	Policía	**Police**
Privé Interdit au public	Privat	Privado	**Private**
Tirez	Ziehen	Tirad	**Pull**
Appuyez Poussez	Drücken	Empuje	**Push**
Réception	Empfang Rezeption	Recepción	**Reception**
Réservations Locations	Reservierungen	Reservas	**Reservations**
Réservé	Reserviert Belegt	Reservado	**Reserved**
Soldes	Ausverkauf Schlußverkauf	Rebajas Liquidación Saldos	**Sale**
Dégustation	Kostprobe	Degustación	**Sampling** (*of wine etc*)
Libre-service	Selbstbedienung	Autoservicio	**Self-service**
Service (non) compris	Bedienung (nicht) inbegriffen	Servicio (no) incluido	**Service (not) included**
Fumeurs	Raucher	Fumadores	**Smokers**
En promotion	Sonderangebot	Oportunidad	**Special offer**
Téléphone	Fernsprecher Telefon	Teléfono	**Telephone**
Vente de billets Guichet	Kasse	Taquilla	**Ticket office**
Toilettes	Toiletten	Servicios Aseos Retrete	**Toilets**
À louer	Zu vermieten	Se alquila	**To let**
Hôtel de ville Mairie	Rathaus	Ayuntamiento	**Town Hall**
Libre	Frei	Libre	**Vacant**

Shopping

French	German
Où est le rayon de chaussures/la caisse? *oo ay luh re-yoñ duh shō-sōōr/la kes?*	Wo ist die Schuhabteilung/die Kasse? *vō ist dee **shoo**-ap-tile-oong/dee **kas**-è?*
À quelle heure fermez-vous/ouvrent les magasins? *a kel uhr fer-may-voo/oo-vruh lay ma-ga-zañ?*	Wann machen Sie zu/wann machen die Geschäfte auf? *van **makh**-èn zee tsoo/van **makh**-èn dee gè-**sheft**-è owf?*
Où est-ce que je peux acheter…? *oo es-kuh zhuh puh zash-tay…?*	Wo kann ich … kaufen? *vō kan ikh … **kow**-fèn?*
Je regarde seulement *zhuh ruh-gard suhl-moñ*	Ich schaue mich nur um *ikh **show**-è mikh noor oom*
Je cherche un chapeau *zhuh shersh uñ sha-pō*	Ich hätte gerne einen Hut *ikh **he**-tè **gern**-è **ine**-èn hoot*
Est-ce que je peux voir le chapeau en vitrine/ce chapeau-là? *es-kuh zhuh puh vwahr luh sha-pō oñ vee-treen/suh sha-pō-la?*	Kann ich den Hut aus dem Schaufenster sehen/den Hut dort sehen? *kan ikh dayn hoot ows daym **show**-fen-stèr **zay**-èn/dayn hoot dort **zay**-èn?*
Non, l'autre *noñ, lō-truh*	Nein, den anderen *nine, dayn **an**-dè-rèn*
Je n'aime pas celui-là *zhuh nem pa suh-lwee-la*	Er gefällt mir nicht *er gè-**felt** meer nikht*
J'aime celui-ci *zhem suh-lwee-see*	Dieser hier gefällt mir ***dee**-zèr heer gè-**felt** meer*
Est-ce que vous avez quelque chose de plus petit/de plus grand/de moins cher? *es-kuh voo za-vay kel-kuh shōz duh plōō puh-tee/duh plōō groñ/duh mwañ sher?*	Haben Sie etwas Kleineres/Größeres/Billigeres? ***hah**-bèn zee **et**-vas **kline**-èr-ès/**grur's**-èr-ès/**bil**-ig-èr-ès?*
Je prendrai celui-ci/celui-là/l'autre *zhuh proñ-dray suh-lwee-see/suh-lwee-la/lō-truh*	Ich nehme diesen hier/diesen da/den anderen *ikh **nay**-mè **dee**-zèn heer/**dee**-zèn da/dayn **an**-dè-rèn*
J'ai acheté ça ici, hier *zhay ash-tay sa ee-see, yer*	Ich habe das gestern hier gekauft *ikh **hah**-bè das **ges**-tèrn heer gè-**kowft***
Est-ce que vous pouvez me le changer? *es-kuh voo poo-vay muh luh shoñ-zhay?*	Können Sie es mir umtauschen? ***kur'n**-èn zee es meer **oom**-tow-shèn?*
Est-ce que vous pouvez me le reprendre contre remboursement? *es-kuh voo poo-vay muh luh ruh-proñ-druh koñ-truh roñ-boors-moñ?*	Können Sie mir mein Geld zurückgeben? ***kur'n**-èn zee meer mine gelt tsoo-**rōōk**-gay-bèn?*

Spanish

¿Dónde está la sección de zapatos/la caja? **don**-day es-**ta** la sek-**thyon** day tha-**pa**-tōs/la **ka**-kha?	**Where is the shoe department/the checkout?**
¿Cuándo cierra/abren las tiendas? **kwan**-dō **thye**-rra/**a**-bren las **tyen**-das?	**When do you close/do the shops open?**
¿Dónde puedo comprar...? **don**-day **pway**-dō kom-**prar**...?	**Where can I buy...?**
Sólo estoy mirando **sō**-lō es-**toy** mee-**ran**-dō	**I'm just looking**
Estoy buscando un sombrero es-**toy** boos-**kan**-dō oon som-**bray**-rō	**I'm looking for a hat**
¿Puede enseñarme el sombrero del escaparate/aquel sombrero de allí? **pway**-day en-se-**nyar**-may el som-**bray**-rō del es-ka-pa-**ra**-tay/a-**kel** som-**bray**-rō day a-**lyee**?	**Can I see the hat in the window/that hat over there?**
No, el otro nō, el **ō**-trō	**No, the other one**
No me gusta nō may **goos**-ta	**I don't like it**
Me gusta ésto may **goos**-ta **es**-tō	**I like this one**
¿Tienen algo más pequeño/más grande/más barato? **tyay**-nen **al**-gō mas pay-**kay**-nyō/mas **gran**-day/mas ba-**ra**-tō?	**Have you got anything smaller/larger/cheaper?**
Me llevo éste/ése/el otro may **lyay**-bō **es**-tay/e-say/el **ō**-trō	**I'll take this one/that one/the other one**
Hé comprado éste aquí ayer ay kom-**pra**-dō **es**-tay a-**kee** a-**yer**	**I bought this here yesterday**
¿Pueden cambiármelo? **pway**-den kam-**byar**-may-lō?	**Can you change it?**
¿Pueden devolverme el dinero? **pway**-den day-bol-**ber**-may el dee-**nay**-rō?	**Can you refund my money?**

Paying

French	German
Ça coûte combien, ça? *sa koot koñ-byañ, sa?*	Wieviel kostet das? *vee-**feel kos**-tèt das?*
C'est trop cher pour moi *say trŏ sher poor mwah*	Das ist mir zu teuer *das ist meer tsoo **toy**-èr*
Ça fait combien en tout? *sa fay koñ-byañ oñ too?*	Was macht das? *vas makht das?*
Le service et la TVA sont compris? *luh ser-vees ay la tay-vay-ah soñ koñ-pree?*	Sind Bedienung und Mehrwertsteuer inbegriffen? *zint bè-**dee**-noong oont **mayr**-vert-shtoy-èr **in**-bè-grif-èn?*
Est-ce qu'il y a des suppléments? *es-keel ya day sŏŏ-play-moñ?*	Gibt es irgendwelche Preiszuschläge? *gipt es **ir**-gènt-vel-khè **prise**-tsoo-shlay-gè?*
Est-ce qu'il y a une réduction pour un groupe/les étudiants/le troisième âge? *es-keel ya ŏŏn ray-dook-syoñ poor uñ groop/lay zay-tŏŏ-dyoñ/luh trwah-zyem azh?*	Gibt es Preisermäßigung für Gruppen/für Studenten/für Rentner? *gipt es **prise**-èr-may-si-goong fŏŏr **groo**-pen/fŏŏr shtoo-**den**-tèn/fŏŏr **rent**-nèr?*
Est-ce que vous exigez des arrhes? *es-kuh voo zeg-zee-zhay day zar?*	Muß ich eine Anzahlung machen? *moos ikh **ine**-è **an**-tsah-loong **makh**-èn?*
Est-ce que je paie d'avance ou après? *es-kuh zhuh pay da-voñs oo a-pre?*	Zahle ich im voraus oder später? ***tsah**-lè ikh im fŏr-**ows** ŏ-dèr **shpay**-tèr?*
Est-ce que vous pourriez m'écrire le prix, s'il vous plaît? *es-kuh voo poor-yay may-kreer luh pree, see voo play?*	Könnten Sie den Preis bitte aufschreiben? ***kur'n**-tèn zee dayn prise **bit**-è **owf**-shrye-bèn?*
Est-ce que vous acceptez les chèques de voyage? *es-kuh voo zak-sep-tay lay shek duh vwah-yazh?*	Nehmen Sie Reiseschecks? ***nay**-mèn zee **rye**-zè-sheks?*
Je désire payer avec une carte de crédit *zhuh day-zeer pe-yay a-vek ŏŏn kart duh kray-dee*	Ich möchte mit meiner Kreditkarte bezahlen *ikh **mur'kh**-tè mit **mine**-èr kre-**deet**-kar-tè bè-**tsahl**-èn*
Est-ce que je peux avoir une addition avec le détail/un reçu? *es-kuh zhuh puh za-vwahr ŏŏn a-dee-syoñ a-vek luh day-tye/uñ ruh-sŏŏ?*	Kann ich eine detaillierte Rechnung/eine Quittung haben? *kan ikh **ine**-è day-tye-**yeer**-tè **rekh**-noong/**ine**-è kvi-toong **hah**-bèn?*
Je n'ai pas assez d'argent *zhuh nay pa za-say dar-zhoñ*	Ich habe nicht genug Geld bei mir *ikh **hah**-bè nikht gè-**nook** gelt bye meer*
Vous avez fait une erreur en me rendant la monnaie *voo za-vay fet ŏŏn e-ruhr oñ muh roñ-doñ la mo-nay*	Sie haben mir falsch herausgegeben *zee **hah**-bèn meer falsh hè-**rows**-gè-gay-bèn*

Paying

Spanish

¿Cuánto es eso? *kwan-tŏ es e-sŏ?*	**How much is that/are those?**
Es demasiado caro *es day-ma-sya-dŏ ka-rŏ*	**It's too expensive for me**
¿Cuánto hace eso? *kwan-tŏ a-thay e-so?*	**What does that come to?**
¿Incluye servicio e impuestos? *een-kloo-yay ser-bee-thyŏ ay* *eem-pwes-tŏs?*	**Are service and tax included?**
¿Hay algún recargo? *a-ee al-goon ray-car-gŏ?*	**Is there any extra charge?**
¿Hay descuento para grupos/ estudiantes/jubilados? *a-ee des-kwen-tŏ pa-ra groo-pŏs/* *es-too-dyan-tays/khoo-bee-la-dŏs?*	**Is there a reduction for a** **group/students/senior citizens?**
¿Tengo que pagar un depósito? *teng-gŏ kay pa-gar oon* *day-po-see-tŏ?*	**Do I pay a deposit?**
¿Le pago por adelantado o después? *lay pa-gŏ por a-day-lan-ta-dŏ ŏ* *des-pwes?*	**Do I pay in advance or** **afterwards?**
¿Puede escribirme el precio, por favor? *pway-day es-kree-beer-may el* *pray-thyŏ, por fa-bor?*	**Could you write the price down,** **please?**
¿Aceptan cheques de viaje? *a-thep-tan che-kays day bya-khay?*	**Do you accept traveller's** **cheques?**
Querría pagar con tarjeta de crédito *kay-rree-a pa-gar kon tar-khay-ta day* *kre-dee-tŏ*	**I want to pay by credit card**
¿Puede darme una factura detallada/un recibo? *pway-day dar-may oo-na fak-too-ra* *day-ta-lya-da/oon ray-thee-bŏ?*	**Can I have an itemized bill/a** **receipt?**
No tengo dinero suficiente *nŏ teng-gŏ dee-nay-rŏ soo-fee-* *thyen-tay*	**I haven't enough money**
Me ha dado usted mal el cambio *may a da-dŏ oos-ted mal el kam-byŏ*	**You've given me the wrong** **change**

Food & Drink

French	*German*
Je voudrais une livre de tomates *zhuh voo-dray zōōn lee-vruh duh* *to-mat*	Ich hätte gerne ein Pfund Tomaten *ikh **he**-tè **gern**-è ine pfoont* *to-**mah**-tèn*
Je voudrais une bouteille de vin blanc sec/de vin du pays *zhuh voo-dray zōōn boo-tye duh vañ* *bloñ sek/duh vañ dōō pay-ee*	Ich hätte gerne eine Flasche trockenen Weißwein/hiesigen Wein *ikh **he**-tè **gern**-è ine-è **flash**-è* ***trok**-èn-èn **vise**-vine/**hee**-zig-èn vine*
Je voudrais une bouteille d'eau minérale gazeuse/non gazeuse *zhuh voo-dray zōōn boo-tye dō* *mee-nay-ral ga-zuhz/noñ ga-zuhz*	Ich hätte gerne eine Flasche Mineralwasser/Mineralwasser ohne Kohlensäure *ikh **he**-tè **gern**-è ine-è **flash**-è mi-nay-* ***rahl**-vas-èr/mi-nay-**rahl**-vas-èr **ō**-nè* ***kō**-lèn-zoy-rè*
Je voudrais un grand pain (*general*)/une baguette (*French stick*) *zhuh voo-dray zuñ groñ pañ/zōōn* *ba-get*	Ich hätte gerne ein Brot *ikh **he**-tè **gern**-è ine brōt*
Je voudrais trois tranches de jambon *zhuh voo-dray trwah troñsh duh* *zhoñ-boñ*	Ich hätte gerne drei Scheiben Schinken *ikh **he**-tè **gern**-è drye **shye**-bèn* ***shing**-kèn*
Je voudrais deux côtes d'agneau *zhuh voo-dray duh kōt dan-yō*	Ich hätte gerne zwei Lammkoteletts *ikh **he**-tè **gern**-è tsvye **lam**-kot-è-lets*
Deux cents grammes de pâté, s'il vous plaît *duh soñ gram duh pa-tay, see voo* *play*	Zweihundert Gramm Leberpastete, bitte ***tsvye**-hoon-dèrt gram **lay**-bèr-pas-* *tay-tè, **bit**-è*
Un litre de lait, s'il vous plaît *uñ lee-truh duh lay, see voo play*	Einen Liter Milch, bitte ***ine**-èn **lee**-tèr milkh, **bit**-è*
Quatre morceaux de gâteau, s'il vous plaît *ka-truh mor-sō duh ga-tō, see voo play*	Vier Stücke Torte, bitte *feer **shtōō**-kè **tor**-tè, **bit**-è*
Un pot de confiture *uñ pō duh koñ-fee-tōōr*	Ein Glas Marmelade *ine glahs mar-mè-**lah**-dè*
Une boîte de petits pois *ōōn bwat duh puh-tee pwah*	Eine Dose Erbsen *ine-è **dō**-zè **erp**-sèn*
Deux paquets de biscuits *duh pa-kay duh bees-kwee*	Zwei Pakete Kekse *tsvye pa-**kay**-tè **kek**-sè*
Un quart de fromage *uñ kar duh fro-mazh*	Ein Viertel Käse *ine **fir**-tèl **kay**-zè*
Six œufs *see zuh*	Ein halbes Dutzend Eier *ine **hal**-bès **doot**-sènd **eye**-èr*
Qu'est-ce que c'est? *kes-kuh say?*	Was ist das? *vas ist das?*

Spanish

Querría medio (kilo) de tomates *kay-**rree**-a **may**-dyō (**kee**-lō) day to-**ma**-tays*	**I would like a pound of tomatoes**
Querría una botella de vino blanco seco/de vino del país *kay-**rree**-a **oo**-na bo-**te**-lya day bee-nō **blang**-kō **say**-kō/day **bee**-nō del pa-**ees***	**I would like a bottle of dry white wine/local wine**
Querría una botella de agua mineral con gas/sin gas *kay-**rree**-a **oo**-na bo-**te**-lya day **a**-gwa mee-nay-**ral** con gas/seen gas*	**I would like a bottle of sparkling/still mineral water**
Querría una barra de pan *kay-**rree**-a **oo**-na **ba**-rra day pan*	**I would like a loaf of bread**
Querría tres lonchas de jamón *kay-**rree**-a tres **lon**-chas day kha-**mon***	**I would like three slices of ham**
Querría dos chuletas de cordero *kay-**rree**-a dōs choo-**lay**-tas day cor-**day**-rō*	**I would like two lamb chops**
Doscientos gramos de paté, por favor *dōs-**thyen**-tōs **gra**-mōs day pa-**tay**, por fa-**bor***	**200 grammes of pâté please**
Un litro de leche, por favor *oon **lee**-trō day **lay**-chay, por fa-**bor***	**A litre of milk please**
Cuatro porciones de tarta, por favor *kwa-trō por-**thyo**-nays day **tar**-ta, por fa-**bor***	**Four pieces of cake please**
Un tarro de mermelada *oon **ta**-rrō day mer-may-**la**-da*	**A jar of jam**
Una lata de guisantes *ōō-na **la**-ta day gee-**san**-tays*	**A tin of peas**
Dos paquetes de galletas *dōs pa-**kay**-tays day ga-**lyay**-tas*	**Two packets of biscuits**
Cien gramos de queso *thyen **gra**-mōs day **kay**-sō*	**A quarter of cheese**
Media docena de huevos ***may**-dya do-**thay**-na day **way**-bōs*	**Half-a-dozen eggs**
¿Qué es esto/son estos? *kay es **es**-tō/son **es**-tōs?*	**What is that/are those?**

Food & Drink

Fruit, Vegetables & Herbs

French	German	Spanish	
la pomme *la pom*	der Apfel *der **ap**-fèl*	la manzana *la man-**tha**-na*	**apple**
l'abricot *la-bree-kō*	die Aprikose *dee a-pri-**kō**-zè*	el albaricoque *el al-ba-ree-**ko**-kay*	**apricot**
l'artichaut *lar-tee-shō*	die Artischocke *dee ar-ti-**shok**-è*	la alcachofa *la al-ka-**chō**-fa*	**artichoke**
les asperges *lay zas-perzh*	der Spargel *der **shpar**-gèl*	los espárragos *lōs es-**pa**-rra-gōs*	**asparagus**
l'aubergine *lō-ber-zheen*	die Aubergine *dee ō-ber-**zhee**-nè*	la berenjena *la bay-ren-**khay**-na*	**aubergine** **(eggplant)**
l'avocat *la-vō-ka*	die Avocado *dee a-vō-**kah**-dō*	el aguacate *el a-gwa-**ka**-tay*	**avocado**
la banane *la ba-nan*	die Banane *dee ba-**nah**-nè*	el plátano *el **pla**-ta-nō*	**banana**
le chou *luh shoo*	der Kohl *der kōl*	el repollo *el ray-**pol**-yō*	**cabbage**
les carottes *lay ka-rot*	die Möhren *dee **mur**-èn*	las zanahorias *las tha-na-**ōr**-yas*	**carrots**
le chou-fleur *luh shoo-fluhr*	der Blumenkohl *der **bloo**-mèn-kōl*	la coliflor *la ko-lee-**flor***	**cauliflower**
le céleri *luh sayl-ree*	der Stangen- sellerie *der **shtang**-èn- ze-lè-ree*	el apio *el **ap**-yō*	**celery**
les cerises *lay suh-reez*	die Kirschen *dee **kir**-shèn*	las cerezas *las thay-**ray**-thas*	**cherries**
l'endive *loñ-deev*	die Chicorée *dee shi-ko-**ray***	la achicoria *la a-chee-**kor**-ya*	**chicory**
la ciboulette *la see-boo-let*	der Schnittlauch *der **shnit**-lowkh*	los cebollinos *lōs thay-bol-**yee**-nōs*	**chives**
les courgettes *lay koor-zhet*	die Zucchini *dee tsoo-**kee**-nee*	los calabacines *lōs ka-la-ba-**thee**-nays*	**courgettes** **(zucchini)**
le concombre *luh koñ-koñ-bruh*	die Gurke *dee **goor**-kè*	el pepino *el pay-**pee**-nō*	**cucumber**
les haricots verts *lay a-ree-kō ver*	die grünen Bohnen *dee **grōō**-nèn **bō**-nèn*	las judías verdes *las khoo-**dee**-as **ber**-days*	**French beans**
l'ail *lye*	der Knoblauch *der **knōp**-lowkh*	el ajo *el **a**-khō*	**garlic**
le pamplemousse *luh poñ-pluh-moos*	die Pampelmuse *dee **pam**-pèl-moo-zè*	el pomelo *el po-**may**-lō*	**grapefruit**

French	German	Spanish	
les raisins *lay ray-zañ*	die Trauben *dee **trow**-bèn*	las uvas *las **oo**-bas*	**grapes**
le poivron vert *luh pwa-vroñ ver*	der grüne Paprika *der **grōō**-nè **pa**-pri-ka*	el pimiento verde *el pee-**myen**-tō **ber**-day*	**green pepper**
le poireau *luh pwah-rō*	der Porree *der **po**-ray*	el puerro *el **pway**-rrō*	**leek**
le citron *luh see-troñ*	die Zitrone *dee tsi-**trō**-nè*	el limón *el lee-**mon***	**lemon**
la laitue *la lay-tōō*	der Kopfsalat *der **kopf**-za-lat*	la lechuga *la lay-**choo**-ga*	**lettuce**
la courge *la koorzh*	der Kürbis *der **kōō**r-bis*	el calabacín *el ka-la-ba-**theen***	**marrow** **(squash)**
le melon *luh muh-loñ*	die Melone *dee me-**lō**-nè*	el melón *el may-**lon***	**melon**
la menthe *la moñt*	die Minze *dee **min**-tsè*	la hierbabuena *la yer-ba-**bway**-na*	**mint**
les champignons *lay shoñ-peen-yoñ*	die Champignons *dee **sham**-peen- yons*	los champiñones *los cham-peen- **yo**-nays*	**mushrooms**
l'oignon *lon-yoñ*	die Zwiebel *dee **tsvee**-bèl*	la cebolla *la thay-**bol**-ya*	**onion**
l'orange *lo-roñzh*	die Orange *dee o-**ran**-zhè*	la naranja *la na-**rang**-kha*	**orange**
le persil *luh per-see*	die Petersilie *dee pay-tèr-**zee**-li-yè*	el perejil *el pay-ray-**kheel***	**parsley**
la pêche *la pesh*	der Pfirsich *der **pfir**-zikh*	el melocotón *el may-lō-ko-**ton***	**peach**
la poire *la pwahr*	die Birne *dee **bir**-nè*	la pera *la **pay**-ra*	**pear**
les petits pois *lay puh-tee pwah*	die Erbsen *dee **erp**-sèn*	los guisantes *los gee-**san**-tays*	**peas**
l'ananas *la-na-na*	die Ananas *dee **a**-na-nas*	la piña *la **peen**-ya*	**pineapple**
la prune *la prōōn*	die Pflaume *dee **pflow**-mè*	la ciruela *la theer-**way**-la*	**plum**
la grenadine *la gruh-na-deen*	der Granatapfel *der gra-**naht**-ap-fèl*	la granada *la gra-**na**-da*	**pomegranate**
la pomme de terre *la pom duh ter*	die Kartoffel *dee kar-**tof**-èl*	la patata *la pa-**ta**-ta*	**potato**
les radis *lay ra-dee*	die Radieschen *dee ra-**dees**-khèn*	los rábanos *los **ra**-ba-nos*	**radishes**
les framboises *lay froñ-bwaz*	die Himbeeren *dee **him**-bay-èr-èn*	las frambuesas *las fram-**bway**-sas*	**raspberries**

Food & Drink

French	German	Spanish	
le poivron rouge *luh pwah-vroñ roozh*	der rote Paprika *der rō-tè pa- pri-ka*	el pimiento rojo *el peem-yen-tō rō-khō*	**red pepper**
la sauge *la sōzh*	der Salbei *der zal-bye*	la salvia *la salb-ya*	**sage**
les épinards *lay zay-pee-nar*	der Spinat *der shpi-naht*	la espinaca *la es-pee-na-ca*	**spinach**
			squash = marrow
les fraises *lay frez*	die Erdbeeren *dee ert-bay-èr-èn*	las fresas *las fray-sas*	**strawberries**
l'estragon *les-tra-goñ*	der Estragon *der es-tra-gon*	el estragón *el es-tra-gon*	**tarragon**
le thym *luh tañ*	der Thymian *der tōō-mi-yahn*	el tomillo *el to-meel-yō*	**thyme**
les tomates *lay to-mat*	die Tomaten *dee tō-mah-tèn*	los tomates *los to-ma-tays*	**tomatoes**
la pastèque *la pas-tek*	die Wasser- melone *dee va-sèr-me- lō-ne*	la sandía *la san-dee-a*	**watermelon**
			zucchini = courgettes

Groceries & Household

French	German	Spanish	
les petits pots (pour bébés) *lay puh-tee pō (poor bay-bay)*	die Babynahrung *dee bay-bee- nah-roong*	la comida para bebés *la ko-mee-da pa-ra bay-bays*	**baby food**
la bière *la byer*	das Bier *das beer*	la cerveza *la ther-bay-tha*	**beer**
les biscuits *lay bees-kwee*	die Kekse *dee kek-sè*	las galletas *las gal-yay-tas*	**biscuits**
le pain *luh pañ*	das Brot *das brōt*	el pan *el pan*	**bread**
le beurre *luh buhr*	die Butter *dee boo-tèr*	la mantequilla *la man-tay-keel-ya*	**butter**
le fromage *luh fro-mazh*	der Käse *der kay-zè*	el queso *el kay-sō*	**cheese**
le cidre *luh see-druh*	der Apfelwein *der ap-fèl-vine*	la sidra *la see-dra*	**cider**
le café *luh ka-fay*	der Kaffee *der ka-fay*	el café *el ka-fay*	**coffee**
la crème *la krem*	die Sahne *dee zah-nè*	la nata *la na-ta*	**cream**
les œufs *lay zuh*	die Eier *dee eye-èr*	los huevos *los way-bōs*	**eggs**
la farine *la fa-reen*	das Mehl *das mayl*	la harina *la a-ree-na*	**flour**

French	German	Spanish	
les cornichons *lay kor-nee-shoñ*	die Gewürz- gurken *dee ge-**vōōrts**- goor-kèn*	los pepinillos *los pay-pee- **neel**-yōs*	**gherkins**
la confiture *la koñ-fee-tōōr*	die Marmelade *dee mar-mè- **lah**-dè*	la mermelada *le mer-may-**la**-da*	**jam (jelly)**
la margarine *la mar-ga-reen*	die Margarine *dee mar-ga- **ree**-nè*	la margarina *la mar-ga-**ree**-na*	**margarine**
le lait *luh lay*	die Milch *dee milkh*	el leche *el **lay**-chay*	**milk**
la moutarde *la moo-tard*	der Senf *der zenf*	la mostaza *la mos-**ta**-tha*	**mustard**
l'huile *lweel*	das Öl *das ur'l*	el aceite *el a-**the**-ee-tay*	**oil**
les olives *lay zo-leev*	die Oliven *dee o-**lee**-vèn*	las aceitunas *las a-the-ee- **too**-nas*	**olives**
le poivre *luh pwah-vruh*	der Pfeffer *der **pfe**-fèr*	la pimienta *la peem-**yen**-ta*	**pepper**
le lait en poudre (*pour bébés*) *luh lay oñ poo-druh* (*poor bay-bay*)	das Milchpulver (*für Babys*) *das **milkh**-pool-fèr* (*fōōr bay-bees*)	el leche en polvo (*infantil*) *el **lay**-chay en **pol**- bō (*een-fan- **teel***)	**powdered milk** (*for baby*)
le riz *luh ree*	der Reis *der rise*	el arroz *el a-**rroth***	**rice**
le sel *luh sel*	das Salz *das zalts*	la sal *la sal*	**salt**
la lessive *la le-seev*	das Waschpulver *das **vash**-pool-fèr*	el jabón en polvo *el kha-**bon** en **pol**-bō*	**soap powder**
la soupe *la soop*	die Suppe *dee **zoo**-pè*	la sopa *la **so**-pa*	**soup**
le sucre *luh sōō-kruh*	der Zucker *der **tsoo**-kèr*	el azúcar *el a-**thoo**-kar*	**sugar**
le thé *luh tay*	der Tee *der tay*	el té *el tay*	**tea**
le papier hygiénique *luh pa-pyay ee- zhyay-neek*	das Toilettenpapier *das tō-a-**le**-tèn-pa- peer*	el papel higiénico *el pa-**pel** ee-khyen- ee-kō*	**toilet paper**
le vinaigre *luh vee-ne-gruh*	der Essig *der **es**-ikh*	el vinagre *el bee-**na**-gray*	**vinegar**
le produit à vaisselle *luh pro-dwee a ve-sel*	das Spülmittel *das **shpōōl**-mit-èl*	el liquido lavava- jillas *el lee-**kee**-dō la-ba- ba-**kheel**-yas*	**washing-up liquid**

Food & Drink

French	German	Spanish	
le vin (rouge/blanc) *luh vañ (roozh/ bloñ)*	der (rote/weiße) Wein *der (rō-tè/vye-sè) vine*	el vino (tinto/ blanco) *el bee-nō (teen-tō/ blang-kō)*	**(red/white) wine**
le yaourt *luh ya-oor*	der Joghurt *der yō-goort*	el yogur *el yō-goor*	**yoghourt**

Meat

French	German	Spanish	
le bœuf *luh buhf*	das Rindfleisch *das rint-flyesh*	la vaca *la ba-ka*	**beef**
le poulet *luh poo-lay*	das Huhn *das hoon*	el pollo *el pol-yō*	**chicken**
la côte *la kōt*	das Kotelett *das kō-tè-let*	la chuleta *la choo-lay-ta*	**chop**
le jambon *luh zhoñ-boñ*	der Schinken *der shing-kèn*	el jamón *el kha-mon*	**ham**
les rognons *lay ron-yoñ*	die Nieren *dee nee-rèn*	los riñones *los reen-yo-nays*	**kidneys**
l'agneau *lan-yō*	das Lamm *das lam*	el cordero *el kor-day-rō*	**lamb**
le foie *luh fwah*	die Leber *dee lay-bèr*	el hígado *el ee-ga-dō*	**liver**
le pâté *luh pa-tay*	die (Leber)pastete *dee (lay-bèr-)pas-tay-tè*	el paté *el pa-tay*	**pâté**
le porc *luh por*	das Schweinefleisch *das shvye-nè-flyesh*	el cerdo *el ther-dō*	**pork**
le salami *luh sa-la-mee*	die Salami *dee za-lah-mi*	el salami *el sa-la-mee*	**salami**
le saucisson *luh sō-see-soñ*	die Wurst *dee voorst*	el salchichón *el sal-chee-chon*	**sausage**
les saucisses *lay sō-sees*	die Würstchen *dee vōōrst-khèn*	las salchichas *las sal-chee-chas*	**sausages**
le bifteck *luh beef-tek*	das Steak *das shtayk*	el biftec *el beef-tek*	**steak**
le veau *luh vō*	das Kalbfleisch *das kalp-flyesh*	la ternera *la ter-nay-ra*	**veal**

Fish & Shellfish

French	German	Spanish	
la praire *la prer*	die Venusmuschel *dee vay-noos-moosh-èl*	la almeja *la al-may-kha*	**clam**
la morue *la mo-rōō*	der Kabeljau *der kah-bèl-yow*	el bacalao *el ba-ka-la-ō*	**cod**
le crabe *luh krab*	die Krabbe *dee kra-bè*	el cangrejo *el kang-gray-khō*	**crab**

Food & Drink

French	German	Spanish	
les langoustines *lay loñ-goos-teen*	die Languste *dee lang-**goos**-tè*	los langostinos *los lang-gos-**tee**-nōs*	**crawfish,** **crayfish**
l'anguille *loñ-gee*	der Aal *der ahl*	la anguila *la ang-**gee**-la*	**eel**
le colin *luh ko-lañ*	der Seehecht *der **zay**-hekht*	la merluza *la mer-**loo**-tha*	**hake**
le hareng *luh a-roñ*	der Hering *der **hay**-ring*	el arenque *el a-**reng**-kay*	**herring**
le homard *luh o-mar*	der Hummer *der **hoom**-èr*	la langosta *la lang-**gos**-ta*	**lobster**
les moules *lay mool*	die Muscheln *dee **moosh**-èln*	los mejillones *los may-kheel-**yo**-nays*	**mussels**
les huîtres *lay zwee-truh*	die Austern *dee **ows**-tèrn*	las ostras *las **os**-tras*	**oysters**
la perche *la persh*	der Flußbarsch *der **floos**-barsh*	la perca *la **per**-ca*	**perch**
le brochet *luh bro-shay*	der Hecht *der hekht*	el lucio *el **loo**-thyō*	**pike**
les crevettes *lay kruh-vet*	die Garnelen *dee gar-**nay**-lèn*	las gambas *las **gam**-bas*	**prawns**
le rouget *luh roo-zhay*	die Meerbarbe *dee **mayr**-bar-bè*	el salmonete *el sal-mo-**nay**-tay*	**red mullet**
le saumon *luh sō-moñ*	der Lachs *der laks*	el salmón *el sal-**mon***	**salmon**
les sardines *lay sar-deen*	die Sardinen *dee zar-**deen**-èn*	las sardinas *las sar-**dee**-nas*	**sardines**
les coquilles Saint- Jacques *lay ko-kee sañ-zhak*	die Jakobsmuscheln *dee **ya**-kōps-moosh- èln*	las vieiras *las bye-**ee**-ras*	**scallops**
la sole *la sol*	die Seezunge *dee **zay**-tsoong-è*	el lenguado *el leng-**gwa**-dō*	**sole**
le sprat *luh sprat*	die Sprotte *dee **shpro**-tè*	el chanquete *el chang-**kay**-tay*	**sprat**
le calmar *luh kal-mar*	der Tintenfisch *der **tin**-tèn-fish*	el calamar *el ka-la-**mar***	**squid**
l'espadon *les-pa-doñ*	der Schwertfisch *der **shvayrt**-fish*	la pez espada *la peth es-**pa**-da*	**swordfish**
la truite *la trweet*	die Forelle *dee for-**el**-è*	la trucha *la **troo**-cha*	**trout**
le thon *luh .toñ*	der Thunfisch *der **toon**-fish*	el atún *el a-**toon***	**tuna**
le turbot *luh tōōr-bō*	der Steinbutt *der **shtine**-boot*	el rodaballo *el ro-da-**bal**-yō*	**turbot**

The Bank

French	German

French banks are usually open from 9 a.m. until 4 p.m. and most close for lunch. You may be told to pick up your currency from a different desk or caisse. You can also change money at hotels, large stores and bureaux de change, but the rate of exchange tends to be less favourable. Those at airports and major railway stations stay open at night and over the weekend.

German banks are usually open from 8 a.m. until 5 p.m. and most close for lunch. You can also change money at hotels and Wechselbüros, but the rate of exchange tends to be less favourable.

Est-ce que vous pouvez me changer ces chèques de voyage/ces billets?
es-kuh voo poo-vay muh shoñ-zhay say shek duh vwah-yazh/say bee-yay?

Kann ich hier diese Reisechecks einlösen/Banknoten umtauschen?
*kan ikh heer **dee**-zè **rye**-zè-sheks **ine**-lur'-zèn/**bank**-nō-tèn **oom**-tow-shèn?*

À combien est la livre sterling/le dollar?
a koñ-byañ nay la lee-vruh ster-leeng/luh do-lar?

Was ist der Kurs für Pfund Sterling/Dollars?
*vas ist der koors fōōr pfoont **ster**-ling/**do**-larz?*

Voici mon passeport
vwah-see moñ pas-por

Hier ist mein Reisepaß
*heer ist mine **rye**-zè-pas*

Je voudrais retirer de l'argent avec ma carte eurochèque
zhuh voo-dray ruh-tee-ray duh lar-zhoñ a-vek ma kart uh-rō-shek

Ich möchte gerne einen Euroscheck einlösen
*ikh **mur'kh**-tè **gern**-è **ine**-èn **oy**-rō-shek **ine**-lur'-zèn*

Je voudrais retirer de l'argent avec ma carte de crédit
zhuh voo-dray ruh-tee-ray duh lar-zhoñ a-vek ma kart duh kray-dee

Ich möchte gerne Bargeld auf meine Kreditkarte haben
*ikh **mur'kh**-tè **gern**-è **bar**-gelt owf **mine**-è kre-**deet**-kar-tè **hah**-bèn*

Vous prenez combien de commission?
voo pruh-nay koñ-byañ duh ko-mee-syoñ?

Wie hoch ist die Bearbeitungsgebühr?
*vee hōkh ist dee bè-**ar**-bye-toongz-gè-**bōōr**?*

Est-ce que vous pouvez contacter ma banque pour arranger un transfert de fonds?
es-kuh voo poo-vay koñ-tak-tay ma boñk poor a-roñ-zhay uñ troñs-fer duh foñ?

Könnten Sie mit meiner Bank eine Überweisung vereinbaren?
*kur'n-tèn zee mit **mine**-èr bank **ine**-è **ōō**-bèr-vye-zoong fer-**ine**-bah-rèn?*

Voilà le nom et l'adresse de ma banque
vwah-la luh noñ ay la-dres duh ma boñk

Hier sind Name und Adresse meiner Bank
*heer zint **nah**-mè oont a-**dres**-è **mine**-èr bank*

The Bank

Spanish banks are usually open from 9 a.m. until 2 p.m., including Saturdays. You can also change money at hotels and oficinas de cambio, but the rate of exchange tends to be less favourable.

¿Pueden cambiarme estos cheques de viaje/estos billetes? *pway-den kam-byar-may es-tōs che-kays day bya-khay/es-tōs bee-lyay-tays?*	**Will you change these traveller's cheques/these notes (bills)?**
¿A cómo está la libra esterlina/el dólar? *a kō-mō es-ta la lee-bra es-ter-lee-na/el do-lar?*	**What is the rate for sterling/ dollars?**
Aquí está mi pasaporte *a-kee es-ta mee pa-sa-por-tay*	**Here is my passport**
Querría hacer efectivo un cheque con la tarjeta de eurocheque *kay-rree-a a-ther ay-fek-tee-bō oon che-kay kon la tar-khay-ta day e-oo-rō-che-kay*	**I would like to cash a cheque with my Eurocheque card**
Querría obtener dinero en efectivo con mi tarjeta de crédito *kay-rree-a' ob-te-ner dee-nay-rō en ay-fek-tee-bō kon mee tar-khay-ta day kre-dee-tō*	**I would like to obtain a cash advance with my credit card**
¿Que comisión cobran ustedes? *kay ko-mee-syon ko-bran oos-tay-days?*	**What is your commission?**
¿Pueden ponerse en contacto con mi banco para pedir una transferencia, por favor? *pway-den po-ner-say en kon-tak-tō kon mee bang-kō pa-ra pay-deer oo-na trans-fe-ren-thya, por fa-bor?*	**Can you contact my bank to arrange for a transfer please?**
Este es el nombre y la dirección de mi banco *es-tay es el nom-bray ee la dee-rek-thyon day mee bang-kō*	**This is the name and address of my bank**

The Post Office

French	German
A large French post office can be confusing with a long row of desks, each providing a specific service. The ones you're most likely to need are those for stamps – timbres au détail – and parcels – colis. If you just want stamps it's simpler to get them in a café with a tobacco counter.	*A German post office can be rather confusing with a long row of desks, each providing a specific service. The ones you're most most likely to need are those dealing with stamps – Briefmarken – and parcels – Pakete.*
C'est combien pour envoyer une lettre en Grande-Bretagne/aux États-Unis? *say koñ-byañ poor oñ-vwah-yay ōōn le-truh oñ groñd-bruh-tan-yuh/ō zay-ta-zōō-nee?*	Wieviel kostet ein Brief nach Großbritannien/in die Vereinigten Staaten? *vee-**feel kos**-tèt ine breef nakh grōs-bri-**tan**-yèn/in dee fer-**ine**-ikh-tèn **shtah**-tèn?*
Six timbres à deux francs, s'il vous plaît *see tañ-bruh a duh froñ, see voo play*	Sechs Briefmarken zu achtzig Pfennig, bitte *zeks **breef**-mark-èn tsoo **akh**-tsikh **pfe**-nikh, bit-è*
Je voudrais six timbres pour cartes postales à envoyer en Grande-Bretagne *zhuh voo-dray see tañ-bruh poor kart po-stal a oñ-vwah-yay oñ groñd-bruh-tan-yuh*	Kann ich sechs Briefmarken für Postkarten nach Großbritannien haben? *kan ikh zeks **breef**-mark-èn fōōr **post**-kar-tèn nahkh grōs-bri-**tan**-yèn **hah**-ben?*
Je voudrais expédier ce colis *zhuh voo-dray zek-spay-dyay suh ko-lee*	Ich möchte dieses Paket aufgeben *ikh **mur'kh**-tè **dee**-zès pa-**kayt** owf-gay-bèn*
Je voudrais envoyer un télégramme *zhuh voo-dray zoñ-vwah-yay uñ tay-lay-gram*	Ich möchte ein Telegramm aufgeben *ikh **mur'kh**-tè ine tay-lay-**gram** owf-gay-bèn*
Un formulaire pour un télégramme, s'il vous plaît *uñ for-mōō-ler poor uñ tay-lay-gram, see voo play*	Kann ich bitte ein Telegramm-formular haben? *kan ikh **bit**-è ine tay-lay-**gram**-for-moo-lar **hah**-bèn?*
Quand est-ce qu'il arrivera? *koñ tes-keel a-ree-vuh-ra?*	Wann kommt es an? *van komt es an?*
Je voudrais envoyer cela en recommandé *zhuh voo-dray zoñ-vwah-yay suh-la oñ ruh-ko-moñ-day*	Ich möchte dies per Einschreiben schicken *ikh **mur'kh**-tè dees per **ine**-shrye-bèn **shi**-kèn*
Un aérogramme, s'il vous plaît *uñ na-ay-ro-gram, see voo play*	Kann ich bitte einen Luftpost-leichtbrief haben? *kan ikh **bit**-è **ine**-èn **looft**-post-lyekht-breef **hah**-bèn?*

Spanish

A large Spanish post office can be rather confusing
with a long row of desks, each providing a specific
service. The ones you're most likely to need are
those dealing with stamps – venta de sellos – and
parcels – paquetes. If you just want stamps it's
simpler to get them from an estanco.

¿Qué franqueo lleva una carta a Inglaterra/a los Estados Unidos? *kay frang-**kay**-ō **lyay**-ba **ōō**-na **kar**-ta a eeng-gla-**te**-rra/a lōs es-**ta**-dōs oo-**nee**-dōs?*	**How much is a letter to Britain/to the United States?**
Seis sellos de veinticinco pesetas, por favor *se-ees se-lyōs day be-een-tee-**theeng**-kō pay-**say**-tas, por fa-**bor***	**Six 2-franc/80-Pfennig/25-peseta stamps please**
¿Me da seis sellos para tarjetas postales a Inglaterra? *may da **se**-ees se-lyōs **pa**-ra tar-**khay**-tas pos-**ta**-lays a eeng-gla-**te**-rra?*	**Can I have 6 stamps for postcards to Britain?**
Quiero enviar este paquete ***kyay**-rō en-**byar es**-tay pa-**kay**-tay*	**I want to send this parcel**
Quiero poner un telegrama ***kyay**-rō po-**ner** oon tay-lay-**gra**-ma*	**I want to send a telegram**
¿Me da un impreso para telegrama, por favor? *may da oon eem-**pray**-sō **pa**-ra tay-lay-**gra**-ma, por fa-**bor**?*	**Can I have a telegram form please?**
¿Cuando llegará? ***kwan**-dō lyay-ga-**ra**?*	**When will it arrive?**
Quiero enviar esto por correo certificado ***kyay**-rō en-**byar es**-tō por ko-**rray**-ō ther-tee-fee-**ka**-dō*	**I want to send this by registered mail**
¿Me da un aerograma, por favor? *may da oon a-ay-rō-**gra**-ma, por fa-**bor**?*	**Can I have an areogramme please?**

Using the Telephone

French	German
To make a telephone call, go to a post office, tell the clerk the number you want, and she will direct you to a box. You need a counter (jeton) for local calls, coins for longer distances and in some cases, as when phoning outside France, she will dial the call herself and charge you afterwards. In some cafés you use jetons or coins, in others you pay afterwards. The latest type of street telephones are in stainless steel and glass boxes.	*To make a telephone call, go to a post office, tell the clerk the number you want, and she will direct you to a box. In some cases, as when phoning outside Germany, she will dial the call herself and charge you afterwards. In some cafés and restaurants you pay after you have made the call. The latest type of street telephones are in stainless steel and glass boxes; a green sign means you can make international calls.*
Je voudrais téléphoner en Grande-Bretagne *zhuh voo-dray tay-lay-fo-nay oñ groñd-bruh-tan-yuh*	Ich möchte gerne nach Großbritannien anrufen *ikh **mur'kh**-tè **gern**-è nakh grōs-bri-**tan**-yèn **an**-roo-fèn*
Est-ce que vous pouvez me donner ce numéro, s'il vous plaît? *es-kuh voo poo-vay muh do-nay suh nōō-may-rō, see voo play?*	Können Sie mir bitte diese Nummer geben? ***kur'n**-èn zee meer **bit**-è **dee**-zè **noo**-mèr **gay**-bèn?*
Je voudrais téléphoner en P.C.V. *zhuh voo-dray tay-lay-fo-nay oñ pay-say-vay*	*Not applicable*
Est-ce que je peux utiliser le téléphone, s'il vous plaît? *es-kuh zhuh puh zōō-tee-lee-zay luh tay-lay-fon, see voo play?*	Kann ich bitte telefonieren? *kan ikh **bit**-è tay-lay-fo-**neer**-èn?*
Est-ce que vous pouvez me faire la monnaie/me donner des jetons, s'il vous plaît? *es-kuh voo poo-vay muh fer la mo-nay/muh do-nay day zhuh-toñ, see voo play?*	Können Sie mir bitte Wechselgeld geben? ***kur'n**-èn zee meer **bit**-è **vek**-sèl-gelt **gay**-bèn?*
Est-ce que je peux parler à ...? *es-kuh zhuh puh par-lay a ...?*	Kann ich bitte mit ... sprechen? *kan ikh **bit**-è mit ... **shprekh**-èn?*
J'ai été coupé *zhay ay-tay koo-pay*	Wir sind unterbrochen worden *veer zint **oon**-tèr-brokh-èn **vor**-dèn*

Things You May Hear

Allô *a-lō*	Hallo *ha-**lō***
Ne quittez pas *nuh kee-tay pa*	Bleiben Sie am Apparat ***blye**-bèn zee am a-pa-**raht***
J'essaie d'obtenir la communication *zhe-say dob-tuh-neer la ko-mōō-nee-kas-yoñ*	Einen Moment, ich verbinde ***ine**-èn mō-**ment**, ikh fer-**bin**-dè*
Je ne peux pas obtenir la communication *zhuh nuh puh pa zob-tuh-neer la ko-mōō-nee-kas-yoñ*	Ich kann diese Nummer nicht erreichen *ikh kan **dee**-zè **noo**-mèr nikht er-**rye**-khèn*

Using the Telephone

To make a telephone call, go to a central telefónica,
tell the clerk the country or place you want, and
she will direct you to a box. You dial the number
yourself and afterwards, but she will charge you afterwards,
but she will connect you for person-to-person and
reversed charge calls. Pay phones in the street and
in bars require coins, but in some bars you pay
after the call and sometimes you still need
telephone tokens (fichas).

Querría hacer una llamada telefónica a Inglaterra kay-**rree**-a a-**ther oo**-na lya-**ma**-da tay-lay-**fo**-nee-ka a eeng-gla-**te**-rra	**I would like to make a phone call to Britain**
¿Puede usted obtenerme este número? **pway**-day oos-**ted** ob-tay-**ner**-may **es**-tay **noo**-may-rŏ?	**Can you get me this number?**
Quiero hacer una llamada a cobro revertido **kyay**-ro a-**ther oo**-na lya-**ma**-da a **ko**-brŏ ray-ber-**tee**-dŏ	**I want to make a reversed charge (collect) call**
¿Puedo usar el teléfono, por favor? **pway**-dŏ oo-**sar** el tay-**lay**-fo-no, por fa-**bor**?	**May I use the telephone please?**
¿Puede cambiarme en monedas/darme una ficha, por favor? **pway**-day kam-**byar**-may en mo-**nay**-das/**dar**-may **oo**-na **fee**-cha, por fa-**bor**?	**Can you give me change/a token please?**
¿Podría hablar con ...? po-**dree**-a a-**blar** kon ...?	**Can I speak to ...?**
Se ha cortada la comunicación say a kor-**ta**-da la ko-moo-nee-ka-**thyon**	**We have been cut off**

Things You May Hear

Diga/dígame **dee**-ga/**dee**-ga-may	**Hello**
No cuelgue/Un momento, por favor nŏ **kwel**-gay/oon mo-**men**-tŏ, por fa-**bor**	**Hold the line**
Estoy intentando ponerle es-**toy** een-ten-**tan**-dŏ po-**ner**-lay	**I'm trying to connect you**
No puedo conseguirle la comunicación no **pway**-do kon-say-**geer**-lay la ko-moo-nee-ka-**thyon**	**I cannot obtain this number**

The Chemist/Druggist

French	German
You should see the If You're Ill *section if anyone is really unwell, but a chemist should be able to help you with minor ailments. There will be an illuminated green cross outside the shop, which might not sell the range of toiletries stocked by chemists at home, and certainly won't sell film – for that you want a photographic shop.*	*You should see the* If You're Ill *section if anyone is really unwell, but a chemist (Apotheke) should be able to help you with minor ailments. There will be an illuminated sign outside, a red A on a white background. He won't sell the range of toiletries stocked by chemists at home – for some of the items on the next pages you'll have to go to a Drogerie.*

Je voudrais quelque chose pour ...
zhuh voo-dray kel-kuh shōz poor ...

Ich hätte gerne etwas gegen ...
*ikh **het**-e **gern**-e et-vas gay-gèn ...*

les gerçures
lay zher-sōōr

rissige Haut
***ris**-i-gè howt*

un rhume
uñ rōōm

Erkältung
*er-**kayl**-toong*

la toux
la too

Husten
***hoo**-stèn*

le rhume des foins
luh rōōm day fwañ

Heuschnupfen
***hoy**-shnoop-fèn*

un mal de tête
uñ mal duh tet

Kopfschmerzen
***kopf**-shmer-tsèn*

les piqûres d'insectes
lay pee-kōōr dañ-sekt

Insektenstiche
*in-**zek**-tèn-shtikh-è*

les pieds douloureux
lay pyay doo-loo-ruh

Fußschmerzen
***foos**-shmer-tsèn*

un mal de gorge
uñ mal duh gorzh

Halsschmerzen
***hals**-shmer-tsèn*

un coup de soleil
uñ koo duh so-lye

Sonnenbrand
***zon**-èn-brant*

une rage de dents
ōōn razh duh doñ

Zahnschmerzen
***tsahn**-shmer-tsèn*

un mal d'estomac
uñ mal des-to-ma

einen verdorbenen Magen
***ine**-en ver-**dor**-bè-nèn **mah**-gèn*

J'en prends combien?
zhoñ proñ koñ-byañ?

Wieviele soll ich nehmen?
*vee-**feel**-è zol ikh **nay**-mèn?*

Combien de fois par jour faut-il les prendre?
koñ-byañ duh fwah par zhoor fō-teel lay proñ-druh?

Wie oft muß ich sie nehmen?
*vee oft moos ikh zee **nay**-mèn?*

Est-ce que les enfants peuvent en prendre?
es-kuh lay zoñ-foñ puhv toñ proñ-druh?

Ist das für Kinder geeignet?
*ist das fōōr **kin**-dèr gè-**ige**-nèt?*

The Chemist/Druggist

Spanish

You should see the If You're Ill section if anyone is
really unwell, but a chemist should be able to help
you with the usual holiday ailments. There will be
an illuminated green cross outside, and a sign
saying FARMACIA. You won't find the range of
toiletries and cosmetics sold by chemists at home,
so for some of the items on the next pages you'll
have to go to a Perfumería or a Droguería.

Querría algo para . . . *kay-**rree**-a **al**-gō **pa**-ra . . .*	**I want something for . . .**
piel agrietada *pyel a-gree-ay-**ta**-da*	**chapped skin**
un resfriado *oon res-free-**a**-dō*	**a cold**
(una) tos *(**oo**-na) tos*	**a cough**
fiebre del heno ***fyay**-bray del **ay**-nō*	**hay fever**
el dolor de cabeza *el do-**lor** day ka-**bay**-tha*	**a headache**
las picaduras de insectos *las pee-ka-**doo**-ras day een-**sek**-tōs*	**insect bites**
pies cansados *pyays kan-**sa**-dōs*	**sore feet**
una garganta irritada ***oo**-na gar-**gan**-ta ee-rree-**ta**-da*	**a sore throat**
quemadura de sol *kay-ma-**doo**-ra day sol*	**sunburn**
dolor de muelas *do-**lor** day **mway**-las*	**toothache**
un trastorno estomacal *oon tras-**tor**-nō es-to-ma-**kal***	**an upset stomach**

¿Cuántas tomo? ***kwan**-tas **tō**-mō?*	**How many do I take?**
¿Cada cuánto las tomo? ***ka**-da **kwan**-tō las **tō**-mō?*	**How often do I take them?**
¿Lo pueden tomar los niños? *lō **pway**-den tō-**mar** lōs **nee**-nyos?*	**Is this safe for children?**

The Chemist/Druggist

French	German	Spanish	
la lotion après-rasage *la lō-syoñ a-pre-ra-zazh*	das Aftershave *das af-tèr-shayv*	el áftershave *el af-ter-shayv*	**aftershave**
l'antiseptique *loñ-tee-sep-teek*	das Antiseptikum *das an-ti-zep-ti-koom*	el antiséptico *el an-tee-sep-tee-kō*	**antiseptic**
l'aspirine *las-pee-reen*	das Aspirin *das as-pi-reen*	la aspirina *la as-pee-ree-na*	**aspirin**
le pansement *luh poñ-suh-moñ*	das Verband *das fer-bant*	la venda *la ben-da*	**bandage**
le démaquillant *luh day-ma-kee-yoñ*	die Reinigungs-milch *dee rye-ni-goongs-milkh*	la leche limpiadora *la lay-chay leem-pya-do-ra*	**cleanser**
le contraceptif *luh koñ-tra-sep-teef*	das Verhütungs-mittel *das fer-hōō-toongs-mit-èl*	el anticonceptivo *el an-tee-kon-thep-tee-bō*	**contraceptive**
le coton (hydro-phile) *luh ko-toñ (ee-dro-feel)*	die Watte *dee va-tè*	el algodón *el al-go-don*	**cotton wool**
le déodorant *luh day-ō-dō-roñ*	der Deodorant *der day-ō-do-rant*	el desodorante *el day-so-do-ran-tay*	**deodorant**
le désinfectant *luh day-zañ-fek-toñ*	das Desinfek-tionsmittel *das dayz-in-fek-tsi-yōns-mit-èl*	el desinfectante *el day-seen-fek-tan-tay*	**disinfectant**
l'eau de Cologne *lō duh ko-lon-yuh*	das Kölnisch Wasser *das kur'l-nish vas-èr*	el agua de colonia *el a-gwa day-ko-lon-ya*	**eau de Cologne**
le calmant *luh kal-moñ*	das Kolikmittel *das kō-lik-mit-èl*	el agua de anís para niños *el a-gwa day a-nees pa-ra nee-nyōs*	**gripe water**
la crème pour les mains *la krem poor lay mañ*	die Handcreme *dee hant-kraym*	la crema de manos *la kray-ma day ma-nōs*	**handcream**
la crème anti-insecte *la krem oñ-tee-añ-sekt*	das Insekten-schutzmittel *das in-zek-tèn-shootsmit-èl*	la loción contra insectos *la lo-thyon kon-tra een-sek-tōs*	**insect repellent**
la pommade rosat *la po-mad rō-za*	die Lippencreme *dee lip-èn-kraym*	el cacao *el ka-ka-ō*	**lipsalve**

124

French	German	Spanish	
la crème hydra-tante *la krem ee-dra-toñt*	die Feuchtig-keitscreme *dee **foykh**-tikh-kites-kraym*	la crema hidratante *la **kray**-ma ee-dra-**tan**-tay*	**moisturiser**
la lime à ongles *la leem a oñ-gluh*	die Nagelfeile *dee **nah**-gèl-fye-lè*	la lima *la **lee**-ma*	**nailfile**
le dissolvant *luh dee-sol-voñ*	der Nagellack-entferner *der **nah**-gèl-lak-ent-**fer**-nèr*	el quitaesmalte *el kee-ta-es-**mal**-tay*	**nail polish** or **varnish remover**
			nipple = teat
les lames de rasoir *lay lam duh ra-zwar*	die Rasierklingen *dee ra-**zeer**-kling-èn*	las cuchillas de afeitar *las koo-**chee**-lyas day a-fe-ee-**tar***	**razor blades**
les épingles de sûreté *lay zay-pañ-gluh duh sōōr-tay*	die Sicherheits-nadeln *dee **zikh**-èr-hites-nah-dèln*	los imperdibles *lōs eem-per-**dee**-blays*	**safety pins**
les serviettes hygiéniques *lay ser-vyet ee-zhyay-neek*	die Damen-binden *dee **dah**-mèn-bin-dèn*	las compresas higiénicas *las kom-**pray**-sas ee-**khye**-nee-kas*	**sanitary towels (napkins)**
le shampooing *luh shoñ-pwañ*	das Shampoo *das **sham**-poo*	el champú *el cham-**poo***	**shampoo**
la crème à raser *la krem a ra-zay*	die Rasiercreme *dee ra-**zeer**-kraym*	la crema de afeitar *la **kray**-ma day a-fe-ee-**tar***	**shaving cream** or **foam**
le savon *luh sa-voñ*	die Seife *dee **zye**-fè*	el jabón *el kha-**bon***	**soap**
le sparadrap *luh spa-ra-dra*	das Heftpflaster *das **heft**-pfla-stèr*	el esparadrapo *el es-pa-ra-**dra**-pō*	**sticking plaster**
le lait solaire *luh lay so-ler*	das Sonnenöl *das **zon**-èn-ur'l*	la loción bronceadora *la lo-**thyon** bron-thay-a-**do**-ra*	**suntan lotion**
les tampons *lay toñ-poñ*	die Tampons *dee **tam**-pons*	los tampones *los tam-**po**-nays*	**tampons**
la tétine *la tay-teen*	der Gummi-sauger *der **goo**-mi-zow-gèr*	la tetina *la tay-**tee**-na*	**teat (nipple)**
les kleenex *lay klee-neks*	die Papiertücher *dee pa-**peer**-tōō-khèr*	los kleenex *lōs **klee**-neks*	**tissues**
le dentifrice *luh doñ-tee-frees*	die Zahnpasta *dee **tsahn**-pas-ta*	la pasta de dientes *la **pas**-ta day **dyen**-tays*	**toothpaste**

Newspapers & Tobacco

French	German
You'll get newspapers at a newsstand (kiosque à journaux), while stationery is generally sold along with books in a librairie-papeterie.	You'll get newspapers at a newsstand (Zeitungskiosk), while stationery is generally sold in a Schreibwarenhandlung.

The simplest way to buy tobacco is from a café-tabac, that is, a café with a red TABAC sign outside. British and American brands are often available along with the stronger French varieties. Wherever tobacco is sold you can also buy stamps – you'll find the phrases in the Post Office section on page 118.

French	German
Est-ce que vous avez des journaux anglais/américains/des cartes postales? *es-kuh voo za-vay day zhoor-nõ zoñ-glay/za-may-ree-kañ/day kart po-stal?*	Haben Sie englische/amerikanische Zeitungen/Postkarten? ***hah**-bèn zee **eng**-lish-è/a-me-ri-**kahn**-ish-è **tsye**-toong-èn/**post**-kar-tèn?*
Je voudrais du papier à lettres/des enveloppes/un stylo/un crayon/du Scotch *zhuh voo-dray dōō pap-yay a le-truh/day zoñ-vlop/zuñ stee-lõ/zuñ kre-yoñ/dōō skotch*	Ich hätte gerne Schreibpapier/Briefumschläge/einen Kugelschreiber/einen Bleistift/Klebstreifen *ikh **he**-tè **gern**-è **shripe**-pa-peer/**breef**-oom-shlay-gè/**ine**-èn **koo**-gèl-shrye-bèr/**ine**-èn **blye**-shtift/**klayp**-shtrye-fèn*
Est-ce que vous vendez des livres de poche anglais/des plans de la ville? *es-kuh voo voñ-day day lee-vruh duh posh oñ-glay/day ploñ duh la veel?*	Führen Sie englische Taschenbücher/Stadtpläne? ***fōōr**-èn zee **eng**-lish-è **tash**-èn-bōō-khèr/**shtat**-play-nè?*
Un paquet de ..., s'il vous plaît *uñ pa-kay duh ..., see voo play*	Eine Schachtel ..., bitte ***ine**-è shakh-tèl ..., **bit**-è*
Avec/sans filtre *a-vek/soñ feel-truh*	Mit/ohne Filter *mit/**ō**-nè **fil**-tèr*

French	German	Spanish	
la boîte d'allumettes *la bwaht da-lōō-met*	die Schachtel Streichhölzer *dee **shakh**-tèl shtryekh-hur'l-tsèr*	la caja de cerillas *la **ka**-kha day thay-**ree**-lyas*	**box of matches**
le cigare *luh see-gar*	die Zigarre *dee tsi-**ga**-rè*	el puro *el **poo**-rõ*	**cigar**
le briquet *luh bree-kay*	das Feuerzeug *das **foy**-èr-tsoyk*	el encendedor *el en-then-day-**dor***	**cigarette lighter**
les cigarettes *lay see-ga-ret*	die Zigaretten *dee tsi-ga-**re**-tèn*	los cigarillos *lõs thee-ga-**ree**-lyõs*	**cigarettes**
le recharge de briquet *luh ruh-sharzh duh bree-kay*	die Gaspatrone *dee **gahs**-pa-trõ-nè*	la carga para encendedor de gas *la **kar**-ga pa-ra en-then-day-**dor** day gas*	**gas (butane) refill**

Spanish

You'll get newspapers at a newsstand (quiosco de periódicos), while stationery is generally sold along with books in a librería-papelería.

Tobacco is sold in estancos, which have a red, yellow and red sign outside saying TABACALERA S.A., as well as in most bars and cafés. British and American brands are available along with the stronger Spanish ones. Estancos also sell stamps – you'll find the phrases you want on page 119.

¿Tiene periódicos ingleses/
americanos/tarjetas postales?
tyay-nay payr-yo-dee-kōs eeng-glay-says/a-may-ree-ka-nōs/tar-khay-tas pos-ta-lays?

**Have you got any English/
American newspapers/
postcards?**

Querría papel de escribir/sobres/un
bolígrafo/un lápiz/cinta adhesiva
*kay-rree-a pa-pel day es-kree-beer/
so-brays/oon bo-lee-gra-fō/oon
la-peeth/theen-ta a-day-see-ba*

**I would like some notepaper/
some envelopes/a pen/a pencil/
some adhesive tape**

¿Venden libros de bolsillo en
inglés/planos de la cuidad?
*ben-den lee-brōs day bol-seel-yō en
een-glays/pla-nōs day la thyoo-dad?*

**Do you sell English
paperbacks/street maps?**

Un paquete de ..., por favor
oon pa-kay-tay day ..., por fa-bor

A packet of ... please

Con/sin filtro
kon/seen feel-trō

With/without filter-tip

French	German	Spanish	
le magazine *luh ma-ga-zeen*	die Zeitschrift *dee tsite-shrift*	la revista *la ray-bees-ta*	**magazine**
la pipe *la peep*	die Pfeife *dee pfye-fè*	la pipa *la pee-pa*	**pipe**
les cure-pipes *lay kŏŏr-peep*	die Pfeifen- reiniger *dee pfye-fèn- rye-ni-gèr*	las escobillas *las es-ko-bee-lyas*	**pipe cleaners**
le tabac pour la pipe *luh ta-ba poor la peep*	der Pfeifentabak *der pfye-fèn- ta-bak*	el tabaco de pipa *el ta-ba-kō day pee-pa*	**pipe tobacco**
la carte (routière) *la kart (roo-tyer)*	die (Straßen-) karte *dee (shtrah-sèn-) kar-tè*	el mapa (de carreteras) *el ma-pa (day ka-rray- tay-ras)*	**(road) map**

Clothing

French	German

Je voudrais une robe/un pull
zhuh voo-dray zōōn rob/zuñ pōōl

Ich hätte gerne ein Kleid/einen Pullover
*ikh **he**-tè **gern**-è ine klite/**ine**-èn poo-**lō**-vèr*

Je porte du quarante
zhuh port dōō ka-roñt

Ich habe Größe vierzig
*ikh **hah**-bè **grur'**-sè **fir**-tsikh*

Je chausse du quarante
zhuh shōs dōō ka-roñt

Ich habe Schuhgröße vierzig
*ikh **hah**-bè **shoo**-grur'-sè **fir**-tsikh*

Est-ce que vous pouvez prendre mes mesures?
es-kuh voo poo-vay proñ-druh may muh-zōōr?

Können Sie mir Maß nehmen?
***kur'n**-èn zee meer mahs **nay**-mèn?*

Est-ce que vous l'avez en bleu?
es-kuh voo la-vay oñ bluh?

Haben Sie das gleiche in blau?
***hah**-bèn zee das **glye**-khè in blow?*

C'est fait en quoi?
say fay toñ kwah?

Was ist das für ein Material?
*vas ist das fōōr ine ma-tay-ri-**yahl**?*

J'aime celui-ci/celui-là/celui qui est en vitrine
zhem suh-lwee-see/suh-lwee-la/ suh-lwee kee e toñ vee-treen

Mir gefällt dieses/das da/das im Schaufenster
*meer gè-**felt dee**-zès/das da/das im **show**-fen-stèr*

Est-ce que je peux l'essayer?
es-kuh zhuh puh le-se-yay?

Kann ich es anprobieren?
*kan ikh es **an**-pro-bee-rèn?*

J'aime/je n'aime pas ça
zhem/zhuh nem pa sa

Es gefällt mir/gefällt mir nicht
*es gè-**felt** meer/gè-**felt** meer nikht*

Cela ne me va pas
suh-la nuh muh va pa

Es paßt nicht
es past nikht

J'en voudrais un plus grand/un plus petit
zhoñ voo-dray zuñ plōō groñ/zuñ plōō puh-tee

Ich hätte gerne ein Größeres/ein Kleineres
*ikh **he**-tè **gern**-è ine **grur'**-sèr-ès/ine **kline**-èr-ès*

Est-ce que c'est tout ce que vous avez?
es-kuh se too skuh voo za-vay?

Haben Sie sonst noch etwas?
***hah**-bèn zee zonst nokh **et**-vas?*

Est-ce que c'est lavable?
es-kuh se la-va-bluh?

Kann man es waschen?
*kan man es **vash**-èn?*

Est-ce que ça rétrécit au lavage?
es-kuh sa ray-tray-see ō la-vazh?

Läuft es ein?
loyft es ine?

Je le prends
zhuh luh proñ

Ich nehme es
*ikh **nay**-mè es*

Clothing

See page 149 for continental clothing sizes

Querría un vestido/un jersey *kay-**rree**-a oon bes-**tee**-dō/oon kher-**se**-ee*	**I would like a dress/sweater**
Uso la talla cuarenta ***oo**-sō la **ta**-lya kwa-**ren**-ta*	**I take a size 40**
Calzo un cuarenta ***kal**-thō oon kwa-**ren**-ta*	**I take a shoe size 40**
¿Puede medirme? ***pway**-day may-**deer**-may?*	**Can you measure me?**
¿Tiene éste en azul? ***tyay**-nay **es**-tay en a-**thool**?*	**Have you got this in blue?**
¿Qué tela es? *kay **tay**-la es?*	**What is the material?**
Me gusta éste/aquél de allí/el del escaparate *may **goos**-ta **es**-tay/a-**kel** day a-**lyee**/el del es-ka-pa-**ra**-tay*	**I like this one/that one there/the one in the window**
¿Puedo probarlo? ***pway**-do pro-**bar**-lō?*	**May I try it on?**
Me gusta/no me gusta *may **goos**-ta/nō may **goos**-ta*	**I like it/I don't like it**
No me vale *nō may **ba**-lay*	**It doesn't fit**
Quiero uno mayor/uno más pequeño ***kyay**-rō **oo**-nō ma-**yor**/**oo**-nō mas pay-**kay**-nyō*	**I want a bigger one/smaller one**
¿No tienen más que ésto? *no **tyay**-nen mas kay **es**-tō?*	**Is this all you have?**
¿Es lavable? *es la-**ba**-blay?*	**Is it washable?**
¿Encogerá? *en-ko-khay-**ra**?*	**Will it shrink?**
Me lo llevo *may lō **lyay**-bō*	**I'll take it**

Clothing

French	German	Spanish	
le chemisier *luh shuh-meez-yay*	die Bluse *dee **bloo**-zè*	la blusa *la **bloo**-sa*	**blouse**
les gants *lay goñ*	die Handschuhe *dee **hant**-shoo-è*	los guantes *lōs **gwan**-tays*	**gloves**
la veste *la vest*	die Jacke *dee **ya**-kè*	la chaqueta *la cha-**kay**-ta*	**jacket**
le jean *luh jeen*	die Jeans *dee jeenz*	los vaqueros *los ba-**kay**-rōs*	**jeans**
le pull *luh pōōl*	der Pullover *der poo-**lō**-vèr*	el jersey *el **kher-se**-ee*	**pullover**
l'imperméable *lañ-per-may-ah- bluh*	der Regenmantel *der **ray**-gèn- man-tèl*	el impermeable *el eem-per- may-**a**-blay*	**raincoat**
les sandales *lay soñ-dal*	die Sandalen *dee zan-**dah**-lèn*	las sandalias *las san-**dal**-yas*	**sandals**
l'écharpe *lay-sharp*	der Schal *der shahl*	el pañuelo *el pan-**yway**-lō*	**scarf**
la chemise *la shuh-meez*	das Hemd *das hemt*	la camisa *la ka-**mee**-sa*	**shirt**
les chaussures *lay shō-sōōr*	die Schuhe *dee **shoo**-è*	los zapatos *lōs tha-**pa**-tōs*	**shoes**
le short *luh short*	die Shorts *dee shorts*	el pantalón corto *el pan-ta-**lon** **kor**-tō*	**shorts**
la jupe *la zhōōp*	der Rock *der rok*	la falda *la **fal**-da*	**skirt**
les chaussures de tennis *lay shō-sōōr duh te-nees*	die Segeltuch- schuhe *dee **zay**-gèl- tookh-shoo-è*	las zapatillas de deporte *las tha-pa-**teel**-yas day day-**por**-tay*	**sneakers**
les chaussettes *lay shō-set*	die Socken *dee **zo**-kèn*	los calcetines *los kal-thay- **tee**-nays*	**socks**
le slip de bain *luh sleep duh bañ*	die Badehose *dee **bah**-dè-hō-zè*	el bañador de hombre *el ban-ya-**dor** day **om**-bray*	**swimming trunks**
le maillot de bain *luh mye-yō duh bañ*	der Badeanzug *der **bah**-dè- an-tsook*	el traje de baño *el **tra**-khay day **ban**-yō*	**swimsuit**
la cravate *la kra-vat*	die Krawatte *dee kra-**va**-tè*	la corbata *la kor-**ba**-ta*	**tie**
le collant *luh ko-loñ*	die Strumpfhose *dee **shtroompf**- hō-zè*	los pantys *los **pan**-tees*	**tights**
le pantalon *luh poñ-ta-loñ*	die Hose *dee **hō**-zè*	los pantalones *los pan-ta-**lo**-nays*	**trousers**
le T shirt *luh tee shert*	das T-Shirt *das **tee**-shirt*	la camiseta *la ka-mee-**say**-ta*	**T-shirt**

French	German	Spanish	
French	*German*	*Spanish*	

Materials

French	German	Spanish	
velours côtelé *vuh-loor kōt-lay*	Cord *kort*	pana *pa-na*	**corduroy**
coton *ko-toñ*	Baumwolle ***bowm**-vo-lè*	algodón *al-go-**don***	**cotton**
fourrure *foo-rōōr*	Pelz *pelts*	pieles ***pye**-lays*	**fur**
dentelle *doñ-tel*	Spitze ***shpit**-sè*	encaje *en-**ka**-khay*	**lace**
cuir *kweer*	Leder ***lay**-dèr*	piel *pyel*	**leather**
lin *lañ*	Leinen ***line**-èn*	hilo *ee-lō*	**linen**
polyester *pol-yes-ter*	Polyester *po-lōō-**es**-tèr*	polyester *po-lee-**es**-ter*	**polyester**
rayonne *re-yon*	Rayon ***re**-yon*	rayón *ra-**yon***	**rayon**
soie *swah*	Seide ***zye**-dè*	seda ***say**-da*	**silk**
daim *dañ*	Wildleder ***vilt**-lay-dèr*	ante ***an**-tay*	**suede**
velours *vuh-loor*	Samt *zamt*	terciopelo *terth-yō-**pay**-lō*	**velvet**
laine *len*	Wolle ***vo**-lè*	lana ***la**-na*	**wool**

Accessories

French	German	Spanish	
la ceinture *la sañ-tōōr*	der Gürtel *der **gōōr**-tèl*	el cinturón *el theen-too-**ron***	**belt**
le bracelet *luh bras-lay*	das Armband *das **arm**-bant*	la pulsera *la pool-**say**-ra*	**bracelet**
les boucles d'oreille *lay boo-kluh do-rye*	die Ohrringe *dee **ōr**-ring-è*	los pendientes *los pend-**yen**-tays*	**earrings**
le sac à main *luh sak a mañ*	die Handtasche *dee **hant**-tash-è*	el bolso *el **bol**-sō*	**handbag (purse)**
le collier *luh kol-yay*	die Halskette *dee **hals**-ke-tè*	el collar *el kol-**yar***	**necklace**
le porte-monnaie *luh port-mo-nay*	der Geldbeutel *der **gelt**-boy-tèl*	el monedero *el mo-nay-**day**-rō*	**purse (UK)**
la bague *la bag*	der Ring *der ring*	el anillo *el a-**neel**-yō*	**ring**
le porte-feuille *luh port-fye*	die Brieftasche *dee **breef**-tash-è*	la cartera *la kar-**tay**-ra*	**wallet**
la montre *la moñ-truh*	die Armbanduhr *dee **arm**-bant-oo-èr*	el reloj *el ray-**lokh***	**watch**

Camera Shop

French	German
J'ai besoin d'un film pour cet appareil-photo/pour cette caméra *zhay buh-zwañ duñ feelm poor set a-pa-rye-fŏ-tŏ/poor set ka-may-ra*	Ich brauche einen Film für diese Kamera/für diese Filmkamera *ikh **brow**-khè **ine**-èn film fŏŏr **dee**-zè **kam**-è-ra/fŏŏr **dee**-zè **film**-kam-è-ra*
Je voudrais une pellicule noir et blanc *zhuh voo-dray zŏŏn pe-lee-kŏŏl nwar ay bloñ*	Ich hätte gerne einen Schwarzweiß-film *ikh **he**-tè **gern**-è **ine**-èn **shvarts**-vise-film*
Je voudrais une pellicule couleur sur papier *zhuh voo-dray zŏŏn pe-lee-kŏŏl koo-luhr sŏŏr pa-pyay*	Ich hätte gerne einen Farbfilm *ikh **he**-tè **gern**-è **ine**-èn **farp**-film*
Je voudrais une pellicule couleur pour diapositives *zhuh voo-dray zŏŏn pe-lee-kŏŏl koo-luhr poor dee-a-po-zee-teev*	Ich hätte gerne einen Diafarbfilm *ikh **he**-tè **gern**-è **ine**-èn **dee**-a-farp-film*
Je voudrais des ampoules de flash *zhuh voo-dray day zoñ-pool duh flash*	Ich hätte gerne Blitzbirnen *ikh **he**-tè **gern**-è **blits**-bir-nèn*
Mon appareil-photo marche mal *moñ na-pa-rye-fŏ-tŏ marsh mal*	Mit meiner Kamera stimmt etwas nicht *mit **mine**-èr **kam**-è-ra shtimt **et**-vas nikht*
Le film est bloqué dans l'appareil *luh feelm ay blo-kay doñ la-pa-rye*	Der Film klemmt *der film klemt*

French	German	Spanish	
le filtre bleu *luh feel-truh bluh*	der Blaufilter *der **blow**-fil-tèr*	el filtro azul *el **feel**-trŏ a-**thool***	**blue filter**
le chargeur *luh shar-zhuhr*	die Filmpatrone *dee **film**-pa-trŏ-nè*	el cartucho *el kar-**too**-chŏ*	**cartridge**
la cassette *la ka-set*	die Filmkassette *dee **film**-ka-se-tè*	el cassette *el ka-**set***	**cassette**
le pose-mètre *luh pŏz-me-truh*	der Belichtungs-messer *der bè-**likh**-toongs-mes-èr*	el fotómetro *el fŏ-**to**-may-trŏ*	**exposure meter**
le flash-cube *luh flash-kŏŏb*	der Blitzwürfel *der **blits**-vŏŏr-fèl*	el cubo de flash *el **koo**-bŏ day flash*	**flash cube**
l'objectif *lob-zhek-teef*	die Linse *dee **lin**-zè*	la lente *la **len**-tay*	**lens**
le protège-lentille *luh pro-tezh-loñ-tee*	die Objektiv-schutzkappe *dee ob-yek-**teef**-shoots-ka-pè*	la tapa de lente *la **ta**-pa day **len**-tay*	**lens cover**
le filtre rouge *luh feel-truh roozh*	der Rotfilter *der **rŏt**-fil-tèr*	el filtro rojo *el **feel**-trŏ **rŏ**-khŏ*	**red filter**

Spanish

Necesito una película para esta cámara/para este tomavistas *nay-thay-**see**-tō **oo**-na pay-**lee**-koo-la **pa**-ra **es**-ta **ka**-ma-ra/**pa**-ra **es**-tay to-ma-**bees**-tas*	**I need a film for this camera/for this cine (movie) camera**
Querría una película en blanco y negro *kay-**rree**-a **oo**-na pay-**lee**-koo-la en **blang**-kō ee **nay**-grō*	**I'd like a black and white film**
Querría una película en color *kay-**rree**-a **oo**-na pay-**lee**-koo-la en ko-**lor***	**I'd like a colour print film**
Querría una película de diapositivas en color *kay-**rree**-a **oo**-na pay-**lee**-koo-la day dee-a-po-see-**tee**-bas en ko-**lor***	**I'd like a colour slide film**
Querría bombillas de flash *kay-**rree**-a bom-**beel**-yas day flash*	**I'd like some flash bulbs**
Mi cámara fotográfica no va bien *mee **ka**-ma-ra fō-tō-**gra**-fee-ka nō ba byen*	**There is something wrong with my camera**
La película está atascada *la pay-**lee**-koo-la es-**ta** a-tas-**ca**-da*	**The film is jammed**

French	German	Spanish	
la pellicule *la pe-lee-kōōl*	die Filmspule *dee **film**-shpoo-lè*	el carrete *el ka-**rray**-tay*	**reel**
le système de rembobinage *luh sees-tem duh roñ-bo-bee-nazh*	der Rückspul-mechanismus *der **rōōk**-shpool-mekh-a-**nis**-moos*	el rebobinado *el ray-bo-bee-**na**-dō*	**rewind mechanism**
l'ombre *loñ-bruh*	die Blende *dee **blen**-dè*	el parasol *el pa-ra-**sol***	**shade**
l'obturateur *lob-tōō-ra-tuhr*	der Verschluß *der fer-**shloos***	el obturador *el ob-too-ra-**dor***	**shutter**
le viseur *luh vee-zuhr*	der Sucher *der **zookh**-èr*	el visor *el bee-**sor***	**viewfinder**
l'objectif grand-angle *lob-zhek-teef groñ-doñ-gluh*	das Weitwinkel-objektiv *das **vite**-ving-kèl-ob-yek-**teef***	la lente gran-angular *la **len**-tay gran-ang-goo-**lar***	**wide-angle lens**
le filtre jaune *luh feel-truh zhōn*	der Gelbfilter *der **gelp**-fil-tèr*	el filtro amarillo *el **feel**-trō a-ma-**reel**-yō*	**yellow filter**

Cleaning & Repairs
Laundry & Dry Cleaning

French	German
A dry cleaner's is une teinturerie or un pressing; sometimes it is combined with une blanchisserie (laundry), which will usually provide a fairly quick service. If you can't wait, and don't mind doing it for yourself, look for une laverie automatique.	*A dry cleaner's is eine Reinigung; sometimes it is combined with eine Wäscherei (laundry), which will usually provide a fairly quick service. If you can't wait, and don't mind doing it yourself, look for ein Waschsalon.*

Est-ce qu'il y a une laverie automatique près d'ici?
es-keel ya ōōn lav-ree ō-tō-ma-teek pre dee-see?

Gibt es hier in der Nähe einen Waschsalon?
*gipt es heer in der **nay**-è **ine**-èn **vash**-za-lon?*

Pouvez-vous nettoyer cette jupe/repasser ce pantalon?
poo-vay-voo net-wah-yay set zhōōp/ruh-pa-say suh poñ-ta-loñ?

Würden Sie bitte diesen Rock reinigen/diese Hose bügeln?
***vōōr**-dèn zee **bit**-è dee-zèn rok **rye**-ni-gèn/**dee**-zè hō-zè bōō-gèln?*

Ceci, c'est une tache de graisse/de sang/de café
suh-see, se tōōn tash duh gres/duh soñ/duh ka-fay

Das ist ein Fettfleck/ein Blutfleck/ein Kaffeefleck
*das ist ine **fet**-flek/ine **bloot**-flek/ine **ka**-fay-flek*

Quand est-ce que mes affaires seront prêtes?
koñ tes-kuh may za-fer suh-roñ pret?

Wann sind meine Sachen fertig?
*van zint **mine**-è **zakh**-èn **fer**-tikh?*

Je les voudrais assez rapidement
zhuh lay voo-dray za-say ra-peed-moñ

Ich brauche sie sehr bald
*ikh **brow**-khè zee zayr balt*

Repairs

C'est cassé/endommagé/déchiré
se ka-say/toñ-do-ma-zhay/day-shee-ray

Das ist kaputt/beschädigt/zerrissen
*das ist ka-**poot**/bè-**shay**-dikht/tser-**ris**-èn*

Est-ce que vous pouvez le réparer?
es-kuh voo poo-vay luh ray-pa-ray?

Können Sie es reparieren?
***kur'n**-èn zee es re-pa-**ree**-rèn?*

Est-ce que vous pouvez refaire les talons/les semelles de ces chaussures?
es-kuh voo poo-vay ruh-fer lay ta-loñ/lay suh-mel duh say shō-sōōr?

Können Sie die Absätze/Sohlen erneuern?
***kur'n**-èn zee dee **ap**-ze-tsè/**zō**-lèn er-**noy**-èrn?*

Est-ce que vous avez une pièce de rechange?
es-kuh voo za-vay zōōn pyes duh ruh-shoñzh?

Haben Sie das Ersatzteil?
***hah**-bèn zee das er-**zats**-tile?*

Est-ce que vous pouvez le faire rapidement?
es-kuh voo poo-vay luh fer ra-peed-moñ?

Können Sie es schnell erledigen?
***kur'n**-èn zee es shnel er-**lay**-di-gèn?*

Pouvez-vous me donner de la colle forte/de la ficelle/une aiguille et du fil?
poo-vay-voo muh do-nay duh la kol fort/duh la fee-sel/ōōn e-gwee ay dōō feel?

Können Sie mir bitte starken Klebstoff/etwas Schnur/Nadel und Faden geben?
***kur'n**-èn zee meer **bit**-è **shtar**-kèn **klayp**-shtof/**et**-vas shnoor/**nah**-dèl oont **fah**-dèn **gay**-bèn?*

A dry cleaner's is una tintorería or un limpieza en
seco; sometimes it is combined with una lavandería
(laundry), which will usually provide a fairly quick
service. If you can't wait, and don't mind doing it
yourself, look for una lavandería automática.

¿Hay una lavandería automática cerca de aquí? *a-ee oo-na la-ban-de-ree-a ow-to-ma-tee-ka ther-ka day a-kee.*	Is there a launderette nearby?
¿Puede limpiar esta falda/planchar estos pantalones? *pway-day leem-pyar es-ta fal-da/plan-char es-tōs pan-ta-lo-nays?*	Will you clean this skirt/press these trousers?
Esta mancha es de grasa/sangre/café *es-ta man-cha es day gra-sa/sang-gray/ka-fay*	This stain is grease/blood/coffee
¿Para cuándo estarán mis cosas? *pa-ra kwan-dō est-ta-ran mees kō-sas?*	When will my things be ready?
Lo necesito urgentemente *lō nay-thay-see-tō oor-khen-tay-men-tay*	I need them in a hurry

Repairs

Esto está roto/estropeado/rasgado *es-tō es-ta ro-tō/es-tro-pay-a-dō/ras-ga-dō*	This is broken/damaged/torn
¿Puede arreglarlo? *pway-day a-rray-glar-lō?*	Can you fix it?
¿Puede ponerme tapas/suelas a estos zapatos? *pway-day po-ner-may ta-pas/sway-las a es-tōs tha-pa-tōs?*	Can you reheel/resole these shoes?
¿Tiene un repuesto? *tyay-nay oon ray-pwes-tō?*	Have you got a replacement part?
¿Puede hacérmelo rápido? *pway-day a-ther-may-lō ra-pee-dō?*	Can you do it quickly?
¿Puede darme pegamento fuerte/una cuerda/aguja e hilo? *pway-day dar-may pay-ga-men-tō fwer-tay/oo-na kwer-da/a-goo-kha ay ee-lō?*	Can you give me some strong glue/some string/a needle and thread?

The Doctor

French	German

If a visit to the doctor is necessary you will have to pay on the spot. Some of the cost of medical treatment is repayable under reciprocal EEC arrangements for British and Irish visitors (form E111 should be obtained before departure), but proper accident and medical insurance is still advisable. Ambulances have to be paid for: there is no central number for you to dial. Normal body temperature on a centigrade thermometer is about 37°, so a reading of 38° means a temperature of 100°.

If a visit to the doctor is necessary you will probably have to pay on the spot. For visitors from Britain and Ireland, some of the cost of medical treatment is repayable under reciprocal EEC agreements (form E111 should be obtained before departure), but proper accident and medical insurance is still advisable. Ambulances also have to be paid for. You will find the number to call at the beginning of the phone book. Normal body temperature on a centigrade thermometer is about 37°, so a reading of 38° means a temperature of 100°.

French	German
Il y a un accident *eel ya uñ nak-see-doñ*	Es ist ein Unfall passiert *es ist ine **oon**-fal pas-**eert***
Appelez une ambulance *ap-lay zoon oñ-bōō-loñs*	Rufen Sie einen Krankenwagen ***roo**-fèn zee **ine**-èn **krang**-kèn-vah-gèn*
Allez chercher un docteur *a-lay sher-shay uñ dok-tuhr*	Holen Sie einen Arzt ***hō**-lèn zee **ine**-èn artst*
Il a perdu connaissance *eel a per-dōō ko-ne-soñs*	Er ist bewußtlos *er ist bè-**voost**-lōs*
Elle est sérieusement blessée *el ay say-ree-yuhz-moñ ble-say*	Sie ist schwer verletzt *zee ist shvayr fer-**letst***
Il faut que je vois le docteur *eel fō kuh zhuh vwah luh dok-tuhr*	Ich muß zum Arzt *ikh moos tsoom artst*
Je me suis coupé/brûlé *zhuh muh swee koo-pay/brōō-lay*	Ich habe mich geschnitten/verbrannt *ikh **hah**-bè mikh gè-**shni**-tèn/fer-**brant***
Je me suis fait mal au bras/à la jambe *zhuh muh swee fay mal ō brah/a la zhoñb*	Ich habe mir den Arm/das Bein verletzt *ikh **hah**-bè meer dayn arm/das bine fer-**letst***
Je suis tombé *zhuh swee toñ-bay*	Ich bin hingefallen *ikh bin **hin**-gè-fal-èn*
Un chien l'a mordue *uñ shyañ la mor-dōō*	Ein Hund hat sie gebissen *ine hoont hat zee gè-**bis**-èn*
Je me suis fait piquer *zhuh muh swee fay pee-kay*	Ich bin gestochen worden *ikh bin gè-**shtokh**-èn **vor**-dèn*
J'ai une douleur ici *zhay ōōn doo-luhr ee-see*	Ich habe hier Schmerzen *ikh **hah**-bè heer **shmerts**-èn*
C'est enflé ici *se toñ-flay ee-see*	Hier ist es geschwollen *heer ist es gè-**shvol**-èn*
C'est enflammé ici *se toñ-fla-may ee-see*	Hier ist es entzündet *heer ist es ent-**tsōōn**-dèt*
Ça me fait mal de marcher/d'avaler/de respirer *sa muh fe mal duh mar-shay/da-va-lay/duh res-pee-ray*	Es tut weh beim Laufen/beim Schlucken/beim Atmen *es toot vay bime **low**-fèn/bime **shloo**-kèn/bime **aht**-mèn*

Spanish

If a visit to the doctor is necessary, you will probably have to pay on the spot, so make sure you are properly insured before you leave. Normal body temperature on a centigrade thermometer is 37°, so a reading of 38° means a temperature of 100°.

Ha habido un accidente a a-**bee**-dō oon ak-thee-**den**-tay	There has been an accident
Llame a una ambulancia **lya**-may a **oo**-na am-boo-**lan**-thya	Call an ambulance
Traiga a un médico **tra**-ee-ga a oon **me**-dee-kō	Get a doctor
Ha perdido el conocimiento a per-**dee**-dō el ko-no-thee-**myen**-tō	He is unconscious
Está gravemente herida es-**ta** gra-bay-**men**-tay ay-**ree**-da	She has been seriously injured
Necesito ver al doctor nay-thay-**see**-tō ber al dok-**tor**	I need to see the doctor
Me he cortado/quemado may ay kor-**ta**-dō/kay-**ma**-dō	I have cut/burnt myself
Me he hecho daño en el brazo/en la pierna may ay **ay**-chō **da**-nyō en el **bra**-thō/en la **pyer**-na	I have hurt my arm/my leg
Me he caído may ay ka-**ee**-dō	I have had a fall
La ha mordido un perro la a mor-**dee**-dō oon **pe**-rrō	She has been bitten by a dog
Tengo una picadura **teng**-gō **oo**-na pee-ka-**doo**-ra	I have been stung
Tengo un dolor aquí **teng**-gō oon do-**lor** a-**kee**	I have a pain here
Tengo esto hinchado **teng**-gō es-**tō** een-**cha**-dō	There is a swelling here
Está inflamado aquí es-**ta** een-fla-**ma**-dō a-**kee**	It is inflamed here
Me duele al andar/al tragar/al respirar may **dway**-lay al an-**dar**/al tra-**gar**/al res-pee-**rar**	It is painful to walk/swallow/breathe

The Doctor

French	German
J'ai mal à la tête/à l'oreille/à la gorge *zhay mal a la tet/a lo-rye/a la gorzh*	Ich habe Kopfschmerzen/Ohren-schmerzen/Halsschmerzen *ikh **hah**-bè **kopf**-shmerts-èn/**ō**-rèn-shmerts-èn/**hals**-shmerts-èn*
J'ai envie de vomir *zhay oñ-vee duh vo-meer*	Mir ist übel *meer ist **ōō**-bèl*
Je crois que c'est une intoxication alimentaire *zhuh krwah kuh se tōōn añ-tok-see-kas-yoñ a-lee-moñ-ter*	Ich glaube, ich habe eine Lebensmittelvergiftung *ikh **glow**-bè, ikh **hah**-bè **ine**-è **lay**-bènz-mi-tèl-fer-**gif**-toong*
J'ai vomi *zhay vo-mee*	Ich habe mich übergeben *ikh **hah**-bè mikh ōō-bèr-**gay**-bèn*
J'ai la diarrhée *zhay la dee-a-ray*	Ich habe Durchfall *ikh **hah**-bè **doorkh**-fal*
Je suis constipé *zhuh swee koñ-stee-pay*	Ich habe Verstopfung *ikh **hah**-bè fer-**shtop**-foong*
Je ne me sens pas bien *zhuh nuh muh soñ pa byañ*	Mir ist schwindelig *meer ist **shvin**-dè-likh*
Je suis allergique à la pénicilline *zhuh swee za-ler-zheek a la pay-nee-see-leen*	Ich bin allergisch gegen Penizillin *ikh bin a-**ler**-gish **gay**-gèn pen-i-tsi-**leen***
J'ai de la tension *zhay duh la toñ-syoñ*	Ich habe zu hohen Blutdruck *ikh **hah**-bè tsoo **hō**-èn **bloot**-drook*
Je suis diabétique/asthmatique *zhuh swee dee-ya-bay-teek/as-ma-teek*	Ich bin zuckerkrank/Ich habe Asthma *ikh bin **tsoo**-kèr-krank/ikh **hah**-bè **ast**-ma*
Je prends ces médicaments *zhuh proñ say may-dee-ka-moñ*	Ich nehme diese Medikamente *ikh **nay**-mè **dee**-zè me-di-ka-**men**-tè*
Est-ce que vous pouvez me donner des médicaments équivalents? *es-kuh voo poo-vay muh do-nay day may-dee-ka-moñ zay-kee-va-loñ?*	Können Sie mir dafür ein deutsches Rezept geben? *kur'n-èn zee meer da-**fōōr** ine **doyt**-shès re-**tsept gay**-bèn?*
Je suis enceinte *zhuh swee zoñ-sañt*	Ich bin schwanger *ikh bin **shvang**-èr*
Je prends la pilule *zhuh proñ la pee-lōōl*	Ich nehme die Pille *ikh **nay**-mè dee **pil**-è*
Est-ce que je dois rester au lit? *es-kuh zhuh dwah res-tay ō lee?*	Muß ich im Bett bleiben? *moos ikh im bet **blye**-bèn?*
Est-ce que je pourrai sortir demain? *es-kuh zhuh poo-ray sor-teer duh-mañ?*	Darf ich morgen ausgehen? *darf ikh **mor**-gèn **ows**-gay-èn?*

Spanish

Tengo dolor de cabeza/dolor de oídos/irritación de garganta *teng-gō do-lor day ka-bay-tha/do-lor day o-ee-dōs/ee-rree-ta-thyon day gar-gan-ta*	**I have a headache/earache/a sore throat**
Siento náuseas *syen-tō na-oo-say-as*	**I feel sick**
Creo que tengo intoxicación por alimentos *kray-ō kay teng-gō een-tok-see-ka-thyon por a-lee-men-tōs*	**I think I have food poisoning**
He vomitado *ay bo-mee-ta-dō*	**I have been sick**
Tengo diarrea *teng-gō dee-a-rray-a*	**I have diarrhea**
Tengo estreñimiento *teng-gō es-tray-nyee-myen-tō*	**I am constipated**
Me siento débil *may syen-tō de-beel*	**I feel faint**
Soy alérgico a la penicilina *soy a-ler-khee-kō a la pay-nee-thee-lee-na*	**I am allergic to penicillin**
Tengo la tensión alta *teng-gō la ten-syon al-ta*	**I have high blood pressure**
Soy diabético/asmático *soy dee-a-bay-tee-kō/as-ma-tee-kō*	**I am a diabetic/an asthmatic**
Estoy tomando estos medicamentos *es-toy to-man-dō es-tōs may-dee-ka-men-tōs*	**I am taking these drugs**
¿Puede darme una receta española para esto? *pway-day dar-may oo-na ray-thay-ta es-pa-nyo-la pa-ra es-tō?*	**Can you give me a French/German/Spanish prescription for them?**
Estoy embarazada *es-toy em-ba-ra-tha-da*	**I am pregnant**
Estoy tomando la píldora *es-toy to-man-dō la peel-do-ra*	**I am on the pill**
¿Tengo que quedarme en la cama? *teng-gō kay kay-dar-may en la ka-ma?*	**Must I stay in bed?**
¿Podré salir mañana? *po-dray sa-leer ma-nya-na?*	**Will I be able to go out tomorrow?**

The Doctor

French	German
Est-ce que je dois aller à l'hôpital?	Muß ich ins Krankenhaus?
es-kuh zhuh dwah za-lay a lo-pee-tal?	*moos ikh ins **krang**-kèn-hows?*
Est-ce que je dois me faire opérer?	Muß operiert werden?
es-kuh zhuh dwah muh fer o-pay-ray?	*moos o-pè-**reert ver**-dèn?*
Voici mon formulaire britannique de sécurité sociale assurance-maladie	Hier ist mein internationaler Krankenschein
*vwah-see moñ for-m**ōō**-ler bree-ta-neek duh say-k**ōō**-ree-tay s**ōō**s-yal a-s**ōō**-roñs-ma-la-dee*	*heer ist mine in-ter-nat-see-**ō-nah**-lèr **krang**-kèn-shine*
Comment est-ce que je me fais rembourser?	Wie werden mir die Kosten zurückerstattet?
ko-moñ tes-kuh zhuh muh fe roñ-boor-say?	*vee **ver**-dèn meer dee **kos**-tèn tsoo-r**ōō**k-er-shta-tèt?*

Parts of the Body

French	German	Spanish	
la cheville *la shuh-vee*	der Knöchel *der **knur'kh**-èl*	el tobillo *el to-**beel**-yō*	**ankle**
le bras *luh brah*	der Arm *der arm*	el brazo *el **bra**-thō*	**arm**
le dos *luh dō*	der Rücken *der **rōō**-kèn*	la espalda *la es-**pal**-da*	**back**
l'os *(pl* les os) *los (lay zō)*	der Knochen *der **kno**-khèn*	el hueso *el **way**-sō*	**bone**
le sein *luh sañ*	die Brust *dee broost*	el pecho *el **pay**-chō*	**breast**
la joue *la zhoo*	die Wange *dee **vang**-è*	la mejilla *la may-**kheel**-ya*	**cheek**
la poitrine *la pwah-treen*	der Brustkorb *der **broost**-korp*	el pecho *el **pay**-chō*	**chest**
l'oreille *lo-rye*	das Ohr *das ōr*	la oreja *la o-**ray**-kha*	**ear**
le coude *luh kood*	der Ellbogen *der **el**-bō-gèn*	el codo *el **kō**-dō*	**elbow**
l'œil *(pl* les yeux) *lye (lay zyuh)*	das Auge *das **ow**-gè*	el ojo *el **ō**-khō*	**eye**
le visage *luh vee-zazh*	das Gesicht *das gè-**zikht***	la cara *la **ka**-ra*	**face**
le doigt *luh dwah*	der Finger *der **fing**-èr*	el dedo *el **day**-dō*	**finger**
le pied *luh pyay*	der Fuß *der foos*	el pie *el pyay*	**foot**
la main *la mañ*	die Hand *dee hant*	la mano *la **ma**-nō*	**hand**
le cœur *luh kuhr*	das Herz *das herts*	el corazón *el ko-ra-**thon***	**heart**

¿Tendré que ir al hospital? *ten-**dray** kay eer al os-pee-**tal**?*	**Will I have to go into hospital?**
¿Hará falta operar? *a-**ra fal**-ta o-pay-**rar**?*	**Will an operation be necessary?**
not applicable	**Here is my E111 form**
not applicable	**How do I get reimbursed?**

Parts of the Body

French	German	Spanish	
le rein *luh rañ*	die Niere *dee **nee**-rè*	el riñón *el reen-**yon***	**kidney**
le genou *luh zhuh-noo*	das Knie *das knee*	la rodilla *la ro-**deel**-ya*	**knee**
la jambe *la zhoñb*	das Bein *das bine*	la pierna *la **pyer**-na*	**leg**
le foie *luh fwah*	die Leber *dee **lay**-bèr*	el hígado *el **ee**-ga-dō*	**liver**
les poumons *lay poo-moñ*	die Lungen *dee **loong**-èn*	los pulmones *los pool-**mo**-nays*	**lungs**
la bouche *la boosh*	der Mund *der moont*	la boca *la **bo**-ka*	**mouth**
le muscle *luh moos-kluh*	der Muskel *der **moos**-kèl*	el músculo *el **moos**-koo-lō*	**muscle**
le cou *luh koo*	der Hals *der hals*	el cuello *el **kwel**-yō*	**neck**
le nez *luh nay*	die Nase *dee **nah**-zè*	la nariz *la na-**reeth***	**nose**
le tibia *luh tee-bya*	das Schienbein *das **sheen**-bine*	la espinilla *la es-pee-**neel**-ya*	**shin**
la peau *la pō*	die Haut *dee howt*	la piel *la pyel*	**skin**
la colonne vertébrale *la ko-lon ver-tay-bral*	die Wirbelsäule *dee **vir**-bèl-zoy-lè*	la columna vertebral *la ko-**loom**-na ber-tay-**bral***	**spine**
l'estomac *les-to-ma*	der Magen *der **mah**-gèn*	el estómago *el es-**to**-ma-gō*	**stomach**
la gorge *la gorzh*	der Hals *der hals*	la garganta *la gar-**gan**-ta*	**throat**
le poignet *luh pwahn-yay*	das Handgelenk *das **hant**-gè-lenk*	la muñeca *la moon-**yay**-ka*	**wrist**

The Dentist

French	German
Il faut que je vois le dentiste *eel fõ kuh zhuh vwah luh doñ-teest*	Ich muß zum Zahnarzt *ikh moos tsoom **tsahn**-artst*
J'ai mal aux dents *zhay mal õ doñ*	Ich habe Zahnschmerzen *ikh **hah**-bè **tsahn**-shmerts-èn*
C'est celle-ci *say sel-see*	Es ist dieser Zahn *es ist **dee**-zèr tsahn*
J'ai une dent de cassée *zhay õõn doñ duh ka-say*	Mir ist ein Zahn abgebrochen *meer ist ine tsahn **ap**-gè-brokh-èn*
Le plombage est parti *luh ploñ-bazh ay par-tee*	Die Plombe ist herausgefallen *dee **plom**-bè ist he-**rows**-gè-fal-èn*
Est-ce qu'il faudra l'arracher? *es-keel fõ-dra la-ra-shay?*	Müssen Sie ihn ziehen? ***mõõs**-èn zee een **tsee**-èn?*
Est-ce que vous allez la plomber? *es-kuh voo za-lay la ploñ-bay?*	Müssen Sie ihn plombieren? ***mõõs**-èn zee een plom-**bee**-rèn?*
Ça fait mal *sa fe mal*	Das tut weh *das toot vay*
Faites-moi une piqûre pour insensibiliser, s'il vous plaît *fet-mwah õõn pee-kõõr poor añ-soñ-see-bee-lee-zay, see voo play*	Bitte geben Sie mir eine Spritze ***bit**-è **gay**-bèn zee meer **ine**-è **shprit**-sè*
Mes gencives sont douloureuses *may zhoñ-seev soñ doo-loo-ruhz*	Mir tut das Zahnfleisch weh *meer toot das **tsahn**-flyesh vay*
Mon dentier est cassé *moñ doñ-tyay ay ka-say*	Mein Gebiß ist kaputt *mine gè-**bis** ist ka-**poot***
Est-ce que vous pouvez le réparer? *es-kuh voo poo-vay luh ray-pa-ray?*	Können Sie es reparieren? ***kur'n**-èn zee es re-pa-**ree**-rèn?*

The Dentist

Spanish	English
Necesito ver al dentista *nay-thay-**see**-tō ber al den-**tees**-ta*	**I need to see the dentist**
Me duele una muela *may **dway**-lay **oo**-na **mway**-la*	**I have toothache**
Es ésta *es **es**-ta*	**It's this one**
Me he roto un diente *may ay **rō**-tō oon **dyen**-tay*	**I've broken a tooth**
Se me ha caído el empaste *say may a ka-**ee**-dō el em-**pas**-tay*	**The filling has come out**
¿Tendré que sacarla? *ten-**dray** kay sa-**kar**-la?*	**Will you have to take it out?**
¿Va a empastarla? *ba a em-pas-**tar**-la?*	**Are you going to fill it?**
Eso duele mucho *e-**sō dway**-lay **moo**-chō*	**That hurts**
Póngame una inyección, por favor ***pong**-ga-may **oo**-na een-yek-**thyon**, *por fa-**bor***	**Please give me an injection**
Me duelen las encías *may **dway**-len las en-**thee**-as*	**My gums hurt**
Se me ha roto la dentadura postiza *say may a **rō**-tō la den-ta-**doo**-ra pos-**tee**-tha*	**My false teeth are broken**
¿Puede arreglarla? ***pway**-day a-rray-**glar**-la?*	**Can you repair them?**

Road Signs
French

French	English
Accotement non stabilisé	Soft verge *or* shoulder
Allumez vos phares	Switch on headlights
Arrêt	Stop
Arrêt interdit	No stopping
Attention	Caution
Autres directions	Other directions
Boue	Mud
Centre ville	City *or* town centre
Chaussée déformée	Uneven road surface
Danger	Danger
Défense de stationner	No parking
Descente dangereuse	Steep hill
Détour	Bend
Déviation	Diversion
Douane	Customs
École	School
Entrée interdite	No entry
Fin d'interdiction de stationner	End of parking restrictions
Gravillons	Loose chippings (gravel)
Impasse	No through road
Klaxonner	Sound your horn
La flèche verte n'est pas prioritaire	The green arrow does not indicate priority
Poids lourds	Trucks
Priorité à droite	Give way to traffic from right
Prudence	Caution
Ralentir	Slow/Reduce speed now
Réservé aux piétons	Pedestrians only
Route barrée	Road closed
Sans issue	No through road
Sauf riverains	Residents only
Secours routier français	Breakdown service
Sens unique	One-way street
Serrez à droite/à gauche	Keep right/left
Sortie d'autoroute	Motorway exit road
Sortie de véhicules/d'usine	Vehicle/factory exit
Stationnement interdit/autorisé	No parking/Parking permitted
Toutes directions	All directions
Travaux	Road works
Trous en formation	Uneven road surface
Un train peut en cacher un autre	One train can conceal a second
Virage dangereux	Dangerous bend
Zone à stationnement réglementé	Controlled parking zone

Achtung	Caution
Achtung! Ein Zug kann einen zweiten verdecken	One train can conceal a second
Ausfahrt	Exit
Ausfahrt freihalten	Exit – Keep clear
Autobahn	Motorway
Der grüne Pfeil bedeutet keine Vorfahrt!	The green arrow does not indicate priority
Einbahn(straße)	One way street
Einfahrt	Entrance
Ende des Parkverbots	End of parking restrictions
Fernlaster	Trucks
Gebührenpflichtige Brücke	Toll bridge
Gefahr	Danger
Gefährliche Kurve	Dangerous bend
Halten verboten	No stopping
Keine Durchfahrt	No through road
Keine Einfahrt	No entry
Kurzparkzone	Short-term parking only
Langsamer fahren	Reduce speed
Maut(brücke)	Toll (bridge)
Nur für Anlieger	Residents only
Pannenhilfe	Breakdown service
Parken verboten	No parking
Privatweg	Private road
Radweg	Cycle track
Raststätte	Service area
Rechts/links fahren	Drive on the right/left
Rechtsvorfahrt	Give way to traffic from right
Rollsplitt	Loose chippings (gravel)
Schlechte Fahrbahn	Uneven road surface
Schulkinder überqueren/ Schülerlotsen	Children crossing
Starkes Gefälle	Steep hill
Straßenwacht	Breakdown service
Umgehungsstraße	By-pass
Umleitung	Diversion
Vorsicht	Caution
Wasser Schutzgebiet	Protected water – do not pollute
Werkausfahrt	Factory exit
Zentrum	City *or* town centre
Zoll	Toll
Zoll/Douane	Customs

Road Signs
Spanish

Aduana	Customs
Alto	Stop
Aparcamiento	Parking
Atención	Caution
Autopista (de peaje)	(Toll) Motorway
Bajada peligrosa	Steep hill
Calzada or **firme deteriorada** or **en mal estado**	Uneven road surface
Callejón sin salida	No through road
Cambio de pista	Change lanes
Camino cerrado	Road closed
Ceda el paso	Give way
Centro urbano	City or town centre
Cerrado al tráfico	Closed to traffic
Circule a su derecha	Keep right
Circule despacio	Slow
Conducir por la derecha/la izquierda	Drive on the right/the left
Curva peligrosa	Dangerous bend
Dejar libre la salida	Exit – keep clear
Desembocadura de una calle	Road junction
Despacio	Slow
Desviación/Desvío	Diversion
Dirección prohibida	No entry
Dirección única	One way street
Disminuir la marcha	Reduce speed
Encender las luces	Switch on headlights
Entrada	Way in
Escuela	School
Estacionamiento	Parking
Fin de la prohibición de estacionar	End of parking restrictions
Fuerte declive	Steep hill
Gravilla	Loose chippings (gravel)
Obras	Road works
¡Pare!	Stop
Peatones	Pedestrians
Peligro	Danger
Precaución	Caution
Prohibida la entrada	No entry
Prohibido aparcar or **detenerse**	No parking
Respetar la precedencia	Give way
Salida	Exit
Salida de fabrica/de camiones	Factory/vehicle exit
Salida de la autopista	Motorway exit road

kilometres	miles		litres	UK gallons	US gallons
1	0.66		5	1.1	1.3
5	3.1		10	2.2	2.6
10	6.2		15	3.3	3.9
20	12.4		20	4.4	5.2
30	18.6		25	5.5	6.5
40	24.9		30	6.6	7.8
50	31		35	7.7	9.1
60	37.3		40	8.8	10.4
70	43.5				
80	49.7				
90	56				
100	62				
110	68.3				
120	74.6				
130	81				
140	87				
150	93.2				
160	100				
200	124				
300	186				
500	310				

Tire pressures

lb/sq in	15	18	20	22	24	26	28	30	33	35
kg/sq cm	1.1	1.3	1.4	1.5	1.7	1.8	2	2.1	2.3	2.5

Conversion Tables
Clothing

As these can be only approximate equivalents, it's best to try clothes on before buying.

Ladies' Wear

Dresses

UK	10	12	14	16	18
US	8	10	12	14	16
France/Germany/Spain	36	38	40	42	44

Sweaters

UK/US	32	34	36	38	40	42
France/Spain	36	38	40	42	44	46
Germany	42	44	46	48	50	52

Menswear

Waist and chest measurements

inches	28	30	32	34	36	38	40	42	44	46	48	50	52	54
centimetres	71	76	81	87	91	97	102	107	112	117	122	127	132	138

Shirts

UK/US	14	$14^{1}/_{2}$	15	$15^{1}/_{2}$	16	$16^{1}/_{2}$	17
France/Germany/Spain	36	37	38	39	41	42	43

Suits

UK/US	36	38	40	42	44	46
Germany/Spain	46	48	50	52	54	56

In France, men's clothing may have the appropriate measurement in centimetres, or a size which is half the centimetre measurement. For instance, a pair of trousers with a 32 inch waist will be either an 80 centimetre waist or a size 40.

Shoes

UK	$4^{1}/_{2}$	5	$5^{1}/_{2}$	6	$6^{1}/_{2}$	7	$7^{1}/_{2}$	8	$8^{1}/_{2}$	9
US	6	$6^{1}/_{2}$	7	$7^{1}/_{2}$	8	$8^{1}/_{2}$	9	$9^{1}/_{2}$	10	$10^{1}/_{2}$
France/Germany/Spain	$37^{1}/_{2}$	38	$38^{1}/_{2}$	39	40	$40^{1}/_{2}$	41	42	$42^{1}/_{2}$	43

Centigrade	Fahrenheit		inches =	cm	
0	32		0.39	1	2.54
5	41		0.79	2	5.08
10	50		1.18	3	7.62
15	59		1.57	4	10.6
17	63		1.97	5	12.7
20	68		2.36	6	15.2
22	72		2.76	7	17.8
24	75		3.15	8	20.3
26	79		3.54	9	22.9
28	82		3.9	10	25.4
30	86		4.3	11	27.9
35	95		4.7	12	30.1
37	98.4		**inches =**		**cm**
38	100				
40	104				
50	122				
100	212				

lb =	kg		feet =	metres	
2.2	1	0.45	3.3	1	0.3
4.4	2	0.91	6.6	2	0.61
6.6	3	1.4	9.9	3	0.91
8.8	4	1.8	13.1	4	1.22
11	5	2.2	16.4	5	1.52
13.2	6	2.7	19.7	6	1.83
15.4	7	3.2	23	7	2.13
17.6	8	3.6	26.2	8	2.44
19.8	9	4.1	29.5	9	2.74
22	10	4.5	32.9	10	3.05
	lb =	**kg**		**feet** =	**metres**

The Time

French	German
Quelle heure est-il? *kel uhr e-teel?*	Wieviel Uhr ist es? *vee-**feel** **oo**-èr ist es?*
Il est ... dix heures *eel ay ... dee zuhr*	Es ist ... zehn Uhr *es ist ... tsayn **oo**-èr*
dix heures cinq/moins cinq *dee zuhr sañk/mwañ sañk*	fünf nach zehn/vor zehn *f**ōō**nf nakh tsayn/f**ō**r tsayn*
dix heures dix/moins dix *dee zuhr dees/mwañ dees*	zehn nach zehn/vor zehn *tsayn nakh tsayn/f**ō**r tsayn*
dix heures et quart/moins le quart *dee zuhr ay kar/mwañ luh kar*	viertel nach zehn/vor zehn ***fir**-tèl nakh tsayn/f**ō**r tsayn*
dix heures vingt/moins vingt *dee zuhr vañ/mwañ vañ*	zwanzig nach zehn/vor zehn ***tsvan**-tsikh nakh tsayn/f**ō**r tsayn*
dix heures vingt-cinq/moins vingt-cinq *dee zuhr vañ-sañk/mwañ vañ-sañk*	fünf vor halb elf/fünf nach halb elf *f**ōō**nf f**ō**r halp elf/f**ōō**nf nakh halp elf*
dix heures et demie *dee zuhr ay dmee*	halb elf *halp elf*
onze heures *oñz uhr*	elf Uhr *elf **oo**-èr*
midi *mee-dee*	zwölf Uhr mittags *tsvur'lf **oo**-èr **mi**-tahks*
minuit *mee-nwee*	zwölf Uhr nachts *tsvur'lf **oo**-èr nakhts*
ce soir *suh swar*	heute abend ***hoy**-tè **ah**-bènt*
ce matin *suh ma-tañ*	heute morgen ***hoy**-tè **mor**-gèn*
cet après-midi *set a-pre-mee-dee*	heute nachmittag ***hoy**-tè **nakh**-mi-tahk*
avant/après trois heures *a-voñ/a-pre trwah zuhr*	vor/nach drei Uhr *f**ō**r/nakh drye **oo**-èr*
à/vers six heures et demie *a/ver see zuhr ay dmee*	um/gegen halb sieben *oom/**gay**-gèn halp **zee**-bèn*
presque cinq heures *pres-kuh sañk uhr*	kurz vor fünf *koorts f**ō**r f**ōō**nf*
dans une heure/une demi-heure *doñ z**ōō**n uhr/**ōō**n duh-mee-uhr*	in einer Stunde/einer halben Stunde *in **ine**-èr **shtoon**-dè/**ine**-èr **hal**-bèn **shtoon**-dè*
il y a deux heures *eel ya duh zuhr*	vor zwei Stunden *f**ō**r tsvye **shtoon**-dèn*

The Time

Spanish

¿Qué hora es? *kay **ō**-ra es?*	**What time is it?**
Son … las diez *son … las dyeth*	**It's … ten o'clock**
las diez y cinco/menos cinco *las dyeth ee **theeng**-kō/**may**-nōs **theeng**-kō*	**5 past/to 10**
las diez y diez/menos diez *las dyeth ee dyeth/**may**-nōs dyeth*	**10 past/to 10**
las diez y cuarto/menos cuarto *las dyeth ee **kwar**-tō/**may**-nōs **kwar**-tō*	**a quarter past/to 10**
las diez y veinte/menos veinte *las dyeth ee **be**-een-tay/**may**-nōs **be**-een-tay*	**20 past/to 10**
las diez y veinticinco/menos veinticinco *las dyeth ee be-een-tee-**theeng**-kō/ **may**-nōs be-een-tee-**theeng**-kō*	**25 past/to 10**
las diez y media *las dyeth ee **may**-dya*	**half past 10**
las once *las **on**-thay*	**eleven o'clock**
las doce (mediodía) *las **do**-thay (may-dyō-**dee**-a)*	**12 o'clock (midday)**
las doce (medianoche) *las **do**-thay (may-dya-**no**-chay)*	**12 o'clock (midnight)**
esta noche ***es**-ta **no**-chay*	**tonight**
esta mañana ***es**-ta ma-**nya**-na*	**this morning**
esta tarde ***es**-ta **tar**-day*	**this afternoon**
antes de/después de las tres ***an**-tays day/des-**pways** day las tres*	**before/after 3 o'clock**
a/hacia las seis y media *a/**a**-thya las **se**-ees ee **may**-dya*	**at/at about half past 6**
casi las cinco ***ka**-see las **theeng**-kō*	**nearly 5 o'clock**
dentro de una hora/media hora ***den**-trō day **oo**-na **ō**-ra/**may**-dya **ō**-ra*	**in an hour/half an hour**
hace dos horas ***a**-thay dōs **ō**-ras*	**two hours ago**

Numbers

French	German	Spanish	
zéro	null	cero	**0**
zay-rō	*nool*	***thay**-rō*	
un/premier	eins/erste	uno/primero	**1(st)**
uñ/pruh-myay	*ines/**er**-stè*	***oo**-nō/pree-**may**-rō*	
deux/-ième	zwei/-tè	dos/segundo	**2(nd)**
duh/duh-zyem	***tsvye**/-tè*	*dōs/say-**goon**-dō*	
trois/-ième	drei/dritte	tres/tercero	**3(rd)**
trwah/trwah-zyem	*drye/**dri**-tè*	*tres/ter-**thay**-rō*	
quatre/quatrième	vier/-te	cuatro/cuarto	**4(th)**
ka-truh/ka-tree-em	***feer**/-tè*	***kwa**-trō/**kwar**-tō*	
cinq/-ième	fünf/-te	cinco/quinto	**5(th)**
sañk/-yem	***fōōnf**/-tè*	***theeng**-kō/**keen**-tō*	
six/-ième	sechs/-te	seis/sexto	**6(th)**
sees/see-zyem	***zeks**/-tè*	*se-ees/**sek**-stō*	
sept/-ième	sieben/siebte	siete/séptimo	**7(th)**
set/-yem	*zee-**bèn**/**zeeb**-tè*	***syay**-tay/**sep**-tee-mō*	
huit/-ième	acht/-e	ocho/octavo	**8(th)**
weet/-yem	***akht**/-è*	*o-chō/ok-**ta**-bō*	
neuf/neuvième	neun/-te	nueve/noveno	**9(th)**
nuhf/nuh-vyem	***noyn**/-tè*	***nway**-bay/no-**bay**-nō*	
dix/-ième	zehn/-te	diez/décimo	**10(th)**
dees/dee-zyem	***tsayn**/-tè*	*dyeth/**de**-thee-mō*	
onze/onzième	elf/-te	once/decimoprimero	**11(th)**
oñz/-yem	***elf**/-tè*	***on**-thay/de-thee-mō- -pree-**may**-rō*	
douze/douzième	zwölf/-te	doce/decimosegundo	**12(th)**
dooz/-yem	***tsvur'lf**/-tè*	***do**-thay/de-thee-mō- -say-**goon**-dō*	
treize/treizième	dreizehn/-te	trece/decimotercero	**13(th)**
trez/-yem	*drye-tsayn/-tè*	***tre**-thay/de-thee-mō- -ter-**thay**-rō*	
quatorze	vierzehn	catorce	**14**
ka-torz	***fir**-tsayn*	*ka-**tor**-thay*	
quinze	fünfzehn	quince	**15**
kañz	***fōōnf**-tsayn*	***keen**-thay*	
seize	sechzehn	dieciséis	**16**
sez	***zekh**-tsayn*	*dyeth-ee-**se**-ees*	
diz-sept	siebzehn	diecisiete	**17**
dee-set	***zeeb**-tsayn*	*dyeth-ee-**syay**-tay*	
dix-huit	achtzehn	dieciocho	**18**
dee-zweet	***akh**-tsayn*	*dyeth-ee-**o**-cho*	
dix-neuf	neunzehn	diecinueve	**19**
dees-nuhf	***noyn**-tsayn*	*dyeth-ee-**nway**-bay*	
vingt/-ième	zwanzig/-ste	veinte/vigésimo	**20(th)**
vañ/-tyem	***tsvan**-tsikh/-stè*	*be-een-tay/bee-**khe**- see-mō*	
vingt-et-un	einundzwanzig	veintiuno	**21**
vañ-tay-uñ	***ine**-oont-tsvan- tsikh*	*be-een-tee-**oo**-nō*	

Numbers

French	German	Spanish	
vingt-deux *vañ-duh*	zweiundzwanzig ***tsvye****-oont-tsvan- tsikh*	veintidós *be-een-tee-**dōs***	**22**
trente/trentième *troñt/-yem*	dreißig/-ste ***drye****-sikh/-stè*	treinta/trigésimo *tre-een-ta/tree-**khe**- see-mō*	**30(th)**
quarante/quaran- tième *ka-roñt/-yem*	vierzig/-ste ***fir****-tsikh/-stè*	cuarenta/cuadra- gésimo *kwa-**ren**-ta/kwa- dra-**khe**-see-mō*	**40(th)**
cinquante *sañ-koñt*	fünfzig ***fōōnf****-tsikh*	cincuenta *theeng-**kwen**-ta*	**50**
soixante *swa-soñt*	sechzig ***zekh****-tsikh*	sesenta *se-**sen**-ta*	**60**
soixante-dix *swa-soñt-dees*	siebzig ***zeep****-tsikh*	setenta *se-**ten**-ta*	**70**
quatre-vingts *ka-truh-vañ*	achtzig ***akh****-tsikh*	ochenta *o-**chen**-ta*	**80**
quatre-vingt-dix *ka-truh-vañ-dees*	neunzig ***noyn****-tsikh*	noventa *no-**ben**-ta*	**90**
cent/-ième *soñ/-tyem*	hundert/-ste ***hoon****-dèrt/-stè*	cien/centésimo *thyen/then-**te**-see-mō*	**100(th)**
cent dix *soñ dees*	hundertzehn ***hoon****-dèrt-**tsayn***	ciento diez *thyen-tō dyeth*	**110**
deux cents *duh soñ*	zweihundert ***tsvye****-hoon-dèrt*	doscientos *dōs-**thyen**-tōs*	**200**
cinq cents *sañk soñ*	fünfhundert ***fōōnf****-hoon-dèrt*	quinientos *kee-**nyen**-tōs*	**500**
mille/millième *meel/-yem*	tausend/-ste ***tow****-zènt/-stè*	mil/-ésimo *meel/-**e**-see-mō*	**1,000(th)**
deux mille *duh meel*	zweitausend ***tsvye****-tow-zènt*	dos mil *dōs meel*	**2,000**
un million *uñ meel-yoñ*	eine Million *ine-è mi-lee-**ōn***	un millón *oon mee-**lyon***	**1,000,000**
un demi *uñ duh-mee*	ein halbes *ine **hal**-bès*	medio ***may**-dyō*	**a half**
un quart *uñ kar*	ein Viertel *ine **fir**-tèl*	un cuarto *oon **kwar**-tō*	**a quarter**
un tiers *uñ tyer*	ein Drittel *ine **drit**-èl*	un tercio *oon **ter**-thyō*	**a third**
dix pour cent *dee poor soñ*	zehn Prozent *tsayn prō-**tsent***	el diez por ciento *el dyeth por **thyen**-tō*	**10%**
le dernier *luh der-nyay*	der letzte *der **let**-stè*	el último *el **ool**-tee-mō*	**the last (one)**

The Calendar

French	German	Spanish	
lundi *luñ-dee*	Montag ***mōn**-tahk*	lunes ***loo**-nays*	**Monday**
mardi *mar-dee*	Dienstag ***deens**-tahk*	martes ***mar**-tays*	**Tuesday**
mercredi *mer-kruh-dee*	Mittwoch ***mit**-vokh*	miércoles ***myer**-ko-lays*	**Wednes- day**
jeudi *zhuh-dee*	Donnerstag ***don**-èrs-tahk*	jueves ***khway**-bays*	**Thursday**
vendredi *voñ-druh-dee*	Freitag ***frye**-tahk*	viernes ***byer**-nays*	**Friday**
samedi *sam-dee*	Samstag ***zams**-tahk*	sábado ***sa**-ba-dō*	**Saturday**
dimanche *dee-moñsh*	Sonntag ***zon**-tahk*	domingo *do-**meeng**-gō*	**Sunday**
vendredi *voñ-druh-dee*	am Freitag *am **frye**-tahk*	el viernes *el **byer**-nays*	**on Friday**
mardi prochain *mar-dee pro-shañ*	nächsten Dienstag ***naykhs**-tèn ***deens**-tahk*	el martes que viene *el **mar**-tays kay **byay**-nay*	**next Tues- day**
hier *yer*	gestern ***ges**-tèrn*	ayer *a-**yer***	**yesterday**
aujourd'hui *ō-zhoor-dwee*	heute ***hoy**-tè*	hoy *oy*	**today**
demain *duh-mañ*	morgen ***mor**-gèn*	mañana *ma-**nya**-na*	**tomor- row**
le printemps *luh prañ-toñ*	Frühling ***frōō**-ling*	primavera *pree-ma-**bay**-ra*	**spring**
l'été *lay-tay*	Sommer ***zom**-èr*	verano *bay-**ra**-nō*	**summer**
l'automne *lō-ton*	Herbst *herpst*	otoño *o-**to**-nyō*	**autumn (fall)**
l'hiver *lee-ver*	Winter ***vin**-tèr*	invierno *een-**byer**-nō*	**winter**
au printemps *ō prañ-toñ*	im Frühling *im **frōō**-ling*	en la primavera *en la pree-ma-**bay**-ra*	**in spring**
en été *oñ nay-tay*	im Sommer *im **zom**-èr*	en el verano *en el bay-**ra**-nō*	**in sum- mer**
janvier *zhoñ-vyay*	Januar ***yan**-oo-ar*	enero *ay-**nay**-rō*	**January**
février *fay-vree-ay*	Februar ***fay**-broo-ar*	febrero *fay-**bray**-rō*	**February**
mars *mars*	März *merts*	marzo ***mar**-thō*	**March**
avril *a-vreel*	April *a-**pril***	abril *a-**breel***	**April**

French	German	Spanish	
mai	Mai	mayo	**May**
me	*mye*	***ma**-yŏ*	
juin	Juni	junio	**June**
zhwañ	***yoo**-nee*	***khoo**-nyŏ*	
juillet	Juli	julio	**July**
zhwee-yay	***yoo**-lee*	***khoo**-lyŏ*	
août	August	agosto	**August**
oot	*ow-**goost***	*a-**go**-stŏ*	
septembre	September	setiembre	**Septem-ber**
sep-toñ-bruh	*zep-**tem**-bèr*	*se-**tyem**-bray*	
octobre	Oktober	octubre	**October**
ok-to-bruh	*ok-**tŏ**-bèr*	*ok-**too**-bray*	
novembre	November	noviembre	**Novem-ber**
no-voñ-bruh	*nŏ-**vem**-bèr*	*no-**byem**-bray*	
décembre	Dezember	diciembre	**Decem-ber**
day-soñ-bruh	*day-**tsem**-bèr*	*dee-**thyem**-bray*	
au mois de juin	im Juni	en junio	**in June**
ŏ mwah duh zhwañ	*im **yoo**-nee*	*en **khoo**-nyŏ*	
le six juillet	der sechste Juli	el seis de julio	**July 6th**
luh see zhwee-yay	*der **zekh**-stè **yoo**-lee*	*el **se**-ees day **khoo**-lyŏ*	
la semaine prochaine	nächste Woche	la semana próxima	**next week**
la smen pro-shen	***naykh**-stè **vo**-khè*	*la say-**ma**-na **prok**-see-ma*	
le mois dernier	letzten Monat	el mes pasado	**last month**
luh mwah der-nyay	***let**-stèn **mŏ**-nat*	*el mes pa-**sa**-dŏ*	

Public Holidays

New Year's Day	January 1st
Epiphany	January 6th *(Ger, Aus, Sw, Sp)*
St. Joseph's Day	March 19th *(Sp)*
Good Friday	*(Ger, Sw, Sp)*
Easter Monday	*(Fr, Ger, Aus, Sw)*
Labour Day	May 1st *(Fr, Ger, Aus)*
Ascension Day	*(Fr, Ger, Aus, Sw)*
Whit Monday	*(Fr, Ger, Aus, Sw)*
Corpus Christi	*(Ger, Aus, Sp)*
National Holiday	July 14th *(Fr)*
St. James's Day	July 25th *(Sp)*
Assumption Day	August 15th *(Fr, Sp, Aus)*
Hispanidad	October 12th *(Sp)*
National Day	October 26th *(Aus)*
All Saints' Day	November 1st *(Fr, Ger, Aus, Sp)*
Armistice Day	November 11th *(Fr)*
Repentance Day	November 21st *(Ger)*
Feast of the Immaculate Conception	December 8th *(Aus, Sp)*
Christmas Day	December 25th
St. Stephen's Day	December 26th *(Ger, Aus, Sw)*

Descriptions

French	German	Spanish	

First of all, a list of colours:

French	German	Spanish	
beige *bezh*	beige *bayzh*	beige *be-ees*	**beige**
noir *nwar*	schwarz *shvarts*	negro *nay-grō*	**black**
bleu *bluh*	blau *blow*	azul *a-thool*	**blue**
brun *bruñ*	braun *brown*	marrón *ma-rron*	**brown**
crème *krem*	creme(farben) *kraym(-far-bèn)*	crema *kray-ma*	**cream**
fauve *fōv*	hellbraun *hel-brown*	pardo claro *par-dō kla-rō*	**fawn**
doré *do-ray*	gold *golt*	dorado *do-ra-dō*	**gold**
vert *ver*	grün *grōōn*	verde *ber-day*	**green**
gris *gree*	grau *grow*	gris *grees*	**grey**
mauve *mōv*	violett *vee-ō-let*	malva *mal-ba*	**mauve**
orange *o-roñzh*	orange *o-ran-zhè*	naranja *na-rang-kha*	**orange**
rose *rōz*	rosa *rō-za*	rosa *rō-sa*	**pink**
violet *vee-o-le*	lila *lee-la*	morado *mo-ra-dō*	**purple**
rouge *roozh*	rot *rōt*	rojo *rō-khō*	**red**
argenté *ar-zhoñ-tay*	silber *zil-bèr*	plateado *pla-tay-a-dō*	**silver**
ocre *o-kruh*	gelbbraun *gelp-brown*	canela *ka-nay-la*	**tan**
blanc *bloñ*	weiß *vise*	blanco *blang-kō*	**white**
jaune *zhōn*	gelb *gelp*	amarillo *a-ma-ree-lyō*	**yellow**

and a few other useful adjectives:

French	German	Spanish	
mauvais *mō-vay*	schlecht *shlekht*	malo *ma-lō*	**bad**
joli *zho-lee*	schön *shur'n*	hermoso *er-mō-sō*	**beautiful**
grand *groñ*	groß *grōs*	grande *gran-day*	**big**

Descriptions

French	German	Spanish	
bon marché *boñ mar-shay*	billig ***bil**-ikh*	barato *ba-**ra**-tō*	**cheap**
froid *frwah*	kalt *kalt*	frío ***free**-ō*	**cold**
sombre *soñ-bruh*	dunkel ***doong**-kèl*	oscuro *o-**skoo**-rō*	**dark**
cher *sher*	teuer ***toy**-èr*	caro ***ka**-rō*	**dear**
difficile *dee-fee-seel*	schwierig ***shvee**-rikh*	difícil *dee-**fee**-theel*	**difficult**
facile *fa-seel*	leicht *lyekht*	fácil ***fa**-theel*	**easy**
rapide *ra-peed*	schnell *shnel*	rápido ***ra**-pee-dō*	**fast**
bon *boñ*	gut *goot*	bueno ***bway**-nō*	**good**
haut *ō*	hoch *hōkh*	alto ***al**-tō*	**high**
chaud *shō*	heiß *hise*	caliente *ka-**lyen**-tay*	**hot**
intéressant *añ-tay-re-soñ*	interessant *in-tay-re-**sant***	interesante *een-tay-ray-**san**-tay*	**interest-ing**
long *loñ*	lang *lang*	largo ***lar**-gō*	**long**
nouveau *noo-vō*	neu *noy*	nuevo ***nway**-bō*	**new**
vieux *vyuh*	alt *alt*	viejo ***byay**-khō*	**old**
court *koor*	kurz *koorts*	corto ***kor**-tō*	**short**
lent *loñ*	langsam ***lang**-zam*	lento ***len**-tō*	**slow**
petit *puh-tee*	klein *kline*	pequeño *pay-**kay**-nyō*	**small**
affreux *a-fruh*	schrecklich ***shrek**-likh*	terrible *tay-**rre**-blay*	**terrible**

Index